4TH EDITION

Wanted TO BUY

A listing of serious buyers paying CASH for everything collectible!

COLLECTOR BOOKS
A Division of Schroeder Publishing Co., Inc.

The current values in this book should be used only as a guide. They are not intended to set prices, which vary from one section of the country to another. Auction prices as well as dealer prices vary greatly and are affected by condition as well as demand. Neither the Editors nor the Publisher assumes responsibility for any losses that might be incurred as a result of consulting this guide.

All ink drawings are by Beth Summers.

Searching For A Publisher?

We are always looking for knowledgeable people considered to be experts within their fields. If you feel that there is a real need for a book on your collectible subject and have a large, comprehensive collection, contact us.

COLLECTOR BOOKS
P.O. Box 3009
Paducah, Kentucky 42002-3009

Additional copies of this book may be ordered from:

Collector Books
P.O. Box 3009
Paducah, Kentucky 42002-3009

@ $9.95. Add $2.00 for postage and handling.

Copyright: Schroeder Publishing Co., 1993

Printed by IMAGE GRAPHICS, INC., Paducah, Kentucky

Introduction

This book was compiled to help put serious buyers in contact with the non-collecting sellers all over the country. Most of us have accumulated things that are not particularly valuable to us but could very well be of interest to one of the buyers in this book. Not only does this book list the prices that collectors are willing to pay on thousands of items, it also lists hundreds of interested buyers along with the type of material each is buying. *Wanted To Buy* is very easy to use. The listings are alphabetically arranged by subject, with the interested buyer's name and address preceding each group of listings. In the back of the book, we have included a special section which lists the names and addresses of over 250 buyers along with the categories that they are interested in. When you correspond with these buyers, be sure to enclose a self-addressed, stamped envelope if you want a reply. If you wish to sell your material, quote the price that you want or send a list. Ask if there are any items on the list that they might be interested in and the price that they would be willing to pay. If you want the list back, be sure to send a S.A.S.E. large enough for it to be returned.

Packing and Shipping Instructions

Special care must be exercised in shipping fragile items in the mail or U.P.S. Double-boxing is a must when shipping glass and china pieces. It is extremely important that each item be wrapped in several layers of newspaper. First, put a four-inch layer of wadded newspaper in the bottom of the box. Secondly, start placing the well-wrapped items on top of the crushed newspaper, making certain that each piece of glass or china is separated from the others. Make sure that there are at least four inches of cushioning newspaper or foam between each item. When the box is nearly full, place more cushioning material on top of the contents and then seal the box.

Finally, place this box and contents in a large box cushioned again with a at least four inches of newspaper on all four sides, top and bottom. This double-boxing is very important. Our Postal Service and United Parcel Service are efficient; however, we must pack well just in case there is undue bumping in handling.

When shipping coins and precious metals, be sure to register your shipment and request a return slip so that you will know that the buyer received the goods, as well as the date that they were delivered. All material should be insured for full value. Remember, always use strong boxes, lots of packing and good shipping tape.

ADDING MACHINES AND CALCULATORS

I buy old adding machines and calculators. Most of those I want are small desk-drawer models. I usually avoid the big monsters most often seen at flea markets. The ones I want were made from 1890 to 1920. Machines should be in good, operable condition. Please give details on condition, with photo if possible, and send SASE for reply.

Darryl Rehr
2591 Military Ave.
Los Angeles, CA 90064; 310-477-5229

We Pay

Adix	85.00
Alpina	100.00
Burkhardt	250.00
Calcumeter	85.00
Curta	75.00
Grant	850.00
Locke Adder	85.00
Millionaire	400.00
Rapid Computer	50.00
Spalding	850.00
Thomas Arithometre	850.00

ADVERTISING

Porcelain signs are found in a wide variety of sizes and colors. Some are flat; others have a flange. They are found in square, circular, and rectangular shapes as well as irregular forms known as diecuts.

The basic manufacturing process of these beautiful signs was to start with an iron or steel sheet; then fired-on coatings of a powdered glass-like material were added to them. Porcelain signs are usually heavy and are noticeably thicker than painted signs.

Many porcelain signs were manufactured before 1900, but production continued into the 1960s. None of the original manufacturers are left, but there are many reproductions around in cheap, thin imitations. With a little comparison to an authentic original porcelain advertising sign, you should be able to tell the difference.

Listed here are a few of my wants with buying prices.

Michael Bruner
6980 Walnut Lake Rd.
W Bloomfield, MI 48323

We Pay

Adams Express Co., one-sided, red, white & green **250.00**
Beech-Nut Candy, rectangular, one-sided, 5x28" **600.00**
Brazil Beer, rectangular, one-sided, curved corners...............................**650.00**
Dakota Central Telephone Co., red, white & blue, 18x18" **550.00**
De Laval Cream Separator, two-sided, about 20x30"...............................**600.00**
Dr. Pepper, rectangular, one-sided, about 12x26" **100.00**
Hanna's Green Seal Paints, two-sided, shows paint can..........................**175.00**
Koolmotor, round, two-sided, 14"..**200.00**
Peninsular Stoves, curved, one-sided **375.00**
Railway Express, Packages Received Here, two-sided **175.00**
Sapolin Paints, rectangular, two-sided, shows girl **250.00**
Socony Gasoline, two-sided, red, white & blue..**200.00**
Stork Beer, rectangular, one-sided, curved corners.................................**225.00**
Texaco, flanged, diecut, about 16x24" **350.00**
Texaco, No Smoking, black background, one-sided...................................**550.00**
Western Union Telegraph, oval, two-sided, shows globe **375.00**
Wells Fargo & Co. flanged, two-sided, red, white & blue..........................**475.00**
Wisconsin Official Garage, round, flanged, two-sided...............................**200.00**

Advertising

Advertising by means of signs has been done for many years. Two broad categories of signs would be **collector and decorator signs**. Collector signs have been known to sell for thousands of dollars. The Campbell soup sign which looks like the American flag is the most famous – bringing over eighty thousand dollars. Decorator signs are used in restaurants to provide the desired atmosphere. I'm interested in both types and in any quantity. Below are some prices that I'll pay.

Dave Beck
P.O. Box 435
Mediapolis, IA 52637

We Pay

Fern Glen Rye, self-framed tin	**2,000.00**
Fiddle & Bow Flour, porcelain	**500.00**
Coca-Cola, triangular	**400.00**
Coca-Cola, w/bottle, 24" dia	**200.00**
Pepsi-Cola, w/two dots	**50.00+**
Seed or Feed Signs	**15.00-50.00**
Ocean Liner, self-framed tin	**400.00+**

I collect **cigar store figures, trade signs, and any related literature (catalogs, photos, bills of sale, etc.)**. I buy, broker, and sell. Call or write (enclosing a photo).

Dr. 'Z'
1350 Kirts, Suite 160
Troy, MI 48084; 313-244-9426

Trade Signs **We Pay**

Spectacles	**500.00-1,500.00**
Drug Store	**500.00-1,500.00**
Pawn Shop	**500.00-1,500.00**
Watch Shop	**250.00-2,500.00**

Advertising trademark character story display figures are wanted. These may be made of plaster, composition, plastic or wood and depict cartoonish-advertising characters. Items wanted include story displays and statuettes, promotional banks, figural ashtrays, and bobbin' heads. Items of the 1930s through the 1970s are of particular interest. Examples of characters include

Speedy Alka Seltzer, Reddy Kilowatt, Whitman's Messenger, Elsie, Esquire Man, Pep Boys, and other various chefs and company servicemen. Listed below is a sampling of items sought. Send a description of your item with price, or call to leave a message.

Warren Dotz
2999 Regent St.
Berkeley, CA 94705; 510-652-1159

We Pay

Reddy Kilowatt Store Display	**100.00-500.00**
Speedy Alka Seltzer Bank	**100.00-300.00**
Speedy Alka Seltzer Store Display	**500.00-1,000.00**
Mido Watch Robot Store Display	**500.00-1,000.00**
B.P.R. Whiskies Store Display	**500.00-650.00**
Philip Morris Johnny	**500.00-650.00**
Poll Parrot Bobbin' Head	**150.00-200.00**
Philips 66 Bobbin' Head	**150.00-200.00**
Otto Orkin Bank	**100.00**
Hoover Vacuum Grit Bank	**100.00**

Wanted: **advertising pocket mirrors and sharpening stones** promoting tobacco, motorcycles, vacuum cleaners, marshmallows, cream separators, coffee, shoes, sodas, beer companies, or any thing else – surprise me! Only mint condition items are wanted, please, and a photocopy is a must. State your resonable price, or send insured for my offer. Prices paid usually range from $5.00 to $50.00 per item.

Clayton Zeller
Rd. #2, Box 46
Grand Forks, ND 58201; 701-772-4995

Trade or advertising cards were given away in the late 1900s and early 1900s by almost all companies (local and national) to advertise their products or services. They range from simple, printed cards to colorful, elaborate ones. Families collected them and often pasted them in albums. I will buy in bulk lots at ten cents each for small cards and twenty-five cents each for large cards and will pay the postage. Small lots will be priced on an individual basis. Do not send cards until you contact me with a brief description of the types of cards you have and the total number. I will let you know if I am interested.

We Pay

Old Serving Trays ....50.00+
Old Signs (metal & cardboard) ....25.00+
Old Calendars..50.00+
Bookmarks..35.00+
Watch Fobs...40.00+
Thermometers ....20.00+
Seltzer Bottles ....25.00+
Toys or Games...5.00+
Playing Cards ....10.00+
Syrup Bottles..50.00+
Ink Blotters...2.00+
Clocks ....30.00+
Pocket Mirrors...50.00+
Fans ....5.00+
Coupons ....1.00+
Trade Cards ....10.00+
Posters ....15.00+
Rare Items ....1,000.00-5,000.00+

AMERICAN DINNERWARE

    I deal in **pattern, Depression, kitchen, and '50s glassware, American china, stoneware, linens, and interesting odds and ends.** I collect Hazel Atlas Fine Ribbed and Chevron cobalt items, colored soda fountain glassware, children's root beer mugs, and odd pieces of clear pattern glass (especially children's mugs). I need several pieces of Blair Gay (green) Plaid and Bauer Gloss

Pastel Kitchenware (a.k.a. Wide Ring and Saturn). I can't afford to pay more than book prices for anything. Minor chips are okay if prices are reduced. Write for a more extensive want list. Send want lists, and I will hunt for your need.

Tori Adams
664 Jay St.
Gallup, NM 87301; 505-722-4019 (evenings)

We Pay

Bauer Gloss Pastel Kitchenware, #6 mixing bowl, not green	**35.00**
Blair Gay Plaid, plate, 10"	**8.00**
Blair Gay Plaid, plate, 8" or 8½"	**6.50**
Blair Gay Plaid, plate, 6"	**2.50**
Blair Gay Plaid, pitcher, small utility	**12.00**
Blair Gay Plaid, platter	**12.00**
Hull House & Garden Mirror Brown, plate, 8½"	**4.00**
Hull-Type (McCoy?), salad plate, pie plate form, 7"	**3.00**

We are looking for the following **patterns of Lenox** to complete our own settings of china:

Flower Song – place settings and serving pieces
Eclipse – serving pieces
Oak Leaf – place settings and serving pieces

We are also looking for and adding to our collection of **Lenox figurines (not the newer issues), vases, etc.** Anything we don't have in our collection is wanted. These are not for resale. Please call or write if you have any questions.

Bill & Beverly Rhodes
N 4820 Whitehouse
Spokane, WA 99205; 509-328-8399

ANIMAL DISHES

I buy covered animal dishes. I prefer the original ones but will consider the reproductions if they are American made. See my list here for some of my first choices:

Boar's Head, Atterbury, dated
Cat on Tall Hamper, Greentown, chocolate
Dome Rabbit, Greentown, chocolate
Dolphin w/Serrated Edge, Greentown, chocolate
Chick & Eggs on Round Compote, Atterbury (but would consider
    Westmoreland)
Rabbit, Atterbury, large, dated, 9"
Setter Dog on Square Base w/Gun, Bag, Etc., Vallerysthal
Block Swan, Challinor, Taylor & Co.
Breakfast Set, Vallerysthal
Jack Rabbit, Flaccus, clear
Dolphin on Sauce Dish, Westmoreland, 7¼" long
Powder Jars, Jeannette Glass Co.

I am willing to pay a fair price based on condition and age. Slag glass animals of any color are also wanted. I prefer Imperial Glass or Westmoreland but will consider others.

Robert & Sharon Thoerner
15549 Ryon Ave.
Bellflower, CA 90706; 310-866-1555

We Pay

Animal Dishes...**10.00-200.00**

ART DECO AND ART NOUVEAU

Art Deco and Art Nouveau

I am a private collector interested in all types of Art Deco and Art Nouveau items. Below is just a partial listing of those items I am looking to purchase. Please write or call with your information. I pay top dollar and guarantee a fast response to your correspondence.

John S. Zuk
666 Plainfield Ave.
Berkeley Heights, NJ 07922; 908-464-8252

We Pay

Frankart Castings (nudes, animals, etc.)	**100.00+**
Nuart Castings	**100.00+**
Hall, Red Wing, Fiesta, or Russel Wright China	**5.00+**
Frankoma, Gonder, or Weller China	**5.00+**
Roseville Pottery	**50.00+**
Chase Chromeware	**5.00+**
Faberware	**5.00+**
Tiffany Glass & Bronzeware	**200.00+**
Galle Glassware	**200.00+**
Lalique	**300.00+**
Pairpoint Lamps	**500.00+**
Handel Lamps	**500.00+**
Tiffany Lamps	**500.00+**
Signed Lamp Bases	**250.00+**
Bronze Lamps & Statues	**100.00+**

Collector buying Art Deco and Art Nouveau objects will pay top prices for:

Bronzes	Glass Items
Marble Statues	Tiffany
Porcelain Figurines	Decorator Pieces
Lamps	

I am interested in purchasing one piece or collections. You may call collect.

Brian Margolis
66 Waterloo St.
Winnipeg, Manitoba
Canada R3N-0S2
204-958-8000 (days) or 204-488-1188 (evenings)

I will buy any Art Deco piece! Items sought include nude lady figurines, geometric items (bookends with stairsteps, etc.), prints or originals by Louis Icart (also Maxfield Parrish and Ernesto Vargas), calendars with ladies, jewelry, table flatware, mercury balls, playing cards with ladies and animals, lady head vases, etc. Write or call.

Jean Griswold
1371 Merry Lane
Atlanta, GA 30329; 404-321-4033

ART GLASS

I am currently buying **all types of art glass including both expensive and inexpensive pieces**. All art glass does not need to be signed to have value to a collector. Items signed Galle, Daum Nancy, Tiffany, Lalique, and Murano; reverse-painted lamps; and good unsigned pieces are what I'm interested in buying. There are many counterfeit pieces on the market today that can only be authenticated through examination, but I can usually tell the value of an item from a photo. Listed below are prices I would be willing to pay.

Kimball M. Sterling
125 W Market
Johnson City, TN 37604; 615-928-1471

	We Pay
Galle Cameo	300.00-10,000.00
Lalique Perfumes	100.00-2,000.00
Other Perfumes	20.00-2,000.00
Loetz	50.00-800.00
Murano	25.00-500.00
Tiffany Vases	100.00-2,000.00
Anything Pretty	20.00+

Lamps	We Pay
Handel	500.00-10,000.00
Jefferson	500.00-1,200.00
Pairpoint	500.00-8,000.00
Tiffany	1,000.00-60,000.00
Lamp Bases	50.00-500.00

_____

My purchases of beautiful American antique glass pieces are for enjoyment only. If you have **pretty colored tumblers or water pitcher and tumbler sets**, give me a telephone call or send me a picture. I am especially searching for a very deep fuchsia Diamond Quilted Amberina water pitcher. We have the tumblers and hope to complete a matched set.

Victorian colored glass pitcher and tumbler sets as well as selected art glass pieces are wanted in the following:

Agata	New England Glass Co.
Amberina	Northwood
Burmese	Opalescent
Cranberry	Peachblow
Hobbs Brockunier	Sandwich
Mother of Pearl	U.S. Glass
Mt. Washington	Wheeling

I would also be interested in unique, hard-to-find, beautiful, single tumblers of any kind. Pattern molded or blown glass wanted!

Scott Roland
P.O. Box 262
Schenevus, NY 12155; 607-638-9543

We Pay

Victorian Art Glass ....**up to full market value**

ART POTTERY

    I am buying art pottery vases and wall pockets such as those made by Hull, Abingdon, and Camark. I will consider Roseville and Weller art pottery also if the price is right. I prefer pastel colors and flower motifs. Below I have listed some sample items I may be interested in. All items must be in excellent condition. Please send inquiries to:

Vintage Charm
P.O. Box 26241
Austin, TX 78755

We Pay

Hull, Wall Pockets	**25.00+**
Hull, Rosella Vase	**20.00+**
Hull, Magnolia Vase, glossy	14.00+
Hull, Butterfly Urn	**13.00+**
Camark, Vase (w/mark or paper label)	**10.00+**

AUTOGRAPHS

I seek autographs of famous people, especially businessmen and early financiers and inventors. Items such as letters, stocks, bonds, documents, etc. are wanted. Other famous persons not listed but whose autographs are wanted are: Jay Cooke, George Eastman, Henry Ford, Charles Crocker, and Frank W. Woolworth.

David M. Beach
Paper Americana
P.O. Box 2026
Goldenrod, FL 32733
407-657-7403 or FAX 407-657-6382

Autograph	We Pay
Jay Gould	150.00-1,000.00
John D. Rockefeller	200.00-1,200.00
Andrew Carnegie	200.00-1,000.00
Daniel Drew	150.00-500.00
'Commodore' C. Vanderbilt	250.00-1,500.00
James Fisk, Jr.	250.00-1,000.00
Hetty H.R. Green	250.00-800.00
J.P. Morgan	150.00-500.00
Leland Stanford	200.00-1,000.00

AUTUMN LEAF

I am buying Autumn Leaf china made by Hall. Mostly wanted are completer pieces, tin items, glasses, tablecloths, etc. I will pay fair prices for good pieces depending on condition and rarity.

Brent Dilworth
89 W Pacific
Blackfoot, ID 83221; 208-785-7109

AVIATION

I am buying **World War I (circa 1914-18) aviation items**. I would be interested in one item or a collection. I seek both U.S. and foreign items (British, French, German, etc.). Also wanted are pilot log books, I.D. cards, books, photos, aircraft instruments, souvenir items, helmets, etc. Please get my offer before you sell.

Dennis Gordon
1246 N Ave.
Missoula, MT 59801; 406-549-6280

We Pay

Pilot Wings & Badges	**100.00+**
Uniforms	**200.00+**
Flying Jackets & Suits	**200.00+**
Fabric Insignia (from aircraft)	**250.00+**
Medals	**50.00+**
Squadron Pins	**200.00+**

I am buying **commercial aviation items**. I prefer items from the 1920s through the 1970s, whether a single piece or a collection. Listed below are some of the things am seeking. I also want anything old and unusual.

John R. Joiner
245 Ashland Trail
Tyrone, GA 30290

We Pay

Pilot Wings	25.00+
Pilot Hat Emblems	25.00+
Flight Attendant Wings	25.00+
Flight Attendant Hat Emblems	25.00+
Timetables	3.00+
Playing Cards	1.00+
Post Cards	50¢
Anniversary Pins	5.00+
Pilot Manuals	25.00+
Maintenance Manuals	25.00+
Display Models	50.00+
Early Signs	20.00+
Dining Service Items	1.00+
Posters	5.00+

AVON

I buy Avon items – mostly Christmas plates, representative glassware items, and other glass collectibles. I also collect L.E. Smith glassware, lady head vases, character dolls, and flea market-type items (if the price is right).

Tammy Rodrick
R.R. #2, Box 163
Sumner, IL 62466

We Pay

Christmas Plates, 1973 through 1983, ea **5.00**
Mother's Day Plates, ea...**1.00+**
Cape Cod Goblets or Plates, ea **2.00**
Cape Cod Serving Pieces, ea...**5.00**
George & Martha Washington Candle Holders, pr...**5.00**
Mt. Vernon Candle Holder, pr..**5.00**
Blue Delft Pitcher & Bowl, 1972...**3.00**
Victoriana Pitcher & Bowl, green or blue, ea..**3.00**
Powder Tins, ea...**1.00**
Avon Lady Stemware, set of 12...**10.00**
92nd Anniversary Plate, 1978, set of 8 ....**20.00**
Liberty Bell or Independence Hall Plates, 1976, ea.......................................**5.00**
Town House Canisters, set of 4 ....**20.00**
Currier & Ives Pieces, ea **5.00**
Radios, ea **5.00**
N.A.A.C. or Hastings Bottles, ea..**5.00**
Chess Pieces, ea..**1.00**
Steins, dating from 1976 to present, ea...**5.00-10.00**
Steins, Ceramarte & Gertiz, ea **5.00-10.00**
L.E. Smith Glass, ea **1.00-5.00**
Lady Head Vases, ea **1.00-5.00**

———————————————

Avon **Cape Cod** pieces are wanted to add to my collection. These pieces are made of ruby red pressed glass. Items need not have original contents (cologne, candle, etc.) or boxes to be of interest. Plates and bowls of all sizes, water and wine goblets, mugs, salt and pepper shakers, sugar bowls, creamers, pie plates, pie servers, candlesticks, bells, cruets, etc. are wanted.
Listed below are some examples of prices paid.

L. Fay Holycross
1202 Seventh St.
Covington, IN 47932; 800-292-3703

We Pay

Bell..**4.00**
Bowl, large serving...**6.00**

Bowl, dessert **2.50**
Cruet **2.50**
Plate, dessert or salad **2.50**
Plate, dinner **3.50**
Water Goblet...**4.00**
Wine Goblet...**2.50**
Pie Plate...**7.50**
Pie Server **6.00**
Pitcher **10.00**
Candlestick, short, pr..**6.00**
Candlestick, tall, pr..**8.00**
Butter Dish, w/lid **7.50**
Mug, pedestal base...**2.50**
Sugar Bowl **4.00**
Creamer **4.00**

BADGES

Collector looking to purchase any and all state hunting, fishing, and chauffeur's badges. I especially want southern state badges from North Carolina, Georgia, Florida, Virginia, Alabama, Mississippi, South Carolina, Tennessee, and Louisiana. Advise what you have. Examples of some prices paid for any year are listed. Immediate payment for any badges purchased. These prices are for badges with complete pins and in good, undamaged condition.

Howard Share
4349 La-Vale Ct.
Clemmons, NC 27012; 919-766-6579

We Pay

Alabama Fishing, from 1910-40 ....35.00+
Alabama Fishing, prior to 1920..100.00+
Alabama Non-Resident ....100.00+
Alabama Hunting...35.00+
Alabama Chauffeur ....50.00+
Alabama Chauffeur, prior to 1920...300.00+
Alaska Chauffeur..75.00+
Alaska Fishing..35.00+
Arizona Fishing..30.00+
Arkansas Fishing..20.00+
California Chauffeur ....25.00+
California Fishing ....25.00+
Connecticut Fishing..20.00+
Delaware Fishing ....20.00+
Florida Chauffeur..50.00+
Florida Chauffeur, prior to 1920 ....200.00+
Florida Fishing..25.00+
Georgia Chauffeur 50.00
Georgia Chauffeur, prior to 1920...300.00+
Georgia Hunting..35.00+
Georgia Fishing, county or state...35.00+
Georgia Non-Resident..100.00+
Hawaii Chauffeur..75.00+
Idaho Chauffeur ....20.00+
Kansas Chauffeur ....25.00+
Kansas Fishing ....25.00+
Louisiana Chauffeur...35.00+
Louisiana Fishing, county or state ....35.00+
Louisiana Hunting ....50.00+
Louisiana Non-Resident ....100.00+
Maine Fishing ....15.00+
Michigan Chauffeur, prior to 1920...35.00+
Michigan Fishing, prior to 1920..75.00+
Mississippi Chauffeur...35.00+
Mississippi Fishing...50.00+
Mississippi Non-Resident...100.00+
Montana Chauffeur ....25.00+
Montana Fishing ....25.00+
New Hampshire Chauffeur, prior to 1920...25.00+
New Hampshire Fishing..25.00+
North Carolina Chauffeur ....35.00+
North Carolina Chauffeur, prior to 1930..100.00+
North Carolina Chauffeur, prior to 1920..300.00+
North Carolina Hunting..35.00+
North Carolina Fishing, county...35.00+
North Carolina Fishing, state...45.00+

North Carolina Trapping ....**100.00+**
North Carolina Non-Resident **100.00**
North Carolina Non-Resident Trapping...**300.00+**
North Carolina Combo Hunting & Fishing..**50.00+**
Oklahoma Chauffeur, prior to 1930 ....**25.00+**
Oklahoma Fishing...**25.00+**
Oregon Chauffeur, prior to 1930 ....**35.00+**
Oregon Fishing...**25.00+**
Pennsylvania Chauffeur, prior to 1910 ....**75.00+**
Pennsylvania Fishing, prior to 1920 ....**25.00+**
South Carolina Fishing...**25.00+**
Tennessee Chauffeur, prior to 1920 ....**50.00+**
Tennessee Hunting ....**30.00+**
Tennessee Fishing..**25.00+**
Texas Chauffeur ....**30.00+**
Texas Fishing ....**30.00+**
Utah Chauffeur...**25.00+**
Utah Fishing...**25.00+**
Virginia Fishing ....**25.00+**
Virginia Non-Resident ....**75.00+**
Any State Chauffeur Badge, dated prior to 1910............................**75.00-500.00**

BANKS

Mechanical and still banks bought, brokered (sold for you at a small commission, i.e., 5% to 10% of the sale price), and sold. I will buy broken banks, catalogs, packages (boxes, wooden or cardboard), and trade cards. I am a collector/dealer and have references; let me be your agent. 'Honesty, Integrity, Top Dollar' is my motto and the way I do business.

Dr. 'Z'
1350 Kirts, Suite #160
Troy, MI 48084; 313-244-9426

We Pay

Mechanical Banks	**100.00-10,000.00**
Still Banks	**25.00-10,000.00**
Packages	**25.00-750.00**

Banks copyrighted by Warner Brothers and produced by Metal Moss Manufacturing Company are wanted. These banks depict popular Warner Brothers characters and were introduced in 1936 and continued through the late 1940s. The symbol W.B.C. appears on the tree trunk or barrel and on the green base. The character's name is either painted or embossed on the base as well. Three keys of heavy metal were made to go with the bank. Only mint-condition banks are wanted. Prices listed below are for complete banks with original key.

Clayton D. Zeller
Rt. #2, Box 46
Grand Forks, ND 58203; 701-772-4995

We Pay

Porky Pig	**60.00**
Petunia Pig	**50.00**
Bugs Bunny	**55.00**
Daffy Duck	**50.00**
Sniffles	**45.00**
Beaky Buzzard	**45.00**
Elmer Fudd	**50.00**

BARBED WIRE

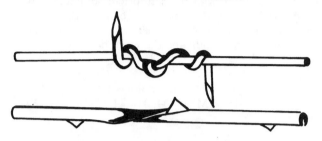

In 1868 Michael Kelly, a New York blacksmith, produced the first successful barbed wire. By 1892 over seven hundred separate patents had been issued to inventors eager to cash in on the 'barbed wire boom.' Today the collecting of these 'slender strands of history' is avidly pursued by thousands of collectors nationwide. (See *Flea Market Trader* published by Collector Books.)

Collectible specimens must be at least eighteen inches long. Wires must be in good condition: no broken or missing barbs and not severly rusted. Values range from a low of twenty-five cents per 'cut' to a high of $300.00. A photo of the wire or a two-inch length with one barb is helpful in making definite identification. I will buy the following wires. Postage costs will be refunded if a sample is sent.

John Mantz, Executive Director
American Barbed Wire Collectors Society
1023 Baldwin Rd.
Bakersfield, CA 93304; 805-397-9672

We Pay

Reynold's 'Necktie,' single-strand wire, Patent 1878, ea................................**1.00**
Stubbe's 'Small Plate,' two-strand wire, Patent 1883, ea **2.50**
Hodge's 'Spur Rowel,' two-strand wire, Patent 1887 (barb has 8- or 10-pointed
    wheel), ea **4.00**

BASEBALL

We are always buying baseball collectibles: cards, photos, balls, autographs, programs, etc. Also wanted are post cards, stamps, coins, comic books, and almost any other collectible. The older the item the better! Only collectibles in excellent condition are wanted.

Windmill Antiques
315 SW 77th Ave.
N Lauderdale, FL 33068

Cards

We Pay

1952 Willie Mays, Topps	100.00+
1952 Mickey Mantle, Topps	2,000.00+
1952 Mickey Mantle, Bowman	200.00+
1952 Yogi Berra, Topps	50.00+

Ephemera and Baseballs

We Pay

Autographed Baseballs, ea	up to 500.00+
Babe Ruth Autographed Baseball	200.00+
Cigarette Cards, old, ea	25.00+
Candy or Gum Cards, old, ea	25.00+

Programs, ea ....**1.00-1,000.00+**
Photos, ea ....**1.00-100.00+**

I collect the following baseball items:

Books & Magazines (1956 or earlier)
Board Games
Wire Photos & Negatives
All-Star Programs & Yearbooks
Baseball Cards (1974 or earlier, stars & commons)

I would also be interested in similar items relating to football, basketball, and hockey (pre-1975) only. Please describe fully; send photocopies, when appropriate, and your price. Enclose SASE for speedy reply. No phone calls please.

G.F. Wade
1320 Ethel St.
Okemos, MI 48864-3009

BATTERSEA BOXES

Call me to discuss these magnificent little boxes. I prefer motto boxes but will buy, sell, and collect all enamel boxes.

John Harrigan
1900 Hennepin
Minneapolis, MN 55403; 612-872-0226

BEATLES MEMORABILIA

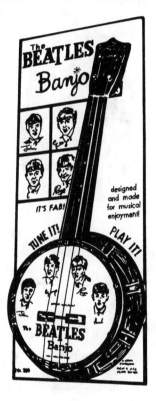

We collect Beatles memorabilia. We are looking for fan club items from the 1960s. We are also interested in trading cards, dolls, puzzles, toys, glasses and jewelry – almost anything Beatles except records. Price is determined by item and condition.

Michael & Deborah Summers
3258 Harrison St.
Paducah, KY 42001

BEDROOM ACCESSORIES AND DRESSER DOLLS

I am interested in buying Victorian, Art Nouveau, and Art Deco dresser dolls, powder boxes, dresser trays, pin trays, hatpin holders, hair receivers, and any item used in grooming milady. These can be made in a variety of materials from china, pottery, glass, or metals. I'm interested in all. Below is a list of prices – although I could possibly pay more depending on the condition and rarity. No collect calls.

K. Hartman
7459 Shawnee Rd.
N Tonawanda, NY 14120; 716-693-4143

We Pay

Dresser Dolls	**up to 100.00**
Dresser Pin Trays	**up to 50.00**
Enameled Compacts	**up to 50.00**
Figural Dresser Lamps	**up to 50.00**
Hatpin Holders	**up to 100.00**
Pincushion Dolls	**up to 100.00**
Sterling Items	**up to 100.00**
Beveled Mirrors, 3-part	**up to 100.00**

Ring Boxes & Trees ....**up to 50.00**
Powder Boxes ....**up to 50.00**
Perfume Bottles ....**up to 100.00**
Picture Frames, small ....**up to 50.00**

BILLIARDS & POOL HALL GAMES

BILLIARDS

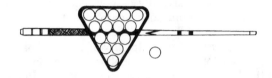

If you have something that is pre-WWII and was used in the old halls or homes, I would like to buy it. Listed below are some items and what I will pay for the common pieces – for the unusual, I pay more!

Mike Gross
P.O. Box 8661
Portland, OR 97286

We Pay

Trophies ....**20.00+**
Balls, ivory **30.00**
Balls, composition ....**3.00+**
Cues, 2-pc, w/manufacturer or player name...............................**50.00+**
Cues, 1-pc, w/manufacturer or player name...............................**10.00+**
Match Safes, spring-lid type..**45.00+**
Match Safes, U-shape type ....**15.00+**
Trade Token, w/town & state ....**4.00+**
Trade Token, without town & state..**2.00**
Books, hardcover ....**20.00+**
Books, softcover ....**5.00+**
Manufacturer Catalogs...**35.00+**
Prints **20.00**
Magazine Ads...**2.00+**
Bottle Openers..**3.00+**
Toys ....**25.00+**

Tins..**15.00+**
Pocket Mirror, w/picture ....**50.00+**
Pocket Mirror, without picture..**20.00+**
Post Cards, comic..**3.00+**
Post Cards, real photo ....**10.00+**

I am buying 1970s or earlier-brand custom pool, billiard, and snooker cues with decoration or inlay work. They must be straight and in good condition, although they need not have their tips or bottom bumpers.

I am also buying 1930s or earlier pool tables with decoration, carving or inlay work. They must basically be complete and in good condition. (The condition of the cloth and cushions will not affect their values.) Not all brands will be considered; price paid depends on condition, brand, decoration, and quality of workmanship. If you have proof the cue or pool table once belonged to a top player (national or international), this would add to its value. Caution! If the cue has been refinished, its value may have been lowered.

Also wanted are cue racks and ball racks. I am buying 1930s or earlier cue and ball racks with decoration, carving, or inlay work. They must be in good condition.

Alan D. Conway
1696 W Morton Ave.
Porterville, CA 93257; 209-782-0505

We Pay

Pool Cues, brand name, 1970s or earlier, w/decoration or inlay work ....**25.00+**
Pool Tables, brand name, 1930s or earlier, w/decoration or inlay.........**350.00+**
Cue Racks, 1930s or earlier, w/decoration or inlay work ....**15.00+**
Ball Racks, 1930s or earlier, w/decoration or inlay work ....**15.00+**

BLACK AMERICANA

Wanted: Black Americana (especially Black Mammy cookie jars, kitchen items, salt and pepper shakers, spice sets, teapots, egg timers, linens, sewing items, and toothbrush holders). I also want children's items and books (such as *Little Black Sambo*), Golliwogs, toys, old folk-art dolls, Beloved Belindy items, Black advertising items (including anything Aunt Jemima, Cream of Wheat, Coon Chicken Inn, and any tins or signs), and pre-1950s books (fiction, poetry, cookbooks, or humor). I buy Black American images only — no African items.

Judy Posner
R.D. #1, Box 273 WB
Effort, PA 18330; 717-629-6583

We Pay

Unusual Black Salt & Pepper Shakers	**40.00+**
Mammy (as maid) Cookie Jar	**300.00+**
Mammy w/Watermelon Teapot	**150.00+**
Vintage *Little Black Sambo* Book	**35.00+**
Aunt Jemima Plate	**50.00**
Coon Chicken Inn Salt & Pepper Shakers	**100.00+**
Various Flour & Grain Sacks w/Black Images	**50.00+**
Black Spice Shakers on Rack	**75.00+**
Mammy Lamp	**75.00+**
Various Wall Pockets w/Black Images	**50.00+**
Various Head Vases w/Black Images	**30.00+**

I am buying anything pertaining to the Black culture for a future museum.

Irene M. Houdek
Rt. 2, Box 231
Cresco, IA 52136; 319-547-2474

We Pay

Advertising Item, pin, etc., ea	**3.00+**
Art	**Call or Write**
Cookie Jar, old, mint condition	**50.00+**
Post Card	**50¢**
Valentine	**50¢**
Little Black Sambo Item	**5.00+**
Mammy Item	**3.00+**
Toys or Dolls	**Call or Write**
Anything Old or Unusual	**Call or Write**

BLACK CATS

I collect black cats made on red clay with high-gloss black glaze and painted-on red bow ties. There are some I'm especially interested in finding, and I'll list those below. But if you have any that are especially unique, I may want to buy those as well. The items that I will list were imported (from Japan) by the Shafford Company. You'll probably find similar pieces with yellow eyes or gold whiskers, but the ones I'm pricing below have green eyes lined in white and white whiskers and eyelashes. I prefer cats whose paint is still in good condition (the white washes off easily) and the prices I'm quoting are for examples in mint or near-mint paint. Cats with only 50% of the original paint remaining are going to be worth only 50% of my prices. These are pieces that I don't already have in my collection, and I'm willing to pay top price to get them.

Sharon Huxford
1202 Seventh St.
Covington, IN 47932; 800-292-3703

We Pay

Spice Set, 3 tiers of canisters (w/embossed cat faces) on a triangular (this is important) wooden rack..**200.00**
Measuring Cup Set, 4 small cups (w/embossed cat faces) hanging from a wooden rack w/a large painted-on black cat face in the center **125.00**
Spice Set, wireware cat face w/marble eyes, 4 black ceramic shakers hang from hooks along the bottom **150.00**
Nesting Trays, flat cat faces in graduated sizes with the largest having a rattan handle **75.00**
Salt & Pepper Shaker, long stretched-out cat w/salt in one end, pepper in the other (green eyes, not jewelled) **50.00**
Bank, head lifts off, tiny padlock at neck **65.00**

BLACK (BLACK AMETHYST) GLASS

Some specific items wanted are given below.

Marge Dozier
1835 Southeast Dr.
Point Pleasant, NJ 08742; 908-892-8441

We Pay

Hen on Basket, w/white head...**25.00**
Hen on Basket, marked Westmoreland **15.00**

Box, square, ornate, w/lid...**25.00**
Powder Horn Tumbler **15.00**
Slipper, L.E. Smith or Westmoreland, ea...............................**15.00**
Lotus Candle, marked Westmoreland **28.00**

THE BLUE MOON GIRL

The Blue Moon girl was the logo for Blue Moon silk stockings sold by the Largman-Gray Company. We are interested in any original item, advertising, or promotional giveaway with the Blue Moon girl logo. Photocopies or close-up photos are most helpful. I will make offers and answer all replies.

Bill Sinesky
7228 McQuaid Rd.
Wooster, OH 44691

BLUE RIDGE

I am buying sets or single dishes with people, birds, farm scenes, bouquets of flowers, or flower wreaths. Blue Ridge china has a hand-painted underglaze pattern and was made by Southern Potteries, Inc.

Robert R. Sabo
2248 Lakeroad Blvd. NW
Canton, OH 44708

We Pay

Artist Signed Pieces...200.00+
Turkey Platters...100.00+
Demitasse Pot..50.00+
Demitasse Cup & Saucer..10.00
Character Jugs..200.00+
Pitchers...25.00+
Boxes...25.00+
Chocolate Pots...25.00+
Vases...25.00+
Christmas Dinner Sets...25.00+
Thanksgiving Dinner Sets..25.00+
Children's Pieces..25.00

I would like to buy Blue Ridge china. Pieces must not have any chips or cracks.

G.D. Johnson
7565 Roosevelt Way NE
Seattle, WA 98115; 206-524-1698

We Pay

Teapot..50.00+
Coffeepot..35.00+
Vase..30.00+
Pitcher..30.00+

I am buying all types of Blue Ridge pottery. Pieces need to be in mint condition. I would also like to buy other pottery such as **Harker's Cameo, Fiesta, Lu Ray, etc**. Some examples of prices paid are listed here.

Christina Caldwell
Rt. 1, Box 336
Hawkins, TX 75765; 903-769-3862

	We Pay
Plates	7.00+
Shakers	20.00+
Teapots	50.00+
Pitchers	30.00+

I collect American pottery dinnerware: **Fiesta, Blue Ridge, and Frankoma**. I prefer accessory pieces of Blue Ridge in more elaborate designs (bowls, cups, etc.). Some pieces I am interested in are listed below. Only pieces without chips, cracks, or imperfections are wanted. Send pictures and/or descriptions of what you have. Please see my listing under Fiesta.

M.C. Wills
103 Virginia St.
Dyess, AFB, TX 79607

Blue Ridge	**We Pay**

Fruit Bowl	3.00+
Cup & Saucer Set	10.00+

BLUE WILLOW

We are buying Blue Willow pieces from the 1800s to the present – one piece, entire sets, or collections. Unusual items are especially wanted. Also pieces of **older carnival glass**, no reproductions or 1960s pieces, in any color or pattern are wanted. Prices paid vary according to color, style, or pattern.

The Antique Emporium
P.O. Box K
214 S State St.
Athens, WV 24712; 304-384-7800

We Pay

Blue Willow Child's Set	**40.00+**
Place Setting, 4 or 6-piece	**50.00+**
Canister Set	**25.00+**
Lamps	**25.00+**
Teapot or Tea Set	**25.00+**
Demitasse Set	**30.00+**
Carnival Punch Set	**30.00+**
Carnival Water Set	**30.00+**
Nappy (miscellaneous bowls, etc.), ea	**5.00+**

BOOKS

All books are a fascinating blend of intrinsic and extrinsic – the book as knowledge and the book as object. Here at the shop in Redlands, California, we focus on books of lasting value, both inside and out. We carry fine and unusual books and are always interested in obtaining notable volumes in the following varied categories: Literature; Americana, Modern Art and Architecture; Signed and Inscribed Books; Early Printing (pre-1800); Limited Editions;

Science and Medicine; Alcoholics Anonymous; Books with Original Art or Photographs; many others as well. In addition we purchase and sell a variety of autograph materials (letters, manuscripts, signed photographs, documents, etc.) from persons of note in all fields.

Below you will find examples of prices I will pay for these books in good original condition. All your quotes will be answered, but we do ask that you describe fully the book's condition, publication information, etc., and include a SASE. Thank you in advance.

Paul Melzer Fine and Rare Books
12 E Vine St.
Redlands, CA 92373; 714-792-7299

Alcoholics Anonymous   **We Pay**

(Wilson, Bill) *Alcoholics Anonymous*. NY, 1939-55 ....**25.00-2,000.00**

Exploration   **We Pay**

Dixon, George. *A Voyage Round the World*. London, 1989 ....**825.00**
Lewis & Clark. *History of the Expedition*. Philadelphia, 1814, 2 vols ...**2,200.00**
National Geographic. (any from 1910 or earlier) **8.00-75.00**

Illustrated Books   **We Pay**

Chagall, Marc. *Illustrations for the Bible*. NY, 1960 ....**1,800.00**
Chagall, Marc. *Jerusalem Windows*. NY, 1962 ....**500.00**
(Matisse) Joyce, James. *Ulysses*. NY, 1935, ltd edition **1,200.00**
(Picasso) Aristophanes. *Lysistrata*. 1934, ltd edition **1,000.00**

Literature   **We Pay**

Austin, Jane. *Sense & Sensibility*. London, 1811 or 1813, 3 vols **850.00**
Crane, Stephen. *Red Badge of Courage*. NY, 1895 ....**300.00**
Defoe, Daniel. *Robinson Crusoe*. London, 1919-20, 3 vols **3,500.00**
London, Jack. *The Cruise of the Dazzler*. NY, 1902 ....**300.00**
Melville, Herman. *Moby Dick*. NY, 1851, 3 vols **2,800.00**
Melville, Herman. *The Whale*. London, 1851, 3 vols...........................**5,500.00**
Wright, Harold Bell. *To My Sons*. NY, 1934 ....**750.00**

I am buying books on **gun and hardware store catalogs featuring guns, knives, and fishing tackle**. I prefer hardbound books from 1900 to 1970 – one book or complete collections.

Robert Lappin
Box 1006
Decatur, IL 62525; 217-428-2973

Subject	We Pay
Colt	20.00+
Winchester	25.00+
Miscellaneous Guns	5.00+
Gunsmithing, before 1940	10.00+
Gunsmithing, before 1920	20.00+
Hardware Store (hardcover)	20.00+
Gun, Fishing, or Hunting, ea	20.00+
Advertising Pieces, ea	20.00+
Any Unusual Related Material	Call or Write

I buy old, used and rare books. Single good items or collections, **early Ohio histories, books about Indians, early Americana, and Western Americana** are wanted. I'm also interested in **old magazines and paper ephemera**, the earlier the better. Of particular interest are books on hunting, shooting, fishing, reloading, and early magazines and paper ephemera on these subjects. I also want **briar or meerschaum pipe collections**.

If you have old books, paper, or pipes not listed below please call. I may have an interest in them or be able to be of assistance. If you get the answering machine, please leave your message and phone number. The following list is a brief sample of items. The wide range of prices reflects the condition, edition, subject, author, etc.; age doesn't always make it valuable. (For me the book would have to be printed in the 1600s to have age affect value. Some recent books and material have more value than older ones.)

C.L. Roberts
Reader's & Smoker's Den
36-42 N 4th St., P.O. Box 1162
Zanesville, OH 43702-1162
800-354-5704 or 614-455-2376

Author or Illustrator	We Pay
Grey, Zane; reprint w/dust jacket	5.00-75.00
Grey, Zane; first edition w/dust jacket	15.00-150.00
Grey, Zane; book without dust jacket	3.00-25.00
King, Stephen; first edition w/dust jacket	5.00-100.00
Naylor, James Ball; book or pamphlet	5.00-40.00

Books

Schneider, Norris; book or pamphlet..5.00-15.00
Christy, Howard Chandler; book, large format.............................10.00-100.00
Christy, Howard Chandler; print, poster or picture......................20.00-200.00

Publisher	We Pay

Winchester Press, w/dust jacket...3.00-15.00
Arkham House Press...5.00-50.00
Other Publishers, modern first edition w/dust jacket, 1950 to date...5.00-50.00

Other Wants	We Pay

Early Books, leather bound, especially pre-1850, ea.........................5.00-500.00
Books, leather bound, sets or singles, 1850 to present, ea...............5.00-300.00
Magazines, 1910-50s, ea..3.00-10.00
Pipes, briar (GBD, Dunhill, Wilmer, Saseni, Comoy, etc.), ea............5.00-50.00
Pipes, meerschaum, ea...5.00-200.00

I have a general bookstore and purchase books on all subjects but am particularly interested in titles and subjects noted below. The condition of the books is most important, so quote only those books that are complete and in excellent shape. When quoting please give title, author, publisher, date of publication, illustrator, and number of pages – the more information the better.

Robert L. Merriam
Rare, Used & Old Books
Newhall Rd.
Conway, MA 01341

	We Pay

Mary P. Wells Smith (author)..7.50+
Deerfield, MA (anything)..Write
American Revolution ....Write
Civil War ....Write
Leather-Bound Books, before 1850 ....Write
American Tract Society Moral Tales...2.50+
Juveniles, before 1920 ....Write
Antiques, specialized subjects ....Write
Decorative Arts ....Write

Wellerdt's Books has been in existence since January of 1992. Before that we were avid readers and collectors. As such we give an interesting thought on society's problems of today: these stem from the lack of reading or the inability to read a book. So much is to be gained from the reading of a book – for instance, feelings, thoughts, emotions, and insight.

We do a lot of quoting and mail order. We sell and collect **modern first editions**.

Wellerdt's
3700 S Osprey Ave., Ste. 214
Sarasota, FL 34239; 813-365-1318

We Pay

Woolf, Virginia; *Letters of Virginia Woolf*, Harcourt Brace World or Hogarth, Vol. 4 only (1928-1932), VG or better w/dust jacket **15.00-25.00**
Wooly, Leonard; *Beginning Again*, Harcourt Brace World, 1st American edition, 1964, VG or better w/dust jacket..**10.00-15.00**

I purchase **used books, CDs, cassettes, and audio books**. Most items must be in excellent condition.

Marsha Lambert
1200 W University
Lafayette, LA 70506

We Pay

CDs ....**2.00+**
Cassettes ....**50¢+**
Audio Books...**30¢+**
Hardcovers **1.00**

Books wanted: **collections and anthologies of cartoonists from 1890 to 1960**. I am interested only in books that are a collection of the cartoons of a single artist, not general collections of cartoons, comic books, or recent reprints.

'Early Editions' listed here need only be early; first editions must be in fine condition (tight, minimal wear, no stains, etc.) with dust covers (if they were issued with them). Prices may be higher if either the condition of the book or dust cover is mint, if the book is signed, or if it is signed and has a hand-drawn cartoon. Other books, including more recent artists' earlier works, are also wanted – especially signed or hardbound first editions. These books are wanted for private collection, not resale; trades are okay.

Abolone Cove Rare Books
7 Fruit Tree Rd.
Portuguese Bend, CA 90274

Cupples & Leon Series, Early Editions   We Pay

Bringing Up Father	**20.00+**
Dolly Dimples	**20.00+**
Mutt & Jeff	**24.00+**
Moon Mullins	**28.00+**
Joe Palooka	**30.00+**
Little Orphan Annie	**25.00+**
Smitty	**20.00+**
Harold Teen	**22.00+**
Nebs	**25.00+**
Keeping Up w/the Joneses	**24.00+**
Tillie the Toiler	**25.00+**
Toonerville Trolly	**30.00+**
The Gumps	**22.00+**
Barney Google	**25.00+**
Winnie Winkle	**22.00+**

Other Early Editions   We Pay

Popeye	**50.00+**
John McCutcheon	**25.00+**
Clare Briggs	**24.00+**

First Editions By: We Pay

Addams, Charles	**15.00+**
Alain	**15.00+**
Arno, Peter	**15.00+**
Corbean, Sam	**15.00+**
Darrow, Whitney Jr.	**8.00+**
Day, Chon (drew Brother Sebastion)	**5.00+**
Fisher, Ed	**8.00+**
Giovannetti, Pericle L.	**12.00+**
Hamilton, William	**18.00+**
Hoff, Syd	**10.00+**
Hokinson, Helen	**12.00+**

Kelly, Walt (drew Pogo)...**15.00+**
Ketcham, Hank (drew Dennis the Menace) ....**9.00+**
Key, Ted (drew Hazel) ....**8.00+**
Kovarsky, Anatol ....**10.00+**
Partch, Virgil (drew VIP) ....**5.00+**
Petty, Mary...**15.00+**
Price, George ....**15.00+**
Shafer, Burr..**7.00+**
Stevenson, James..**12.00+**
Syverson, Henry..**5.00+**
Taylor, Richard ....**13.00+**
Wilson, Gahan...**12.00+**

I am buying **books and American clocks.** I prefer clocks made between 1830 and 1940 with original keys whenever possible. I am also interested in **hardbound books on all subjects with special interest in clocks, the Pacific Northwest, cowboy art, and children's illustrators.** Below are some of the items I am seeking.

Norma Wadler
P.O. Box 418 - S 7th & Pacific
Long Beach, WA 98631; 206-642-3455

Book Subject   **We Pay**

Flora & Fauna of the Pacific Northwest ....**5.00+**
Settling of Southwestern Washington State ....**5.00+**
Clocks ....**5.00+**

Book Illustrator   **We Pay**

Borien, Edward ....**15.00+**
Clarke, Harry ....**10.00+**
Parrish, Maxfield..**10.00+**
Rackham, Arthur...**10.00+**
Russell, Charles..**15.00+**

I am buying **Western Americana genre books and ephemera relating to the American West** including ranching, trapping, cowboys and Indians, outlaws, frontiersmen, settlers, etc. I especially want unusual titles by individual presses. Also wanted are **children's books that are thirty years old or older.**

Listed below are some specific books sought.

Carroll Burcham
5546 17th Place
Lubbock, TX 79416

Author or Illustrator	We Pay
J. Evetts Haley	up to 75.00
J. Frank Dobie, 1st editions	up to 75.00
Harold Bell Wright, *To My Sons*	100.00+
Kate Greenaway	20.00+
Kate Douglas Wiggin	15.00+
Alcoholics Anonymous, 1st 16 printings, any	25.00+

We are purchasing **children's books having from four to thirty-two pages with color plates** by such publishers as Raphael Tuck and McLoughlin Brothers. Books must be pre-1925 and not torn. They can be on linen, linenette, or common paper. Send a list of your books for sale.

Arthur Boutiette
410 W Third St.
Suite 200
Little Rock, AR 72201

	We Pay
Common Paper	5.00-75.00
Linenette	10.00-85.00
Linen	20.00-125.00
Ethnic or Negro Stories	30.00-225.00

I am looking for books from the **International Correspondence School (I.C.S.)**. These date from the early 1900s and are large, leather-bound books on all topics. Examples of titles are given here.

Jack Zimmerly, Jr.
c/o 11711 Sharp Rd.
Waterford, PA 16441; 814-796-2510

I.C.S. Reference Library 7.00-12.00
I.C.S. Technical Library 7.00-12.00

I am looking for *Little Blue Books*. Haldeman Julius Publications of Girard, Kansas, printed 1,773 different titles in a series called *Little Blue Books*. These books were 3½" by 5" in size and had blue paper covers. The covers are often missing on the books found today. The number of pages may vary from thirty-two to one hundred twenty-eight. *Little Blue Books* sold for five cents and were written by many authors about almost any subject imaginable. When writing please describe your book, its condition, and what you want for it.

Judy Wilson
Flamingo's
10125 River Acres Rd.
Scott, AR 72142

We buy and sell used books. Of particular interest to us are **Thomas Alva Edison and Henry Ford material (especially biographies), any Florida items (especially of the Southwest area), and 'the more-unusual-the-better' items.** Please call or send list for formal bid on individual items or large lots.

We have over 12,000 books in stock. If you have been looking for an out-of-print book, please contact our shop. We have a vast selection on hand and offer a search service. Give us a call and find out why 'Book' is our first name! Dealer and private party inquiries are welcome.

The Book Den South
2249 First St.
Ft. Myers, FL 33901; 813-332-2333

BOTTLES

Before 1900 all bottles were made by hand. These can usually be distinguished from machine-made bottles by looking at the seams on each side.

Seams on a machine-made bottle go from the bottom right up to the top of the lip. If the seam ends lower on the bottle, if there is no seam at all, or if there are perpendicular seams, the bottle is collectible; and I might be interested in purchasing it.

I will consider **almost any type of handmade bottle, except fruit jars and milk bottles**. The most desirable are those which match one or more of the following descriptions:

> Embossed lettering indicating manufacturer and/or product
> Embossed design or picture
> Pontil mark (rough gouge on underside of bottle where glassblowing rod was broken off)
> Free-blown (no seams but with pontil mark)
> Bottles stating Cure or Bitters
> Unusual shape
> Unusual color or shade (most bottles are aqua, clear, green, or amber)

Bottles without any of the characteristics listed are probably of little interest or value, even if they are handmade. Presence of a label adds to the value; presence of contents usually does not. Condition is critical. I will not purchase any bottle with cracks, deep scratches, chips, bruises, or with a condition known as sick glass (a milky haze that will not clean off). Iridescent glass is also not wanted. On the other hand, bubbles or other interesting factory-made imperfections are fine.

Please send a full description with a drawing or photo if possible of whatever you have, one bottle or hundreds. I will respond to all communications. If I don't buy it, I will give you an informal appraisal. The huge variety of collectible bottles makes it hard to estimate prices without seeing a specific item, but the listing below will give a general idea of prices paid. Please note that prices are minimums for the more collectible bottles in each category. The majority in each category bring less – but give me the chance to make an offer in any case. Add at least $10.00 or more for pontiled bottles.

Michael Engel
29 Groveland St.
Easthampton, MA 10127; 413-527-8733

Type	We Pay
Medicine (especially cures)	10.00+
Food or Household, ea	5.00+
Bitters	25.00+
Perfume	10.00+
Whiskey	10.00+
Peppersauce or Pickle (elaborate design), ea	20.00+

We are especially interested in **American-made bottles from before 1900 which feature embossed product names or full labels.** Americans bottled countless products during the 1880s. We are interested in any type of bottle, from food to medicine to alcoholic beverages. These might be clear, amber, aqua, blue, green, or milk glass. No machine-made bottles, please. The prices below are starting prices for the pieces we need; your bottle could easily be worth more to us. Please contact us for prices paid for specific items. Please enclose a SASE for a response. We will also appraise bottles for a fee.

Steve Ketcham
P.O. Box 24114
Edina, MN 55424; 612-920-4205

We Pay

Historical Flasks	**50.00+**
Bitters	**25.00+**
Barber Bottles	**50.00+**
Patent Medicines	**10.00+**
Inks	**10.00+**
Figurals	**25.00+**
Beers	**5.00+**
Whiskeys	**10.00+**
Bar Decanters	**25.00+**
Sodas	**10.00+**
Fruit Jars	**25.00+**
Poisons	**10.00+**
Miniatures	**15.00+**

Wanted: **bottles embossed with city and state or state alone** with no chips or cracks. Advise as to what you have and quantity. Prices paid are listed below.

Krol's Rock City
Star Rt. 2, Box 15A
Deming, NM 88030

We Pay

Milk, round quart, marked any state in circle **5.00**
Druggist, Pharmacy or Apothecary, ea..**2.00**
Hutchinson Soda, any state, ea **5.00**
Whiskey, round, amber, ⅕-size, ea...**3.00-5.00**
Coca-Cola or Pepsi, amber, ea **4.00**
Ink or Poison, old, ea **1.00-5.00**

I buy **perfume bottles from the Victorian era to the 1940s**. Original boxes are a plus. I especially like unusual bottles and Czechoslovakian bottles with figurals. Schiaparelli bottles are purchased also.

The Curiosity Shop
P.O. Box 964
Cheshire, CT 06410; 203-271-0643

BOXES

We collect **Victorian-era boxes which held collars and cuffs; gloves; brush, comb, and mirror sets; shaving sets; neckties; etc. Also photograph and autograph albums are wanted**. The items we collect have lithographs affixed to the front or top of the piece. The lithographic prints usually show scenes or people. We prefer those which show close-up views of children or ladies but will consider others. The print and, in some cases, the entire box or album is covered with a thin layer of clear celluloid. In other instances part of the box or album will be covered with an abstract or floral print paper or colorful velvet material.

We are interested only in pieces in top condition – no cracked celluloid, split seams, or missing hardware. Condition of the interior of the boxes or albums is not as important as condition of the outside. We are not interested in 'French Ivory' celluloid boxes or solid celluloid dresser sets.

Mike & Sherry Miller
303 Holiday Dr.
R.R. 3, Box 130
Tuscola, IL 61953; 217-253-4991

We Pay

Boxes, small	**40.00-75.00**
Boxes, medium	**50.00-100.00**
Boxes, large	**85.00-200.00**
Photograph Albums	**50.00-175.00**
Musical Photograph Albums	**100.00-250.00**
Autograph Albums	**25.00-75.00**

I collect **old ring boxes made of plastic, leather, velvet, metal, etc.,** that usually have a jeweler's name inside the lid. Jewelers also furnished boxes for pins, earrings, necklaces, and bracelets which I am also interested in. I will pay $2.00 and up plus postage for these boxes (depending on age, condition, and material). Even if no jeweler's name appears on the box, I still may be interested if it is unusual or interesting in some way. Please send description, photo, sketch, or photocopy along with asking price. All replies will be answered that include an SASE; otherwise, only those that I am interested in will be answered.

Diane Wilson
P.O. Box 561
Wexford, PA 15090

Down through the ages, boxes and containers have been as useful as they are today. They have been used to hold jewelry, documents, Bibles, sewing needs, candles, desk items, cigars, knives, hats, trinkets, tobacco, tea, sugar, salt, and any other conceivable thing. Small containers were used for snuff, matches, scents, beauty patches, rings, etc. Boxes and containers were made of wood, enamels, bronze, silver, gold, brass, pewter, ivory, porcelain, glass, cloisonne, and any combination thereof.

I am in the market for **nice, old boxes and containers**. I like figurals, enamels, art glass, jewelry boxes, vanity cases, and anything that is well-made, of good quality, unusual, or 'special.' Price range is wide and can go from a few dollars to a few hundred and up depending on the item. Describe carefully, noting any damage, and do include a SASE for reply along with a photo of the item if at all possible.

Betty Bird
107 Ida St.
Mount Shasta, CA 96067

BRONZES

I am buying all bronze figures of people and animals, vases, inkwells and lamps made before 1940. Wanted: single bronzes or an entire collection. The following is a listing of items I am seeking.

Stephen R. Carter
2101 Sheffield Ct.
Mobile, AL 36693; 205-666-1631

We Pay

Statues, 24" or taller	500.00-2,500.00
Statues, 24" or smaller	150.00-1,500.00
Animals, large	500.00-7,500.00
Animals, small	100.00-1,000.00
Vases	50.00-3,500.00
Inkwells w/Figures	100.00-300.00
Rare Items	up to 25,000.00

Collector buying Art Deco and Art Nouveau statues (bronze, bronze and ivory, or marble and bronze) will pay top price for one piece or a collection. Also wanted are articles on decorative bronzes. You may call collect.

Brian Margolis
66 Waterloo St.
Winnipeg, Manitoba
Canada R3N-0S2
204-958-8000 (days) or 204-488-1188 (evenings)

BUFFALO POTTERY

We wish to buy Buffalo pottery: Deldare, Blue Willow, jugs and pitchers, game and fish sets, as well as their advertising and commercial ware. Deldare ware is easily distinguished by the masterful use of hand-tinted scenes on the natural olive-green color of the body of the ware and generally portrays village and hunting scenes. Emerald Deldare, made with the same olive-green body (and generally employing the same body shapes) depicts historical scenes and is highlighted with an Art Nouveau border or decoration. Additionally, Buffalo Pottery produced Blue Willow ware, a series of jugs and pitchers, and served the needs of industry with its fine line of commercial ware for hotels, restaurants, railroads, steamships, and various government agencies. We respond to all offerings by telephone or letter.

Buffalo Pottery

Fred & Lila Schrader
2025 Highway 199 (Hiouchi)
Crescent City, CA 95531; 707-458-3525

Deldare
We Pay

Bowl, 9"	**225.00+**
Candlestick or Candle Holder	**225.00+**
Humidor	**375.00+**
Mug, various sizes	**200.00+**
Pitcher, various sizes	**250.00+**
Tankard	**400.00+**
Teapot, various sizes	**200.00+**
Vase, various styles & sizes	**250.00+**

Pitchers and Jugs
We Pay

Cinderella Jug, w/good gold decoration	**200.00+**
Gloriana, mono- or poly-color	**225.00+**
Geranium Jug, various sizes	**100.00+**
Rip van Winkle	**300.00+**
Roosevelt Bears, various sizes	**300.00**

Blue Willow
We Pay

Cup & Saucer (coffee, tea, or demi)	**10.00+**
Pitcher, various sizes & styles	**75.00+**
Platter, various sizes	**75.00+**
Teapot, Coffeepot, Chocolate Pot, ea.	**85.00+**

Commercial Ware
We Pay

Cup & Saucer, marked 'B&O R.R.'	**50.00+**
Mug, shaving; Wildroot	**40.00+**
Plate, dinner; marked 'R.I.'	**250.00+**
Plate, dinner; World's Fair, 1939	**75.00+**
Teapot & Lid, for Nathan Strauss	**100.00+**

Miscellaneous
We Pay

Canister w/Lid, various sizes	**25.00+**
Child's Feeding Dish, various decor	**50.00+**
Fish Set (platter & 6 plates)	**200.00+**

Pitcher, Gaudy Willow, various sizes ....**200.00+**
Pitcher, Bluebird, various sizes...**45.00+**
Plate, Gaudy Willow, various sizes...**50.00+**
Teapot, w/original infusor..**75.00+**
Turkey Platter, 18x13" ....**250.00+**

BUTTER PATS

We seek to buy butter pats (butter chips) which were used for the presentation of individual servings of butter at the table. These little 3" (more or less) plates can be found in any material (vitrified china, silver, glass, porcelain, ironstone, or ?) that was used in the manufacture of tableware. The butter pats were in popular service in the home during the Victorian era, and their usage began to wane in the early twentieth century. The use of butter pats in commercial service (hotels, restaurants, railroads, etc.) continued well into the second half of this century. The dairy industry began to offer their butter pre-sliced and wrapped, and that spelled the demise of the commercial use of butter pats.

We prefer those domestic butter pats that carry the manufacturer's name. The commercial butter pats (vitrified china or metal) which incorporate the establishment's logo, name, or copyright design on the top or underside are preferred. We respond to all offerings by telephone or letter.

Fred & Lila Shrader
2025 Highway 199 (Hiouchi)
Crescent City, CA 95531; 707-458-3525

Commercial **We Pay**

Boos Bros. (top mark) ....**8.00+**
Churchill Hotel (top mark) **7.00**
Heinz 57 Varieties (top mark)...**15.00**
New England Steamship Co. (top mark) **35.00**
Puerto Rico Lines (top mark)..**10.00**
Pullman (top mark)...**35.00+**
Sea Cave (top mark) ....**12.00+**
The Senator Hotel (top mark) **12.00**
Winged Streamliner (top logo) **12.00**

Domestic **We Pay**

Blue Willow (Buffalo Pottery) **12.00**
Blue Onion (unmarked) **5.00**
Blue Onion (Meissen) ....**18.00+**
Blue Transfer Print (Johnson, Woods, Franciscan) ....**4.00+**
Flow Blue, various patterns..**12.00+**
Haviland, various patterns ....**9.00+**
Limoges, various manufacturers ....**8.00+**
Majolica, figural ....**20.00+**
Majolica, plain ....**12.00+**
Shelley, various shapes & patterns..**20.00+**
Silverplate, various manufacturers ....**9.00+**
Sterling Silver, various manufacturers ....**12.00+**
Tea Leaf, various manufacturers ....**9.00+**

BUTTONS AND BUCKLES

Historically, buttons have been used to hold articles of clothing in place. Buttons range in design from the most simple to exquisitely ornate ones. Materials used in the manufacture of buttons covers an extremely broad spectrum: glass, ceramic, metal, plastic, wood, animal materials, a combination of these, and much more.

We seek to buy older buttons in good to excellent condition. The following represent a sampling of buttons we seek to buy. We respond to all offerings.

Fred & Lila Shrader
2025 Hwy. 199 (Hiouchi)
Crescent City, CA 95531; 707-458-3525

We Pay

Celluloid, various sizes & designs...**1.50+**
China, various sizes & designs ....**1.00+**
Enamel, various sizes & designs...**2.00+**
Glass, black or colored, various sizes & designs.......................................**1.00+**
Glass, kaleidoscopes ....**3.00+**
Glass, Moonglow; various sizes & designs ....**75¢**
Horn & Bone, various sizes & designs...**1.00+**
Pearl & Abalone, various sizes & designs...**1.00+**

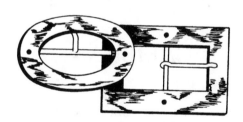

I am interested in purchasing entire contents of **old boxes of buttons, ladies' two-piece dress buckles, ornate shoe buckles, beaded dress trims, elaborate old clothing, etc.** Especially wanted are items with pictorial subjects, unusual construction, or made of materials such as carved horn, pearl, blown glass, etc. Anything is wanted that might be added to my collection or for resale in my vintage button shop. Due to the vast amount of types available, the prices I pay range from as little as 50¢ to as much as $50.00 each. You may ship 'on approval' by your price quote or my offer; or write, describing your item(s).

The Button Lady
E. Gibbons
5153 Plymouth Rd.
Ann Arbor, MI 48105; 313-663-2277

I want to buy beautiful buttons. I prefer handmade or hand-decorated buttons from before 1940. I pay from 50¢ to $12.00 each. Higher prices are paid for those made in the 1800s or before. I would especially like to buy buttons from Civil War uniforms.

Ms. Betty I. Yates
P.O. Box 759
Greeneville, TN 37744-0759

I am a new collector looking for interesting buttons for my collection. Please advise what you have.

Gwen Daniels
18 Belleau Lake Ct.
O'Fallon, MO 63366; 314-281-3190

CAMERAS

I have been buying cameras since 1978 and would like old, quality 35mm cameras such as Nikon, Canon/Sieki, Leitz/Leica, and Zeiss plus stereoscopic '3-D' cameras (with two lenses) such as Stereo Realist, Stereo Wollensack, TDC/Bell & Howell, and others. My View-Master wants are listed elsewhere. Art Deco Kodak cameras, such as the Gift Kodak, colored Folders and Ensembles, Bantam Special, World's Fair, and Scout models are also desired. I buy only wooden movie cameras and only the Polaroid models listed below. I will purchase one item or an entire photo shop; I pay cash and travel if necessary. Please list camera, condition, color, and accessories – I will make offers. A photo and an SASE will help.

Harry Poster
P.O. Box 1883 WB
S Hackensack, NJ 07606

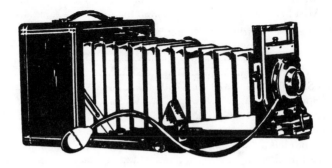

We Pay

Stereo Cameras (Realist, Kodak, Wollensack, Busch, etc.) **50.00-150.00**
Stereoscopic 3-D Slide Viewers (two lenses)....................................**20.00-150.00**
Stereo 3-D Projectors (TDC or Realist w/two lenses) **150.00-650.00**
Early Canon & Nikon Rangefinders..**500.00-5,000.00**
Colored Kodak Folders & Beau Brownies (not black) **25.00-550.00**
Polaroid Models 180, 185, 190, & 195 only **100.00**
Speed Graphics, view cameras, panoramas................................**50.00-2,000.00**
Watch Cameras, motorized, novelty, etc. **50.00-5,000.00**
Dealer Displays or Counter Signs..**Write**

Classic, collectible, and usable cameras are wanted such as Canon, Nikon, Minolta, Leica, Pentax, Fujica, Mamiya, Olympus, Petri, Vivitar, Praktica, Grahplex, Rolleiflex, Yaschica, and others. Prices paid range from ten dollars to thousands for some rare editions of these cameras.

Send list with description of cameras, or call for estimate or information. We **do not** buy Kodak or Polaroid cameras or the modern 'Point and Shoot' auto-focus cameras. We are primarily collectors of cameras of yesteryear that many photographers still prefer and that can be used in the field. We also buy lenses and other accessories. Some examples are listed here with values we pay for cameras in usable condition with lenses.

Gene's Cameras
2603 Artie St. SW, Suite 16
Huntsville, AL 35806; 205-536-6893

We Pay

Canon A-1...**125.00**
Canon AE-1 ....**75.00**

Canon AE-1P **90.00**
Canon AL-1 ....**55.00**
Canon III...**100.00**
Nikon FM **100.00**
Nikon F...**100.00**
Nikon F3 ....**400.00**
Minolta SRT101, 303, X370, or X700 ....**50.00-120.00**
Pentax Spotmatics **40.00-100.00**
Yashicamats 124 or 124G **75.00-125.00**
Olympus OM-1..**90.00**
Leica, all models...**100.00-1,000.00**
Fujicas, all models **40.00-100.00**
Petri Flex **125.00**

CAN OPENERS

     Can openers: the kitchen tools with a cutting-edge blade or slitter that cut open metal cans of vegetables and things like that (no beer can or bottle openers). I am looking for openers that I don't have, complicated or simple, particularly cast iron examples or those that are unique in some manner. Also can opener pictures, photographs, post cards, ads, instructions, etc. are wanted. I would be interested in knowing where the can openers came from and any stories or articles about them as well. Send drawings, copies, or photos first.

Richard M. Bueschel
414 N Prospect Manor Ave.
Mt. Prospect, IL 60056
Phone or FAX 708-253-0791

Can Opener   **We Pay**

Cast Iron, w/patent date & maker name..**35.00+**
Cast Iron, without patent date, w/maker name ....**25.00+**

Cast Iron, without maker, w/patent date ....**15.00+**
Stamped Metal, w/patent & maker, before 1920..**15.00+**
Stamped Metal, without patent, w/maker, before 1920............................**10.00+**
Stamped Metal, without maker, w/patent, before 1920 ....**5.00+**
Any w/intact painted wooden handle (no chips)..**2.50+**
Any w/advertising on handle or elsewhere...**10.00+**

Related Items   We Pay

Advertisement from Magazine, prior to 1920..**5.00+**
Advertisement from Magazine, after 1920...**2.50+**
Display, prior to 1920 ....**5.00+**
Display, after 1920 ....**2.50+**
Instructions ....**5.00+**
Photo, commercial type, showing can opener in use...............................**10.00+**
Photo, snapshot type, showing can opener in use, prior to 1960..............**5.00+**
Post Card, real photo type, showing can opener in any setting...............**15.00+**
Post Card, linen, chrome, or other types, showing can opener in use, ea..**2.50+**

CARNIVAL COLLECTIBLES

Carnival Collectibles

I buy small items from carnival midways, especially chalkware prizes, canes, or items from games. Please send description of item including condition and size.

Tom & Sandy Davis
147 Longleaf Dr.
Blackshear, GA 31516; 912-449-6243

We Pay

Chalkware Items, small	**5.00-15.00**
Chalkware Items, large	**10.00-30.00**
Carnival Canes	**5.00-25.00**
Game Items	**Call or Write**

CARNIVAL GLASS

We are collectors of old carnival glass made circa 1905 through 1930. Some specific items we want are listed below.

John & Sandra Stafford, Sr.
Box 14, 125 E Oak St.
Dalton, WI 53926

We Pay

Book, *Northwood, King of Carnival Glass* ....20.00+
Book, *Millersburg, Queen of Carnival Glass* ....20.00+
Punch Bowl Base, Many Fruits, amethyst (purple) ....**Write**
Punch Cup, Many Fruits, amethyst (purple) ....20.00+
Punch Bowl w/Base, Fashion, marigold ....**Write**

CAST IRON

Collecting **cast iron muffin pans and cast iron broilers** is my passion. To supplement this interest, I also buy, sell, and trade all forms of cast iron cookware. I publish a bimonthly newsletter, *Kettles 'n Cookware*, which covers the full spectrum of cast iron cookware and have had portions of my collection of over two hundred fifty cast iron muffins featured in antique publications nationwide. But no matter what it is, if it's cast iron, I'm interested. I am the 'Pan Man!' The following are examples of prices I will pay.

David G. Smith
P.O. Box B
Perrysburg, NY 14129; 716-523-5154

We Pay

Griswold Wheatstick Pan #2800 ....**500.00**
Griswold Skillet #2 ....**150.00**
Griswold Skillet #13 ....**400.00**

Muffin Pan, heart pattern ....**150.00+**
Griswold Muffin Pan, #10, #11 or #22, ea ....**50.00+**
Wapak Muffin Pan, any **95.00**
G.F. Filley Muffin Pan, #1, #2, #4, or #7, ea ....**150.00+**
Wagner #1 Handled Gem Pan (swirl cups) **250.00**
Waterman Gem Pan, 3-section, any ....**150.00+**
Griswold/Erie Bread Pan, #28, single **450.00**
Griswold/Erie Bread Pan, #26, double **450.00**
Griswold Santa Cake Mold **400.00**

Why does one collect certain things? Appeal, price, appearance – or perhaps it jogs a memory? Is the item something one never had and always wanted? Cast iron evokes many memories from way, way back – when I tripped on the mat under Grandma's parlor stove and broke my mother's doll, to the special star-shaped muffins that were made in my honor.

Needless to say, Waterman, R. & E., and Griswold cast iron pans and molds find a warm welcome at my house. I have a few pieces, but they are neither plentiful nor inexpensive here. This is a bad hobby for a retired person, but I love hearing from other collectors and will answer all letters. Many, many thanks for those received. I have no price knowledge and buy mostly by appeal of the item offered.

My son collects **Greentown chocolate glass in Leaf Bracket and Cactus patterns** (he has more money!) and pays about 50% of book values.

Mrs. Harvey Markley
611 W Beardsley Ave.
Elkhart, IN 46514; 219-522-2135

CATALOGS

I am a doll historian and am looking for primary research material about doll companies. Toy and doll catalogs from any company but especially Ideal, Vogue, American Character, Deluxe Reading, Goldberger, Remco, Uneeda, and Mattel are wanted. Price lists, glossies, store displays, correspondence, *Playthings* magazines, and any other item relating to doll manufacturing would be of interest as well. Also wanted are composition dolls by the Ideal Toy Co. (1907 through 1940s) to buy for my forthcoming book on Ideal dolls.

Judy Izen
208 Follen Rd.
Lexington, MA 02173; 617-862-2994

We Pay

Magazine, *Playthings* ....**20.00+**
Magazine, *Toys & Hobbies* ....**15.00+**
Catalog, any toy company, before 1960 ....**12.00+**
Catalog, any toy company, after 1960 ....**5.00+**
Glossies ....**5.00+**

CHARACTER GLASSES

I buy cartoon and character glasses. I prefer the old, the unusual, and promotional glasses. I will not buy those that are faded or glasses that have been washed in a dishwasher. I also prefer that all the design be within the borders. A sampling of glasses on my want list follows.

Any Wizard of Oz   Al Capp
Older Disney   Jungle Book
Dick Tracy   Canadian Glasses

Sharon Burwash
P.O. Box 2723
West Lafayette, IN 47906

CHILDREN'S DISHES

We buy children's dishes and have special interest in baby plates or sets in good to excellent condition only.

Gary Reed
P.O. Box 342
Fenton, MO 63026

We Pay

Children's Dishes 25.00-1,000.00

CHINA

'Chintz' is the generic name for English china with an allover floral transfer design. This eye-catching china is reminiscent of chintz dress fabric. It is colorful, bright and cheery with its many floral designs and reminds one of an English garden in full bloom. It was produced in England during the first half of this century and stands out among other styles of china. I am interested in **'Chintz' pieces made by Royal Winton, Grimwades, James Kent, Lord Nelson Ware, and Crown Ducal,** among others. Pattern names often found with the manufacturer's name on the bottom of pieces include Anemone, Chelsea, Chintz, Delphinium Chintz, June Roses, Mayfair, Hazel, Eversham, Royalty, Sweet Pea, Summertime, Springtime, and Welbeck, among others.

I am interested in buying individual pieces or complete breakfast, luncheon, or tea sets. Prices vary depending on pattern and manufacturer. All pieces must be in perfect condition, no chips, cracks, crazing, or other damage. I buy all English 'Chintz' pieces and am especially interested in teapots, toast racks, pitchers, wash sets, and other large or unusual pieces. Items of interest are listed here. I hope you tell me about any 'Chintz' china you have for sale.

Biscuit Jars	Jam Jars
Breakfast Sets	Jardineres
Butter Pats	Loving Cups
Candlesticks	Musical Boxes
Candy Dishes	Salt & Pepper Shakers
Cheese Dishes	Sugar & Creamers
Comports	Teapots (all sizes)
Condiment Sets	Toast Racks
Cruets (on stands)	Toilet Sets
Cups & Saucers	Trays
Egg Cups	Vanity Items
Fruit Bowls	Vases
Humidors	Wall Pockets

Marjorie Geddes
P.O Box 5875
Aloha, OR 97007; 503-649-1041

I am buying any old **Haviland** dishes or pottery. I am interested mostly in factory-decorated pieces with flowery designs. Also wanted is **Copeland-Spode 'Mayflower' and Aynsley 'Wild Violets'** china patterns. Examples of prices paid are given here; top prices will be paid for unusual pieces.

Susan Correa
12636 Shirley St.
Omaha, NE 68144
731-8226 or 402-333-7425

Haviland   We Pay

Salt Dip	20.00
Dinner Plate	8.00+
Chocolate Pot	75.00+
Chocolate Cup & Saucer	18.00
Unusual Pieces	**Write or Call**

Copeland-Spode, Mayflower 2/8777   We Pay

Cream Soup, w/handles & underplate, set	30.00
Butter Pat	18.00

Dinner Plate...**20.00**
Fruit Dish **18.00**
Rimmed Soup..**20.00**
Cup & Saucer, set **25.00**
Unusual Pieces ....**Write or Call**

Aynsley **We Pay**

Any Wild Violets Pattern ....**Top Prices**

CHRISTMAS

We want to buy all types of old Christmas items from the 1880s through the 1950s! We buy figural Christmas tree light bulbs, old German figural glass ornaments, German feather trees, old Santas, Belsnickles, cotton batting ornaments, early Santa Claus cookbooks, old light sets in original boxes, bubble light trees, bubble lights, German nativity sets, German stick-leg animals, celluloid figures and toys, lithograph scrap ornaments, papier-mache items and candy containers, hard plastic Santas and toys from the 1940s and 1950s, all types of lighted decorations, and any other unusual old Christmas item. Sample prices are listed. We will answer all letters.

Bob & Diane Kubicki
P.O. Box 33059
W.P.A.F.B., OH 45433; 513-698-3650

We Pay

Belsnickle, German, 8"	250.00-450.00
Bubble Light Santa, plastic	15.00
Bubble Light Tree, green, 18-socket	100.00+
Clockworks Nodder Father Christmas	1,500.00+
Feather Tree, green, 6-foot	300.00+
Lamp, Santa on glass chimney w/black glass base	500.00
Light Bulb, standing figural Indian	250.00+
Light Bulb, green figural Father Christmas	100.00+
Light Bulb, figural Uncle Sam	300.00+
Light Set, early 1920s, boxed	10.00+
Nativity Set, German	35.00-75.00
Ornament, Indian head, German, old glass	125.00+
Ornament, figural cotton girl w/scrap face	75.00+
Ornament, spun cotton fruit, 3"	15.00+
Santa Claus Storybook, 1905	20.00+
Santa, German, w/rabbit fur beard, 8"	200.00+

I am buying **figural Christmas lights.** I am especially looking for clear glass lights with screw bases. I am also looking for milk glass varieties which are unusual. Animals and people are some of the more desirable forms. I am also looking to buy other old Christmas and Halloween items.

Cindy Chipps
4027 Brooks Hill Rd.
Brooks, KY 40109; 502-955-9238

We Pay

Airplane	100.00
Train	100.00
Army Tank	100.00
Soldier & Sailors	110.00
Christmas Tree	100.00
Indian Head	75.00
Howdy Doody Figures	100.00+
Popeye Figures	120.00+

CIGAR BOX LABELS AND

SAMPLE BOOKS

    I am looking for cigar box labels and cigar boxes with a nice label inside the top lid. The approximate size of most inner labels is 6" x 9". The approximate size of most outer labels is 4" x 4". Outer labels are wanted but are not as desirable as the inner labels.

    Here are some themes I particularly seek on these labels and/or boxes:

        Sporting Events
        Scenes of Everyday Life Showing People

Public Service Scenes (firemen, mailmen, policemen, etc.)
Animals Portrayed in Human Roles
Transportation
Humorous Situations or Satire
Weird Situations or Themes
Naughty Women, Nudes, Bathing Beauties, etc.
Women Portrayed in Traditional Men's Roles
Men's Clubs, Gambling, Pool or Card Playing, etc.
Indians, Cowboys, Mining, or Western Themes
Outdoor Scenes (skiing, sledding, fishing, etc.)
Patriotic Themes
Military Leaders, Battles, etc.
Health Claims, Patent Medicines, etc.
Cartoon Characters
Political Candidates

Salesmen's sample books and proof labels are also wanted. Proof labels have alignment lines on them, and some have color bars. I am not interested in the common labels that are available by mail from other dealers; however I may be interested in original packages of labels that are still in factory bundles. I am not interested in cigar bands, unless they have a nice picture on them. Please send photocopies if possible.

David M. Beach
Paper Americana
P.O. Box 2026
Goldenrod, FL 32733
407-657-7403 or FAX 407-657-6382

We Pay

Sample Labels, depending on subject, ea **3.00-50.00**
Cigar Boxes, w/inner lid label, ea **3.00-50.00**

CLOCKS

I buy **antique clocks, especially clocks made before 1890** – single pieces or entire collections. Traveling a distance to view a collection is not a problem. Send photos or call 1-800-277-5275. Below are prices for clocks in original mint condition.

Mark of Time
P.O. Box 15351
Sarasota, FL 34277-1351

We Pay

Welch, Spring & Co.	up to 800.00
S.B. Terry	up to 1,000.00
Eli Terry	up to 2,000.00
English Weight-Driven Wall Clocks	up to 4,500.00
American Weight-Driven Wall Clocks	up to 3,000.00
German Weight-Driven Wall Clocks	up to 3,000.00
English Grandfather Clocks	up to 4,000.00
American Grandfather Clocks	up to 7,000.00
Brewster & Ingrahams	up to 500.00
Fancy Repeating Carriage Clocks	up to 1,000.00
Porcelain-Paneled Carriage Clocks	up to 2,000.00
Ansonia Royal Bonn China Clocks	up to 600.00
Calendar Clocks	up to 2,500.00
Sterling Silver Clocks	up to 600.00
Miniature Clocks	up to 1,000.00
Florence Kroeber	up to 600.00
Ansonia	up to 2,000.00
Seth Thomas	up to 4,000.00
Waterbury	up to 1,500.00

French Statue Clocks...up to 1,500.00
American Fusee Clocks..up to 2,000.00
English Fusee Clocks...up to 2,500.00

———————————————

Collector wants **early weight banjo timepiece clocks and Ithaca and other-maker double-dial calendar clocks**. Also wanted are **cast iron blinking-eye clocks**. Examples of these would be Black man or woman, lion, king sitting on beer keg, elf, dog, etc. Incomplete and non-working, broken examples are wanted also.

Dr. 'Z'
1350 Kirts, Suite #160
Troy, MI 48084; 313-244-9426

We Pay

Banjo Clocks..500.00-3,000.00
Calendar Double-Dial Clocks 500.00-5,000.00
Cast Iron Blinking-Eye Clocks....................................250.00-5,000.00

———————————————

COCA-COLA

I have been collecting Coca-Cola memorabilia since 1975. I collect almost anything made prior to 1969 when the current 'dynamic swirl' logo was introduced. I do not collect ordinary 'hobble skirt' bottles or newspaper or magazine ads. I'm always interested in items in near-mint or mint condition (free of rust, pitting, creases, fading, etc.) such as trays, calendars before 1960, toy cars or trucks, salesman's samples, cartons, small signs, syrup jugs or bottles, thermometers, clocks, and more! I am looking for a straight-sided clear or amber bottle from New Decatur, Alabama, embossed 'Buchheit Bottling Works' with the script Coco-Cola logo.

Please send full description of anything you have for sale along with a photo if possible. Include a stamp for reply. No reproductions wanted!

Terry Buchheit
Rt. 7, Box 62
Perryville, MO 63775

We Pay

Ashtray/Match Holder, 1930-40	**100.00**
Ashtray, 1950s, holds figural bottle lighter or book matches	**35.00**
Bottle, 'Seltzer' w/script logo	**85.00**
Bottle, 'Seltzer' w/etched logo	**100.00**
6-Pack, w/glass bottles, miniature	**25.00**
6-Pack Display Rack, 1930s	**75.00**
Cardboard Carton, 1920s	**40.00**
Cardboard Carton, 1931, shows Santa	**75.00**
Carton, 1940, holds 4 bottles	**30.00**
Cigarette Box, 1936, 50th Anniversary, frosted glass	**100.00**
Salesman's Sample Counter Dispenser, 1960s	**300.00**
Salesman's Sample Cooler, Glascock, 1929	**800.00**
Straws, complete box, 1940s	**50.00**
Syrup Can, 1930s, 1-gal size w/paper label	**40.00**

Playing Card Deck　　　　　　　　　　　　　　　　　　**We Pay**

Any Dated 1939	**70.00**
Nurse, 1943	**25.00**
Operator, 1943	**25.00**
Dancers, 1943	**40.00**

Toy　　　　　　　　　　　　　　　　　　　　　　　　　**We Pay**

Dispenser Bank, 1950s	**100.00**
Dispenser Bank, 1960s	**25.00**
Shopping Basket, 1950s	**75.00**
Stove, child's size, metal	**200.00**
Truck, metal	**up to 200.00**

Tray	We Pay
1910	200.00
1913	200.00
1920	200.00
1921	200.00
1922	200.00
1923	175.00
1924	200.00
1925	150.00
1926	150.00
1929	100.00
1932	125.00
1935	100.00

Vending Machine	We Pay
Cavalier Model 27	350.00
Jacobs Model 26	300.00
Lyons (of New York) Model 500	500.00
Mills Model 400C	100.00
Vendo Model 44	1,000.00
Vendo Model 56	200.00
Vendorlator Model 27	350.00

_____

COFFIN PLATES

The most desirable metal coffin plates are those with elaborate designs (e.g., trees, flowers, and other symbols of grief or new life), and personalized writing – especially name and age or date. Small coffin plates that say 'Our Darling' are common and so are those that say 'At Rest,' 'Mother,' or 'Father.' A rubbing, xerographic copy, or photo would be appreciated. The following are typical prices I will pay for metal coffin plates in reasonable condition (not rusted, but a little tarnish is okay).

Adrienne S. Escoe
4448 Ironwood Ave.
Seal Beach, CA 90740; 310-430-6479

We Pay

'Our Darling,' 4 to 4½" **3.00-5.00**
'At Rest Mother' or 'Father,' w/good border design, ea........................**5.00-7.50**
Personalized, plain border **5.00-7.50**
Personalized, elaborate border **7.50-10.00**

COIN-OPERATED MACHINES

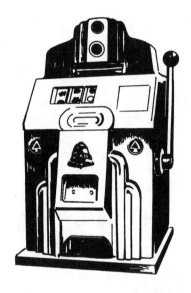

   Slot machines, introduced in San Francisco about 1890, are any machine with a coin slot that involves gambling or speculation. They pay out in either money or tokens. The 1930s and 1940s were the golden years when most bars, gas stations, grocery stores, clubs, and private organizations had them in plain sight for all to play. Throughout most of history, they were illegal except for casinos. Today, ownership is legal in about half of the states – provided they are not used for gambling or illegal purposes.
   The early machines nearly all had wood cases. They came in floor mod-

els as well as counter-top styles. The next type were made of cast metal. Then came the metal fronts and wood sides. The electronic machines are illegal in nearly all states.

There are many others wanted besides the ones listed here, so send photo for information.

Arcade machines used to be in all the penny arcades. They were found by the boardwalks along the shores and were made for amusement only. We all remember the fortuneteller that could move and give you your fortune on a card and the diggers that for a nickle you could maneuver and try to grab a prize with. There were all types of machines to try your strength and some that by turning the crank would flip cards around so fast that they seemed to make movies. Arcade machines were found in amusement parks and carnivals, too. I collect these remembrances of my happy youth.

Thomas J. McDonald
2 Ski Dr.
Neshanic Station, NJ 08853

Arcade Machine	We Pay
Diggers	1,000.00+
Floor Model Fortunetellers (w/figure)	2,000.00+
Mutoscope, cast iron	1,500.00+
Mutoscope, counter-top type, tin or light metal	500.00+
Self-Playing Banjo (coin operated)	5,000.00+
Violin Virtuoso	7,500.00+
Electric Energizer (Spear the Dragon)	1,500.00+
Lion Lung Tester	1,000.00+
Quartoscope (Mills Novelty Co.)	1,500.00+
Owl Lifter (Mills Novelty Co.)	750.00+
The Illusion (how you will become skeleton)	1,000.00+
Harvard Stamper (dispenses tokens)	750.00+
1937 World Series (Rock-Ola Mfg. Co.)	1,500.00+
Play Golf (Chester Pollard Amusement Co.)	1,000.00+
Play the Derby (Pollard)	1,500.00+

Slot Machine	We Pay
Floor Models, wood, 1890-1910	3,000.00+
Counter-Top Models, wood	2,000.00+
Cast Iron Machines, 1910-20	1,500.00+
Average Mills or Jennings, 1920-60	750.00+
Bonus Machines	1,000.00
Baseball Vendor Bell	1,000.00+
Jennings & Mills Golf Ball Vendors	2,000.00
Fey Liberty Bell	50,000.00+

Coin-Operated Machines

Buckley Bones (dice slot machine) ....**3,000.00+**
Bally Spark Plug (horse race slot) ....**2,500.00+**
Mills Futurity, w/counter...**2,000.00+**
Rol-A-Top (Watling Mfg. Co.)..**2,500.00+**

I am a private collector interested in buying **all types of arcade and coin-operated machines in any condition**. Below is a partial listing of items I am looking to purchase. I am also paying finder's fees for assistance in finding these items. Please write or call with your information.

John S. Zuk
666 Plainfield Ave.
Berkeley Heights, NJ 07922

We Pay

Wurlitzer 1015 Jukeboxes...**5,000.00+**
Other Jukeboxes (78rpm & 45rpm)...**500.00+**
Pre-1940 Slot Machines..**900.00+**
Trade Stimulators ....**100.00+**
Gumball Machines...**25.00+**
Pinball Machines ....**100.00+**
Games of Skill..**75.00+**
Player Pianos..**500.00+**
Mills Violano Virtuoso (Coin-Op Violin/Piano)................................**5,000.00+**
Antique (Tube) Radios...**50.00+**

I am interested in buying **all types of coin-operated machines** including slot machines, trade stimulators, vending machines, and skill games. My special interest is pinball machines from the early 1930s. Very early games sat on counter tops, and you simply shot marbles into holes and counted your score. These evolved to include legs and intricate mechanisms to make the games more interesting. Some used batteries to operate devices that gave the balls more action or to pay out coins to skillful players. I pay at least $100.00 for games that are complete and in good working condition. Listed below are some of the prices I will pay for only a few of the more desirable games. Let me know what you have. I also buy games that are rough or incomplete and related advertising and paper items.

I buy certain later pinballs and parts and related items from all later machines. These include back glasses, play boards, advertising material, instruction books, photographs, etc.

Hal O'Rourke
Box 47
Lanexa, VA 23089; 804-966-2278

We Pay

Bingo	**150.00**
Baffle Ball	**200.00**
Ballyhoo	**200.00**
Blue Seal	**250.00**
Five Star Final	**200.00**
Jigsaw (World's Fair)	**600.00**
Register	**300.00**
Official Baseball	**400.00**
World's Series	**500.00**
Games That Pay Out Coins	**200.00+**
Later Pinball Back Glasses	**25.00-100.00**
Play Boards	**10.00-50.00**
Instruction Books	**1.00-5.00**

Other Coin Machines

We Pay

Mills Slot Machines	**500.00-1,500.00**
Jennings Slot Machines	**1,000.00+**
Watling Slot Machines	**1,000.00-4,000.00+**
Trade Stimulators	**100.00-500.00**
Skill Games	**100.00-500.00**

Trade stimulators are counter-top games of chance that do not have an automatic payout. There is an endless variety of spinning wheels of fortune, five-reel poker games, roulette, or dice (single, two-reel, three-reel, or five-reel with fruit or other symbols). Dating from about 1890, they were simple mechanisms since there were no payouts. They started in cigar stores and spread to all types of businesses. The name 'trade stimulator' came from the idea that the merchant hoped you would use your change to play his game. Trade stimulators started to vanish from the market after World War II. During the war, the popular theme was to destroy Hitler, Mussolini, or Tojo; shoot down planes; or bomb ships. The possibility of types of trade stimulators that exist is endless. They have never been a large collectible item, since most collectors preferred slots.

There are many others than the ones listed here that are worth $75.00 to $200.00. I am also looking for all machines made by Clawson Machine Co., of Newark, New Jersey. These machines were made locally and within sight of my home; there is little known about the company or its owner.

Thomas J. McDonald
2 Ski Dr.
Neshanic Station, NJ 08853-9314

We Pay

Horse Race (Seeburg Corp.)	**1,000.00+**
Spark Plug (Bally Mfg.)	**1,500.00+**
Races (Superior Confection Co.)	**2,000.00+**
Rockola Sweepstakes (gum dispenser)	**1,000.00+**
Little Roulette (Caille Brothers)	**3,000.00+**
Domino (Domino Co.)	**2,000.00+**
Little Chief (Charles Fly	**3,500.00+**
Totem (Watling Mfg. Co.)	**2,500.00+**
Square Deal Gum Vendor (Mills Novelty Co.)	**1,500.00+**
The Duo (Charles Fly)	**3,500.00+**
Three Jackpots (Clawson Machine Co.)	**1,000.00+**
The Elk (Paupa & Hochreim)	**2,000.00+**
Play Ball (Caille Bros.)	**2,000.00+**
Automatic Dice (Clawson Machine Co.)	**1,500.00+**
Crap Shooters Delight (F.A. Ruff Co.)	**1,000.00+**
Wizard Clock (Wm. M. White Co.)	**500.00+**
Little Monte Carlo (Mills Novelty Co.)	**1,500.00+**
Lively Cigar Sellers (Clawson Machine Co.)	**500.00+**
The Bicycle (Waddell Wooden Ware Works)	**1,000.00+**
21 Vender (Groetchen Tool Co.)	**350.00+**
Baby Vender (Southern Doll Mfg. Co.)	**400.00+**

COINS

Please send a photo and description – along with condition of coin(s), or send us the coin(s), insured for your protection. We will inspect the coin(s) and make you an offer. If you accept, we will mail you a check. If you do not accept our offer, we will mail back your coin(s) at our expense. Premium prices will be paid for mint, uncirculated coins, rare dates, and low mintages.

Lor-Wal-Weisburd
Antiques-Collectibles
P.O. Box 142
South Jamesport, NY 11970; 516-722-4829

We Pay

Ancient Bronze, Roman or Greek ....3.00-100.00+
Ancient Silver, Roman or Greek ....10.00-200.00+
Ancient Gold, Roman or Greek ....50.00-500.00+
USA $1 to $5 Gold Pieces ....85.00-250.00+
USA $10 Gold Pieces..150.00-500.00+
USA $20 Gold Pieces..300.00-750.00+

COMIC BOOKS

Wanted are any old comic books. They must be in very good condition. Also of interest are **sports collectibles of all kinds** such as post cards, stamps, coins – nearly anything!

Windmill Antiques
315 SW 77th Ave.
N Lauderdale, FL 33068

We Pay

Action Comics #2...300.00+
All Star Comics #1 ....300.00+

Fantastic Four #4 ....50.00+
Captain America #1 ....500.00+
Batman #2 ....300.00+
Superman #5 ....100.00+
The X-Men #1 ....50.00+

I am interested in a little nostalgia, so I am trying to obtain a comic book (or books) from my pre-school days. I would like to obtain one of the comic books titled *Famous Funnies* from the '30s which are now considered collector items, as are the other comics of that era.

My interest in obtaining one of these is purely for my own enjoyment, and I am not concerned about its condition, since I am not a collector and am not interested in reselling. I would prefer one with a cover, but this is not absolutely necessary.

I am basically looking for books that are readable and thus enjoyable. But they don't have to be in a 'normally saleable' condition. Do you have such a copy that might be available for $10.00 or so? If none are available except one in good condition (which would thus be more valuable), I would still welcome it at a reasonable price.

Bob Arriola
4130 Opal Cliff Dr.
Santa Cruz, CA 95062; 408-475-3950

COMIC STRIP ART

Sunday newspaper comics are wanted. Color comics were introduced in the 1890s and continue to the present. I am interested in fine quality pages from bound library volumes, complete comic sections, individual titles, collections, etc. Some prices are noted below, or you may send for a detailed list.

David H. Begin
138 Lansberry Ct.
Los Gatos, CA 95032

We Pay

Buck Rogers, full page, 1930-35	4.00
Flash Gordon, full page, 1934	10.00
Flash Gordon, half page, 1950s	50¢
Yellow Kid, full page, 1890s	100.00
Prince Valiant, full page, 1937	75.00
Prince Valiant, full page, 1937-70	1.00-6.00
Archie, tab, 1946	1.00
Katzenjammer Kids, 1900-02	4.00
Katzenjammer Kids, 1905-09	2.00
Little Nemo, 1905-14	10.00

COMPACTS

We collect ladies' compacts which are in the shape of other objects (figural compacts). We are also very interested in compacts and mesh purse combinations. Some of the manufacturers of these pieces were: Whiting & Davis Co., Napier-Bliss, Evans, R&G Co., and F&B Co.

Only mint or near-mint pieces will be considered. Highest prices are paid for compacts in mint condition complete with puff and original box. Sometimes the mirror will be discolored from age, but that usually does not detract from the compact's desirability.

Below are some of the figural compacts we are seeking for our collection. There are many other figural compacts and mesh vanities not listed that we would also like to find.

Sherry & Mike Miller
303 Holiday Dr.
R.R. 3, Box 130
Tuscola, IL 61953; 217-253-4991

We Pay

Air Balloon	125.00-150.00
Artist's Palatte, by Volupte	75.00-100.00
Beetle	125.00-150.00
Brass Ball w/Dice	60.00-80.00
Camera, by Fillkwik	45.00-60.00
Cigarette Lighter, by Dunhill	75.00-100.00
Coin, by Elgin	125.00-150.00
Cowboy Hat	125.00-150.00
Crown, by Stratton	60.00-80.00
Drum, by Charbert	125.00-150.00
Eight Ball	60.00-80.00
Fan, by Wadsworth	45.00-60.00
Flower Basket, by Zell	60.00-80.00
Guitar, by Samaral	125.00-150.00
Hat	75.00-100.00
Lincoln Penny, by Avon	150.00-200.00
Military Cap	35.00-50.00
Monkey, by Shuco	125.00-150.00
Padlock	45.00-60.00

Piano, by Pygmalion	**125.00-150.00**
Roulette Wheel	**60.00-80.00**
Suitcase	**100.00-125.00**
Vanity Table, by Volupte	**125.00-150.00**
Watch, by Volupte	**35,00-50.00**

Vanity Compact Bags   We Pay

Whiting & Davis Co.	**160.00-450.00**
R&G Co.	**300.00-500.00**

I am interested in buying ladies' vintage compacts for my own personal collection as well as for trade and resale. I am primarily interested in compacts that are odd shaped. For example: pianos, guitars, teddy bears, fans, and monkey forms would be of interest. I can pay $20.00 to $50.00 for these depending on the particular item. I am also interested in boxed sets with a compact and matching jewelry, which is usually a locket or bracelet. These would have a value of $30.00 and up. All must be in excellent condition with little or no wear and have the original puff. Scenic enameled compacts are also wanted. The enamel must not be damaged. I am also buying Stratton and Stratnoid compacts with scenic designs.

Elizabeth Baer
P.O. Box 266
Perry, IA 50220

Compact   We Pay

Figural	**20.00-50.00**
Bracelet Type	**20.00-50.00**
Boxed Set	**30.00+**
Stratton & Stratnoid	**15.00-20.00**

I buy ladies' compacts from the Victorian era to the 1940s. I especially like compacts that are in the shape of something else, such as pianos, hot air balloons, guitars, chairs, vanity tables, cats, roulette tables, etc. I also pay good prices for compacts that are combined with mesh bags. These are usually Victorian up to the 1930s or '40s and are obviously part of the frame or bag, attached to the bag in some way. I also buy unusual celluloid or Bakelite compacts. If a compact is old and unusual, I'm probably interested. I prefer those in only the best condition but also buy 'as is' and pay accordingly.

The Curiosity Shop
P.O. Box 964
Cheshire, CT 06410; 203-271-0643

We Pay

Compacts, in the shape of something else ....75.00+
Compacts, as part of mesh bags...150.00+
Compacts, w/enameling ....45.00+
Compacts, celluloid or Bakelite ....65.00+

I am buying unusual ladies' compacts, colorful Art Deco vanity cases, mesh and beaded purse combination compacts, any gadgety or novelty compacts (in the shape of suitcases, military hats, hands, telephone dials, belt buckles, 8-ball, lady bug, walnut, gun, working camera by Kigu, etc.). Compacts relating to movies such as *The Wizard of Oz* or movie stars such as Shirley Temple are wanted. Automobile-related compacts, Christmas theme, musical and bracelet types, vanities by Volupte among other foreign and novelty types are wanted as well. Compacts must be in good to mint condition; but I have chains and may have mirrors replaced. Prices paid are $40.00 and up, depending on rarity.

Lori Landgrebe
2331 E Main St.
Decatur, IL 62521; 217-423-2254

COOKBOOKS

I am buying cookbooks. I prefer softcover cookbooks, recipe booklets, pamphlets, leaflets, recipe cards, etc. (such as Betty Crocker, Pillsbury, Jell-O, flour companies, cereals, milk, gelatin, canning, bread, shortening, etc.). Pre-1960 items are preferred, but I will consider all. Please send your information listing the title, author, year of publication, and type (i.e., pamphlet, card, etc.).

C. Erling
285 Wilbur Cross Hwy.
Suite #128
Kensington, CT 06037

We Pay

Leaflets ....**50¢+**
Recipe Cards ....**25¢+**
Booklets...**1.00+**
Pamphlets...**75¢+**
Softcover ....**2.00+**
Pillsbury Bake-Off...**3.00+**

I am looking for a Fire-King cookbook that was put out in 1944. The front cover is a plaid-like design with pictures of Fire-King dishes. The back cover has pictures of the actors from the 'Meet Corlis Archer' radio show.

I am also looking for a couple of Pyrex cookbooks. One is dated 1924 and has recipes prepared by Alice Bradley of Farmer's School of Cookery at Boston. The front cover has a picture of a small child wearing an apron and a baker's hat in front of a large glass casserole with the word 'Pyrex' in a curved banner across the top of the book. The other 1920s Pyrex cookbook is titled 'Pyrex Ovenware for Baking and Serving.' The cover shows double pictures, one of a lady taking a dish from the oven and the other of three people eating at a dining table.

Darlene Nossaman
5419 Lake Charles
Waco, TX 76710

We Pay

1944, Fire-King...**6.00**
1924, Pyrex...**8.00**
1920s, Pyrex, 'Pyrex Ovenware for Baking & Serving' **8.00**

COOKIE JARS

Wanted: 1950s-80s figural pottery cookie jars and matching accessories such as salt and peppers, lamps, banks, ironing sprinkler bottles, string holders, and wall pockets. I'm especially interested in those items which depict Disney characters, Black mammys, chefs, and comic and cartoon characters. Personality-related items of any kind are wanted. Below are but a few examples. I will buy any unusual cookie jar – one or an entire collection.

Judy Posner
R.D. #1, Box 273 WB
Effort, PA 18330; 717-629-6583

We Pay

Woody Woodpecker in Birdhouse Cookie Jar **150.00**
Snow White Kneeling w/Bird Cookie Jar...**250.00**
Laurel & Hardy Cookie Jar **200.00**
Superman Cookie Jar **200.00**
Elsie the Cow Lamp **100.00**
Disney Uncle Scrooge Bank...**300.00**
Betty Boop String Holder...**150.00**
Black Butler Salt & Pepper Shakers **150.00**
Basket Handle Black Mammy Cookie Jar..**300.00**
Fred & Wilma Flintstone Bank..**125.00**
Brayton Pottery Peasant Woman Cookie Jar (various styles) **150.00**

I am a collector interested in old and new cookie jars. I particularly like jars made by Abingdon, American Bisque, Brush, Hull, and Regal. The following are examples of prices that I am willing to pay for jars in excellent condition. (I will consider rarer jars with minor damage.) Prices will be higher for jars trimmed in gold. There are many other jars not listed that I am interested in adding to my collection; I can quote you a price on these. I also will consider buying lids and bottoms. If you are not certain of what you have, call or send a photo.

Debbie Yates
P.O. Box 1461
Decatur, GA 30031-1461; 404-377-5145

Abingdon   **We Pay**

Witch **175.00**
Pumpkin **165.00**

Advertising   **We Pay**

Elsie the Cow..**150.00**
Ken-L-Ration Dog..**65.00**

American Bisque   **We Pay**

Elephant w/Baseball Cap or Sailor Elephant, ea **55.00**
Cow Jumped Over Moon Flasher **175.00**
Davy Crockett in Woods **225.00**

Cookie Jars

Mohawk Indian	245.00
Dog w/Toothache	150.00
Any Flintstone (Fred, Wilma, Dino, Rubble House), ea	350.00
Rudolph the Red-Nosed Reindeer	150.00
Sea Bag or Dutch Shoe, ea	95.00
Little Audry	600.00

Brush
We Pay

Formal Pig w/Gold Trim	225.00
Elephant w/Ice Cream Cone	150.00
Peter Pan	200.00
Little Boy Blue	200.00
Little Red Riding Hood	200.00
Fish	150.00
Humpty Dumpty	135.00

Hull
We Pay

Little Red Riding Hood w/Sunflowers on Skirt	200.00
Little Red Riding Hood w/Red-Trimmed Skirt & Stars on Apron	300.00

McCoy
We Pay

Tony Veller	125.00
Dalmations in Rocking Chair	225.00
Apollo	500.00
Stagecoach	350.00
Astronauts	300.00
Uncle Sam's Hat	90.00
Coalby Cat	150.00

Metlox
We Pay

Pinocchio	150.00
Little Red Riding Hood	175.00
Pink Rose	95.00

Miscellaneous
We Pay

Kliban Cat	75.00
Star Wars C3PO	135.00

Red Wing

We Pay

Chef, pink or green, ea **95.00**
King of Tarts **180.00**

Regal

We Pay

Mary Had a Little Lamb **185.00**
Peek-A-Boo Bunny **425.00**
Hubert the Lion **325.00**
Davy Crockett **225.00**

Robinson Ransbottom

We Pay

Cow Over Moon w/Gold Trim **175.00**

Walt Disney

We Pay

Alice in Wonderland, Regal China **650.00**
Snow White **225.00**
Mary Poppins **115.00**
Donald Duck w/Pumpkin **125.00**
Mickey on Drum **125.00**
Bambi, California Originals **175.00**
Pinocchio Hugging Knees, California Originals **175.00**
Pinocchio w/Fishbowl **225.00**
Mickey on Birthday Cake **150.00**

I am interested in cookie jars – originals only, in good condition. I prefer Black, character, or advertising jars as well as any old or unusual jar.

Gene A. Underwood
909 N Sierra Bonita Ave., Apt. 9
Los Angeles, CA 90046-6562; 213-850-6276

Mammy Jars by

We Pay

Brayton ....**150.00+**
Brayton Polka Dot ....**150.00+**
Pearl China ....**250.00+**
Mosaic Tile ....**250.00+**

Cookie Jars

National Silver	125.00
Weller	250.00+
Gilner	250.00+
Metlox	90.00+

Other Jars **We Pay**

Mammy or Butler, basket handle, ea.	250.00+
Topsy, Metlox	85.00+
Black Santa	100.00+
Elephant w/Baby Hat, Brush	100.00
Cow w/Cat, Brush	70.00
Dalmations, McCoy	150.00
Peek-A-Boo, Regal China	200.00+
Joe Carioca, Walt Disney	125.00
Professor Ludwig Von Drake, American Bisque	150.00+
Popeye, U.S.A.	250.00+
Olive Oyl, U.S.A.	250.00+

I buy cookie jars made between the 1930s and 1960s. Most are figural, such as animals, cartoon characters, nursery rhyme characters, Black figures, etc. If possible, send photo and state condition in detail. Enclose SASE for reply.

Kier Linn
2591 Military Ave.
Los Angeles, CA 90064; 310-477-5229

We Pay

Flintstones (any by American Bisque)	400.00-600.00
Popeye, w/hole for pipe	500.00
Swee' Pea	500.00
Peek-a-Boo	500.00
Davy Crockett	100.00
Hippo w/Monkey, Brush	150.00
Teepee, McCoy	125.00
Globe, McCoy	125.00

I'm buying cookie jars. Almost everyone has one – and I want yours. I prefer the figural cookie jars but will buy all kinds. Over the last year, elephants and pigs have become my favorites, and premiums will be paid on certain ones I don't have.

Many cookie jars had accessories such as salt and pepper shakers. These items are wanted, too. Once again, elephants and pigs are my favorites.

All items must be perfect – no cracks or chips. I will buy some with defects but will pay considerably less for them. I will buy one item or a whole collection. When writing, enclose a photograph and list any name, word, or number on the item. Give a price and a phone number where you may be reached.

James Goad
1152A S Eagle Circle
Aurora, CO 80012; 303-745-7068

We Pay

Black Figural Jars	30.00+
Elephant Figural Jars	20.00+
Pig Figural Jars	20.00+
Miscellaneous Figural Jars	10.00+
Glass Jars	5.00+
Miscellaneous Jars	5.00+
Black Figural Salt & Pepper Shakers	5.00+
Elephant Figural Salt & Pepper Shakers	5.00+
Pig Figural Salt & Pepper Shakers	5.00+
Miscellaneous Salt & Pepper Shakers	1.00+

COTTAGE WARE

I'm looking for kitchen items modeled like little English cottages. The ones I want were made by Price Brothers of England and will be so marked. Here are some of the items I need.

Linda Holycross
Rt. 3, Box 21
Veedersburg, IN 47987; 800-292-3703

We Pay

Water Pitcher..**85.00**
Salad Bowl **45.00**
Demitasse Pot **85.00**
Luncheon Plate **15.00**
Egg Cup..**7.50**
Cup & Saucer..**15.00**
Tumbler **7.50**

COUNTRY STORE ITEMS

    I collect old grocery store advertising pieces of almost any kind: bins for bulk grocery items, displays for all manner of grocery items, vending machines, lighted signs, lighted advertising clocks, door push plates, sewing notion items (from scissors displays to spool cabinets and dye displays), almost any kind of advertising art on cardboard with an easel stand. If it was in an old grocery store, I'm interested! Prices for the items will depend on their condition and rarity.

B.J. Summers
Rt. #6, Box 659
Benton, KY 42025

We Pay

Porcelain & Tin Advertising or Utility Signs.....................................**10.00-60.00**
Soft Drink Machines **100.00-300.00**
Tobacco Tins or Glass Jars..**5.00-50.00**
Peanut Jars...**15.00-65.00**
Cracker Jars **10.00-30.00**
Candy Jars **5.00-30.00**
Advertising Chalkboards **5.00-20.00**

I am interested in buying items from old country stores. Anything made before 1960 is of interest. I will buy single pieces or a large quantity. Listed below are some of the things that were found in country stores that are of interest to me. Anything old and unusual is needed as well.

William A. (Bill) Shaw
801 Duval Dr.
Opp, AL 36467

Pre-1960   **We Pay**

Advertising Boxes (wood, cardboard, tin, etc.) **3.00-50.00**
Advertising Signs, cardboard, metal, or neon **1.00-300.00**
Ammunition Boxes, cardboard, full or empty...**5.00+**
Billiard Balls, ivory only **15.00-35.00**
Candy Jars, glass...**10.00+**
Calendars, 1800s-1960...**3.00-50.00**
Counter-top Display Cases, wood & glass or metal & glass......................**75.00+**
Marbles, in cloth or mesh bag **2.00-4.00**
Salesman Samples ....**Write**
Store Stock ....**Write**
Tins...**3.00+**
Tobacco, in cloth pouch or tin **2.00-5.00**

Wanted to buy: Cracker Jack and Checkers items – prizes, store displays, and boxes! Marked items only and no plastic ones.

Old Kilbourn Antiques
Phil Helley
629 Indiana Ave.
Wisconsin Dells, WI 53965; 608-254-8659

We Pay

Prizes, minimum value	**10.00+**
Store Displays, minimum value	**100.00+**
Signs, minimum value	**50.00+**
Boxes, minimum value	**10.00+**

CREDIT CARDS AND
CHARGE ITEMS

Wanted: credit cards or charge items of paper, wood, celluloid, metal, leather, plastic, or fiber. These were used to buy on credit with, and I am especially looking for charge items from before 1960 made of plastic, paper, metal, celluloid, and fiber. Prices quoted are for items in average condition.

Walt Thompson
Box 2541
Yakima, WA 98907-2541
Phone or FAX 409-452-4016

We Pay

American Express Cards, paper or plastic, pre-1960 ....**28.00**
Diners' Club Charge Booklets, pre-1960 ....**25.00**
Any Oil Company, paper, pre-1960 ....**10.00**
Any Oil Company, paper, pre-1930 ....**15.00**
Any Hotel or Restaurant, paper, pre-1950 ....**10.00**
Airline Charge Cards, pre-1970 ....**6.00**
Playboy Club Metal Keys or Cards **10.00**

CZECHOSLOVAKIAN
COLLECTIBLES

At the close of World War I, Czechoslovakia was declared an independent republic and immediately developed a large export industry. The factories produced a wide variety of glassware as well as pottery and porcelain until 1939 when the country was occupied by Germany. I am especially interested in Peasant Art Pottery. The following list reflects prices we will pay. Other items not listed will be considered. Pieces must be marked 'Made in Czechoslovakia.'

Delores Saar
45-5th Ave. NW
Hutchinson, MN 44350; 612-587-2002

Peasant Art Pottery　　　　　　　　　　　　　　　　　　　**We Pay**

Coffee Mug, 4½"	**20.00**
Lamp Base, 12"	**250.00**
Tumbler, 4¼"	**25.00**
Creamer, 3¼"	**30.00**
Compote, 6"	**50.00**
Sugar Bowl, 3¾"	**30.00**
Bowl, 2¾"	**25.00**
Bowl, 2½"	**25.00**

DEPRESSION GLASS

I am paying 60% to 75% of Gene Florence's book price for the following patterns and colors of Depression glass. I am mainly interested in place-setting pieces (plates, cups, saucers, bowls, tumblers, sherbets, etc.) but will consider serving pieces (large bowls, pitchers, etc.). All items must be in mint condition. I will reimburse shipping charges including insurance. See the listing of patterns here; I will also consider other patterns in pink, green, and blue at 50% of book price. Send me a list of what you have to offer, and maybe we can work a deal.

Cameo 'Ballerina' in pink or green	Open Lace in pink
Caprice in blue	Moderntone in cobalt
Cleo in pink	Princess in pink or green
Colonial Knife & Fork in pink or green	Queen Mary in pink
Diane (**not** Diana) in crystal	Rose Point in crystal
Florentine in pink or green	Tea Room in pink or green
Georgian 'Lovebirds' in green	Versailles in blue
June in blue	

Diana McConnell
14 Sassafras Lane
Swedesboro, NJ 08085; 609-467-0685

I have been collecting Depression glass since I was twelve years old. Somewhere along the way, my hobby developed into a business that I enjoy just as much. My mother and I still collect, but I am also buying glassware for resale. All items you offer for sale will be given careful consideration. I prefer glass in excellent condition and pre-priced but will make offers as necessary. I am also interested in odd lids and bottoms of cookie jars and candy jars and sugar bowl lids in various patterns. Some patterns of particular interest are listed here.

American Sweetheart	Cameo
Dogwood	Lace Edge
Mayfair (Hocking)	Princess
Royal Lace	Sandwich (Hocking)

Pamela Wiggins
Depression Delights
6025 Sunnycrest
Houston, TX 77087

I am buying Depression glass in **all colors and patterns**. I will also buy **elegant glass** of the Depression era such as Heisey, Cambridge, Fostoria, Fenton, Tiffin, Imperial, Paden City, Duncan & Miller, etc. **Kitchen glass** items such as juice reamers, canisters, cruets, mixing bowls, refrigerator dishes, butter and cheese dishes, measuring cups, spice sets, rolling pins, etc. are wanted. All items must be in perfect condition – free from chips, nicks, cracks, and scratches. I will pay up to 60% of current book price. Please send a list of what you have to sell and your price.

The Glass Packrat
Pat & Bill Ogden
3050 Colorado Ave.
Grand Junction, CO 81504; 303-434-7452 after 5pm

I am collecting Depression glass in the **Mt. Pleasant pattern by the L.E. Smith Co.** in black amethyst. I particularly want cups and saucers and 8" scalloped plates.

Barbara Craft
202 Lincoln
Emporia, KS 66801

We Pay

Cup & Saucer	**11.00**
Plate, scalloped, 8"	**11.00**

I am wanting to buy **green Cameo, pink Mayfair, Dogwood, pink or monax American Sweetheart, Strawberry, and green saucers for Block Optic**. I will pay half of book price for these patterns and would be interested in anything else you have that is reasonably priced.

Rhonda Hasse
566 Oak Terrace Dr.
Farmington, MO 62640

I am buying **all pink Depression glass**, especially these patterns: Florentine #1, Sharon, and Royal Lace (also wanted in cobalt blue). Etched pink glassware in all patterns and pink kitchenware are sought as well.

Diane Genicola
25 E Adams Ave.
Pleasantville, NJ 08232; 609-646-6140

DIONNE QUINTUPLETS

I am looking for unusual items relating to the Dionne Quintuplets, Dr. Defoe, etc. Listed below are some wants.

Mrs. Donald Hulit
236 Cape Rd.
Standish, ME 04084

We Pay

Bowl, china	**30.00-45.00+**
Cake Plate, china	**75.00-90.00**
Cloth Items, any, ea	**10.00-50.00+**
Lamp, china	**75.00-90.00**
Mug, china	**20.00-35.00**
Pencil Tablet	**15.00+**
Plaster Items, ea	**45.00+**
Post Card, color	**10.00-15.00**
Post Card, sepia	**8.00-12.00**
Soap Dish, 'Good Luck Babies'	**25.00+**
Thermometer Card	**10.00-30.00**
Tray, metal	**45.00+**
Wood Items, ea	**25.00-60.00**
Other Unusual Items	**Write**

DISNEYANA

Disney items I wish to purchase are listed here. Only items in very good shape are wanted, and these prices are negotiable.

Paul J. Baxter
P.O. Box 176
Stronghurst, IL 61480

We Pay

Dopey, dime register bank	**85.00+**
Dopey, pencil sharpener	**60.00+**
Ferdinand the Bull, pencil sharpener	**60.00+**
Ferdinand the Bull, storybook, ca 1938	**65.00+**
Pinocchio, Better Little Book, by Whitman	**45.00+**
Pinocchio, game, The Merry Puppet, ca 1939	**75.00+**
Pinocchio, pencil sharpener	**60.00+**
Pinocchio, scrapbook, by Whitman	**60.00+**
Pinocchio, sheet music	**20.00+**
Snow White & Seven Dwarfs, Big Little Book	**45.00+**
Snow White & Seven Dwarfs, game, ca 1938	**85.00+**
Snow White & Seven Dwarfs, sheet music	**20.00+**

I'm seeking all Disney items from the 1930s through the 1970s with an emphasis on figural ceramic and pottery pieces. I want cookie jars, salt and pepper shakers, baby dishes, figurines, children's tea sets, and teapots. I'm interested in merchandise from all origins and manufacturers: Brayton, Shaw, Goebel, Vernon Kilns, Wade, Wade Heath, Germany, Bavaria, and others. I buy items that relate to Disney's female characters – both heroines and villainesses (e.g., Alice in Wonderland, Cinderella, Snow White, Sleeping Beauty, Tinker Bell, Maleficent, Wicked Queens, Mary Poppins). I buy all Disneyana from one piece to entire collections!

Judy Posner
R.D. #1, Box 273 WB
Effort, PA 18330-717-629-6583

We Pay

Alice in Wonderland Salt & Pepper Shakers	**100.00**
Alice in Wonderland Cookie Jars (various)	**200.00+**
Mickey Mouse Condiment Set	**250.00+**
Snow White Kneeling w/Bird Cookie Jar	**250.00+**
Pinocchio w/Fishbowl Cookie Jar	**150.00+**
Goebel Walrus Decanter	**300.00**
Goebel Figaro Salt & Pepper Shakers	**100.00**
Any Brayton Pottery Disney Figures	**100.00+**
Disney Character Boxed Tea Sets	**150.00+**
Mad Hatter Teapot	**200.00+**
Unusual Disney Salt & Peppers	**50.00+**

DOG COLLECTIBLES

Any dog and fox items are wanted – especially Russian wolfhound and Borzoi dogs. Other breeds we are interested in include English Bulldogs, Afghans, Pugs, Great Danes, Samoyeds, Bull Terriers, Collies, German shepherds, Pomeranians, and Pekingese. Figurines in any material (porcelain, china, small bronzes, cast iron, metal, composition, etc.), plates, mugs, tins, books, prints, cigarette cards, post cards, and thimbles are just some of the items wanted. I will buy, sell, and trade to find wanted breeds.

Cynthia Greenfield
12309 Featherwood Dr. #34
Silver Spring, MD 20904; 301-622-5473

We Pay

Figurines	**50.00+**
Paper Items	**3.00+**
Books	**5.00+**
Plates	**15.00+**

DOLLS

I am interested in buying **Barbie, Ken, Skipper, and Francie dolls and their clothes dating from 1959 to 1966**, a single item or an entire collection. Listed are some of the things I am seeking. Top prices will be paid for rare and unusual items. Boxes and dolls that have not been played with would be worth 50% more than the prices. Prices are currently at an all-time high, so now is the best time to pull those dolls out of the attic.

Irene Davis
27036 Withams Rd.
Oak Hall, VA 23416; 804-824-5259

We Pay

#1 Ponytail Barbie, EX	**1,500.00**
#3 Ponytail Barbie, EX	**300.00**
1961-1963 Ponytail Barbie, EX	**100.00**
Bubble-Cut Barbie, EX	**50.00**
Skipper, EX	**20.00**
Francie, EX	**30.00**
Ken, flocked hair, EX	**30.00**
Wedding Day Outfit, complete	**50.00**
Gay Parisienne Outfit, complete	**400.00**
Mod Fashions, ea	**10.00+**

I enjoy collecting **dolls dating from the 1960s to 1965 and am especially interested in Barbie.** The following is a list of some of the items I am interested in:

Ponytail Barbie   Swirl Ponytail Barbie
Bubble-Cut Barbie   American Girl Barbie

These came in black-and-white striped or solid red bathing suits with sunglasses, gold hoop earrings, and high heels on a black wire stand or a wire stand with a round plastic disk base. Many fashion clothes were produced, and I am interested in clothing with the early 'Barbie' logo label and the accessories that went with these fashions. Also manufactured at the same time was a line of 'Suzy-Goose' furniture made by Mattel for Barbie. The line included a canopy bed and a small single-drawer chest, a vanity and stool, and a tall wardrobe.

I am in a local doll collectors' club, so even if I do not want to buy the particular item you have, I may be able to sell it for you. The price I pay very much depends on the rarity, age, and condition of these dolls. The prices you find in most price guides are for mint-in-box items, and very few little girls left their dolls in the box.

Beth Summers
Rt. #6, Box 659
Benton, KY 42025

Private collector will pay top dollar for **Barbie dolls, friend dolls, clothes, houses, store displays, accessories, and Barbie-related items**. I prefer items made before 1975. Also wanted are Barbie dolls from after 1975, but only those that are mint in box.

Denise Davidson
834 W Grand River Ave.
Williamston, MI 48895; 517-655-2455

I am buying **old dolls, doll parts, and doll heads from 1900 through the 1960s** in any condition. Of special interest are dolls in their original clothes and with their original boxes. I also want unusual dolls. The better the condition, the more I pay!

Dawn Rossi
P.O. Box 484
Canandaigua, NY 14424; 716-394-7083

Dolls & Doll Parts   We Pay

	We Pay
Bisque, w/character face, ea	200.00+
Bisque Doll Head, old, ea	25.00+
Bodies, ball-jointed, ea	35.00+
Bodies, kid, ea	25.00+
Hands, Legs or Feet	10.00+

Composition, ea ....15.00+
Hard Plastic, ca 1950s, ea ....15.00+
Ideal, vinyl, 1960s, 36", ea ....50.00+
Jem Dolls or Clothes...5.00+
Santa Claus (old), ea ....50.00+
Schoenhut, ea...100.00+
Schoenhut Clothes or Shoes, ea ....20.00+
Shirley Temple, 1930s, ea ....100.00+
Shirley Temple, 1950s, ea ....40.00+
Shirley Temple Clothes, ea..20.00+
Shirley Temple Boxes, ea ....20.00+
Toni, in original box, ea..75.00+
1950s Dolls, in original box, ea ....50.00+
Vogue Ginny Dolls, 1950s, ea..25.00+
Wilkins, Baby Dear, ea..20.00+

Accessories and Related Items   We Pay

Boxes, 1950s or earlier..10.00+
Carriages, wicker...25.00+
Clothes, Shoes or Hats, ea..5.00+
Clothes w/Tags, ea ....5.00+
Highchairs ....5.00+
Christening Gowns, child's, ea..20.00+
Baby Clothes or Bonnets, child's, ea...10.00+
Shoes, child's high-button, pr ....10.00+
Teddy Bears w/Doll Heads, ea ....50.00+
Bathing Beauty Figures, ea ....20.00+
Snow Baby Figures (old), ea..20.00+

I will purchase your **Captain Action dolls, uniforms, accessories, Silver Streak car, Action Boy, Dr. Evil, and playsets from the 1966-68 Captain Action doll line made by Ideal Toy Co**. I am interested in any item mint in the original packaging or mint items without packaging. I will also buy entire accumulations of Captain Action stuff, including incomplete outfits and dolls with damage or missing parts. Contact me first to sell one piece or one thousand.

Michael Paquin
That Toy Guy
57 N Sycamore St.
Clifton Heights, PA 19018
215-626-5866 or 215-DYG-TOYS

We Pay

Action Boy, complete uniform, mint..**up to 150.00**
Action Boy, no clothes, undamaged **40.00-75.00**
Captain Action, complete uniform, mint ....**up to 100.00**
Captain Action, no clothes, undamaged..**40.00-60.00**
Dr. Evil, complete uniform, mint..**up to 150.00**
Green Hornet, complete clothes, mint..**up to 500.00**
Action Boy, Captain Action, Dr. Evil, or Green Hornet, original packaging, mint...**200.00-800.00**
Dr. Evil Accessories (gun, sandal, mask, medallion, etc.)................**15.00-30.00**
Green Hornet Accessories..**20.00+**
Uniforms, complete, mint **45.00-300.00**
Uniforms, mint in box **150.00-800.00**
Miscellaneous Box Lots of Captain Action Stuff ....**up to 1,000.00**

I am interested in buying **German pincushion dolls** for my own collection as well as for trade and resale. I am looking for dolls on a cushion with or without legs. No damaged items, please. Any size dolls, large or small, are wanted. Let me know what you have. I can pay $25.00 for more common pieces and more for elaborate dolls.

Elizabeth Baer
P.O. Box 266
Perry, IA 50220

We Pay

German Pincushion Dolls..**25.00+**

I am searching for **Nancy Ann Storybook dolls**. Bisque dolls are preferred, but I'm also interested in plastic. All sizes are wanted in dressed or nude dolls as well as parts. Mint-in-box items or individual accessories such as flowers, hats, ribbons, clothing, booklets, tags, boxes (in red, pink, blue, or gold polka dots), articles written about Nancy Ann Abbot, and advertising items are wanted also. Original doll patterns made from the earliest times to the present along with newspaper and magazines relating to Nancy Ann are sought. Other interests include doll supplies and teddy bears. Items must be original; no photocopy tags, patterns, etc. are wanted. Prices depend on circa of item, its condition, etc. I would like to buy patterns by the box lot.

Noreen Stayton
P.O. Box 379
Doyle, CA 96109-0379

We Pay

Nancy Ann Storybook Doll, MIB ....**18.00-30.00+**
Accessories, ea ....**1.00+**
Doll Pattern, ea...**1.00-10.00+**

_____

I am buying **dolls made of vinyl, hard plastic, bisque, and celluloid**. I am interested in one doll or an entire collection. I prefer hard plastic and bisque dolls. Also bought are doll clothes, accessories, and parts.

Sherry Thornhill
Rt. 1, Box 32
Hawk Point, MO 63349

Material   **We Pay**

Vinyl, ea ....**5.00+**
Hard Plastic, ea ....**20.00+**
Celluloid, ea ....**10.00+**
Bisque, ea ....**75.00+**
Bisque, storybook, ea ....**15.00+**

_____

I am buying **dolls from the 1960s to early 1970s**. Listed below are samples of what I'm interested in purchasing.

Jean Brown
824 N Main
Independence, MO 64050

We Pay

American Character, Black Tressy ....**25.00+**
Hasbro, Leggy Sue, 9" ....**3.00+**
Ideal, Mitzi ....**15.00+**

Ideal, Tiffany Taylor, 11½" ....**5.00+**
Ideal, Black Tiffany Taylor, 11½"...**10.00+**
Kenner, Dana...**10.00+**
Marin, Chiclana Flamenco Dancers ....**5.00+**
Mattel, Brad...**10.00+**
Mattel, Christie...**10.00+**
Mattel, Stacey...**15.00+**
Nancy Ann, 10½" ....**10.00+**
Topper, Dale, 6" ....**3.00+**
Uneeda, Dollkin, 11½" ....**3.00+**

I am buying **Raggedy Ann and Andy dolls, Lulu and Tubby dolls, and their related items** such as paper dolls, purses, soaps, paper goods (no ads), etc. Please call about whatever you have; I will quote you a fair price.

Gwen Daniel
18 Belleau Lake Ct.
O'Fallon, MO 63366; 314-281-3190

We Pay

Raggedy Ann & Andy, early Volland **650.00**
Beloved Belindy, Georgene **500.00**
Beloved Belindy, Knickerbocker...**250.00**
Raggedy Ann Books, all publishers, ea...**10.00-50.00**
Lulu, Georgene...**100.00+**
Tubby, Georgene ....**100.00+**

I am interested in buying **old bisque dolls, doll clothing, and doll furniture**. I also buy bisque heads. Dolls can be without hair or clothing. Please send a photo and price.

Ralonda Lindsay
2504 E Vancouver
Broken Arrow, OK 74014; 918-355-1538

My interests in doll collecting are varied. I want **anything pertaining to the Dionne Quints, Shirley Temple, or Barbie and friends**. I would also like to find a small camel-back trunk as well as other interesting doll items. I will pay according to condition.

I am also interested in **souvenir spoons**. Especially wanted are an old teddy bear spoon and spoons with movie stars. Prices paid depend on condition and whether or not the spoon is sterling. Sterling silver flatware in **Chateau Rose made by Alvin** is sought as well.

Sandi Waddell
2791 County Rd. 302
Durango, CO 81301; 303-247-1568

DOOR PUSH PLATES

I collect porcelain door push plates that were used on entrance doors to grocery stores, drugstores, and any store in general that sold manufacturers' products. They were attached to screen doors where you normally reached out to push the door in or out. The push plate was colorful and advertised the company's product; it often carried the words 'push' or 'pull' as well. Size of the plates varied, but the average was 4" by 7". These were made of enameled steel (more commonly called porcelain). Some examples that exist are: Red Rose Tea, Tetley Tea, Salada Tea, Chesterfield Cigarettes, Dr. Caldwell's Pepsin Syrup, and Vick's.

I buy according to condition. Please send photocopy or photo with a description for a price quote. I will pay $75.00 to $125.00 for nice additions to my collection. I pay the postage.

Betty Foley
227 Union Ave.
Pittsburgh, PA 15202; 412-761-0685

DOORSTOPS

I am an independent filmmaker making a film on the subject of doorstops. It is entitled *Off the Ground and Off the Wall: A Doorstop Documentary.* For my film I have interviewed a number of doorstop collectors as well as the authors of two books about the subject. As a collector of doorstops myself, I am seeking cast iron or bronze frog doorstops (any conditon) to add to my collection. I am interested in any kind of frog that could be used as a doorstop. Ones I am particularly trying to find are listed here.

Gary Roma
23 Foster Rd.
Belmont, MA 02178; 617-489-6360

We Pay

Frog on Mushroom ....up to 125.00
'I Croak for the Jackson Wagon' Frog...up to 100.00
Hubley Bullfrog Garden Ornament..up to 150.00

_____

Duck Decoys

We are buying old duck decoys. Prices paid depend on age and condition. Please call or send photo. Thanks.

J&B Antiques
Jim Franke
3803 Willow St.
Pascagoula, MS 39567; 601-769-0542

_____

EGG TIMERS

I would like to hear from anyone having figural egg timers for sale. Figural egg timers had their most popular production time from about 1930 to the early 1950s, although Goebel has made even more recent ones (into the 1970s).

These tiny figurals range in size from 3" to 5" and can be found in a wide array of shapes – people and animals; a Mammy; a Dutch boy or country girl; or a professional person such as a policeman, chef or chimney sweep. Dogs, roosters, and chicks were popular animal forms. Most were painted in detail, while a few were done in an all-over solid color. Of particular interest to me would be ones marked 'Germany,' 'Japan,' 'Occupied Japan,' or 'Goebel.'

It is still possible to find a figural egg timer with the sand tube intact. This is a plus but is not required for a figural timer to be considered acceptable and collectible. Replacement sand tubes can be easily secured to restore the figural timer to its original appearance. What is important is that the figural itself be in good condition. Since most timers are china and bisque, those with damaging cracks, severe chips, and noticeable repairs are not considered good buys.

Timers missing their sand tubes are easily recognized by a hole either going through the stub of a hand or arm, or some part of the back of the figure. Prices below reflect what I would consider paying for figural timers intact and in excellent to mint condition with production markings as stated earlier. Other timers can and will be considered. A photo is helpful.

Jeannie Greenfield
310 Parker Rd.
Stoneboro, PA 16153

Timer Marked	**We Pay**
Goebel, single or double figure	**25.00-50.00**
German, any type (person, animal, etc.)	**10.00-30.00**
Occupied Japan or Japan, any type (person, animal, etc.)	**5.00-30.00**
Miscellaneous Figural	**5.00-10.00**

EPHEMERA

I am buying **foreign paper currency from any and all countries**. I buy everything from Mexican pesos with a face value of 1/32¢ to German 1920s inflation money when a billion marks couldn't buy a cup of coffee. I also buy **men's magazines and non-sports cards**.

James R. Kruczek
N 11584 Moore Rd.
Alma Center, WI 54611-8301

We Pay

Foreign Paper Money, smaller in size than US dollar ....**up to 10¢**
Foreign Paper Money, same size or larger than US dollar...................**up to 1.00**
Men's Magazines (*Playboy, Penthouse, Oui*) ....**25¢**
Men's Magazines (other titles) ....**up to 1.00**
Non-Sports Cards, any set, any series, per 1,000...**3.00**

EXTENSION CORDS (NOVELTY)

I am looking for old extension cords with figural outlets of animals, flowers, Santa, etc., or anything unusual. I am also interested in old figural garden water sprinklers. Contact to discuss price.

Tom Mattingly
P.O. Box 278
Churchton, MD 20733; 301-261-9522

FANS

I am buying, selling, and restoring all kinds of mechanical fans: unusual ceiling, desk, oscillating, spring-wound, fuel-powered, belt-driven, water-powered, etc.; also wanted are fan catalogs and literature, e.g., G.E., Westinghouse, Emerson. Send photo and price.

The Fan Man, Inc.
1914 Abrams Pkwy.
Dallas, TX 75214; 214-826-7700

We Pay

Common Brass Blade Fans	**25.00+**
Unusual Brass Blade Fans	**50.00+**
Unusual Ceiling Fans (blades not necessary)	**50.00+**
Water or Fuel Powered	**250.00+**
Battery Operated	**100.00+**

FAST FOOD COLLECTIBLES

We buy-sell-trade all fast food memorabilia; however, we specialize in McDonald's® collectibles. We prefer items dated earlier than 1985, whether it be a single piece or a whole collection. The older the item the better. We prefer all items in mint or near-mint condition or mint in package (MIP) when possible. We pay resonable prices, and we trade fair. Send us your want lists and/or your trade lists. Cartoon glasses must be in mint, pristine condition; **PEZ** must be 'without feet' (paying $3.00+), and **Smurfs** need to be in mint or near-mint condition. Listed below are some of the items we are seeking.

Bill & Pat Poe
220 Dominica Circle E
Niceville, FL 32578-4068; 904-897-4163

McDonald's®   We Pay

1985, Melmac Plate, Ronald McDonald w/Grimace in Sailboat.................**3.00+**
Ronald McDonald Figural Telephone..**25.00+**
Ronald McDonald Head, for helium tank..**50.00+**
Garfield or Snoopy, stuffed toy, ea..**10.00+**

Happy Meal® Toys   We Pay

1980, Look-Look Books, any of 4 different ....**3.00+**
1982, Dukes of Hazzard Containers, any of 4 different, ea ....**5.00+**
1982, McDonaldland Express, any of 8 different, ea...................................**3.00+**
1983, Going Places, Hot Wheels, any of 23 different, ea............................**4.00+**
1983, Mystery, all...**2.00**
1984, Lego Building Set, Under 3 (U-3) only, all ....**3.00+**
1985, My Little Pony Charms & Transformers, all colors............................**3.00**
1985, Super Travelers, Lego, 4 different, ea set..**3.00+**
1986, Construct, any ....**4.00+**
1986, Metrozoo, any ....**4.00+**
1986, The Story of Texas, Set 1, 2, 3 or 5 ....**5.00+**
1986, High Flying Kits, any of 3, ea ....**5.00+**
1986, Play Doh (cardboard container w/tin bottom), any color..................**3.00+**
1988, Black History Books, Volume I or Volume II....................................**5.00+**
1988, Fraggle Rock 'Doozers,' any, ea ....**2.00+**
1988, Hot Wheels, '86 P-911, White & '88 Split Window Black.................**3.00+**
1988, Matchbox Super GT, set of 16, any ....**3.00+**
1988, Sportsball, Basketball, w/orange hoop & net...................................**4.00+**
1990, Barbie Hot Wheels (test market), any, ea ....**3.00+**
1990, McDonaldland Craft Kit..**8.00+**

Character Glasses   We Pay

Seattle Seahawks, Milwaukee Brewers..**3.00+**
Philadelphia Eagles, Pittsburgh Steelers...**3.00+**
Houston Livestock & Rodeo...**3.00+**

Texas 'Hook 'Em Horns,' or any story opening ....**3.00+**
Any Special Promotional Glass..**3.00+**

_____

FIESTA

We buy all unusual Fiesta dinnerware pieces in the original eleven colors made from 1936 through 1969. We don't buy any of the new Fiesta which has been made from 1989 to the present. Extreme caution must be used in evaluating old versus new Fiesta in cobalt as the color can be identical. However, the new pieces are significantly smaller than the old when seen side by side. We buy only pieces marked Fiesta (either by mold mark or rubber stamp). We don't buy crazed, chipped, cracked, or factory-defective pieces. We reimburse actual UPS and insurance charges.

Kate's Collectibles
28-US 41 East
Negaunee, MI 49866; 906-475-4443

We Pay

Bowl, fruit; 11¾" ....**75.00+**
Bowl, unlisted salad ....**50.00+**
Candle Holders, tripod, pr..**200.00+**
Carafe w/Lid..**95.00+**
Coffeepot w/Lid ....**80.00+**
Demitasse Cup & Saucer...**30.00+**
Cake Plate (no Kitchen Kraft)...**300.00+**
Marmalade w/Lid...**80.00+**
Mustard w/Lid ....**75.00+**
Syrup w/Lid..**125.00+**
Relish Tray ....**90.00+**
Vase, 8" ....**200.00+**
Vase, 10"...**275.00+**
Vase, 12"...**350.00+**
Advertising Literature, original..**15.00+**
Fiesta Store Display, complete..**400.00+**
Original Packing Carton..**20.00+**
Pieces in Medium Green, ea ....**90% of Book**

I collect American pottery dinnerware: **Fiesta, Blue Ridge, and Frankoma.** I am interested in Fiesta in the five original colors and turquoise. I prefer accessory pieces of Blue Ridge in more elaborate designs (bowls, cups, etc.). I am interested in most Frankoma patterns except Wagon Wheel. Some pieces wanted are listed below. No pieces with cracks, chips, or imperfections please. Send pictures and/or descriptions of what you have. See also my listing under Blue Ridge.

M.C. Wills
103 Virginia St.
Dyess AFB, TX 79607

We Pay

Demitasse Coffeepot	**80.00+**
Demitasse Cup & Saucer, red, cobalt, ivory or turquoise, set, ea	**20.00+**
Demitasse Saucer, green	**8.00+**
Bowl, cream soup	**15.00+**
Tumbler, water, red or cobalt	**15.00+**
Tumbler, juice	**10.00+**
Teapot Lid, yellow, large size	**10.00+**
Mustard	**60.00+**
Marmalade	**60.00+**
Pitcher, 2-pt	**25.00+**

I am buying all pieces of Fiesta dinnerware made by the Homer Laughlin China Company: cups, saucers, plates, bowls, tumblers, water pitchers, etc. All colors are wanted.

Diane Genicola
25 E Adams Ave.
Pleasantville, NJ 08232; 609-646-6140

FIGURINES

I am buying interesting figurines. I prefer pieces from the 1700s through the 1930s. Slightly damaged pieces (restorable) are preferred. I would purchase a single item or by the lot. Animal figurines are of no interest. Please send photo with description of damage (if applicable) and price desired.

Val Arce
23029 Cerca Dr.
Valencia, CA 91354

We Pay

Capo Di Monte	25.00+
Chelsea	25.00+
Coalport	25.00+
Dresden	25.00+
Fabris	25.00+

Goldscheider ....**25.00+**
Haviland ....**25.00+**
Meissen...**25.00+**
Rosenthal..**25.00+**
Royal Dux ....**25.00+**
Royal Rudolstadt..**25.00+**
Royal Worcester ....**25.00+**
Staffordshire...**25.00+**

FIRE DEPARTMENT MEMORABILIA

Always wanted are fire department items from the early 1800s to 1920. I will buy a single piece or an entire collection. Also of interest are early fire engines: hand, steam, and horse-drawn. I want anything related to fire departments except convention ribbons, glass and copper extinguishers, nozzels under four feet long, modern badges, and books written after 1910.

James Piatt
P.O. Box 244
Oakland, NJ 07436

We Pay

History Books, pre-1910 ....**30.00+**
Helmets, early ....**150.00+**
Helmets, w/painted shields..**350.00+**
Helmets, unusual ....**500.00+**
Presentation Items, gold ....**300.00+**
Trumpets, unusual...**500.00+**
Engine Lights, w/colored glass or engraved ....**1,500.00+**
Toys ....**25.00+**
Pocket Watches, gold or silver ....**200.00+**
Shaving Mugs, w/fire theme...**400.00+**
Fire Engine Name Plates..**100.00+**
Gongs, w/wood cases...**500.00+**
Indicator w/Gong (Gamewell) ....**2,000.00+**
Advertising Items for Equipment...**200.00+**
Insurance Items (showing firemen or engines)........................**200.00+**
Magazines, ca 1900 ....**5.00+**
Prints ....**300.00+**
Ambrotypes or Daguerreotypes (showing firemen or equipment)..........**250.00+**

Fire Department Memorabilia

Presentation Items...**100.00+**
Statues of Firemen ....**200.00+**
Catalogs of Equipment ....**50.00+**

I buy fire department-related items such as helmets, nozzles, axes, extinguishers, bells, ladders, etc. – all prices!

Richard C. Price
Professional Land Surveyor
Box 219
Arendtsville, PA 17303; 717-677-6986

FIRE-KING

Issac Collins started the Hocking Glass Company in 1905 near Lancaster, Ohio. In 1937 Hocking merged with the Anchor Cap Corporation and the name was changed to Anchor Hocking Glass Corporation. Fire-King was produced from about 1942 to 1976 and is a trademark of Anchor Hocking Glass Corporation.

Jadite, pink, ivory, white, turquoise blue, azurite, peach lustre, and blue are only a few of the many colors that were used to make glassware with the Fire-King mark. Many of these items were used as premiums in boxes of Quaker Oats. They were also given away at gas stations and theaters to promote customer interest.

I am mostly interested in the Jane Ray pattern in jadite. The ribbed edgings of this pattern make it easy to identify. Pieces must be in mint condition with no nicks, breaks, or scratches. When writing, please send an SASE along with a list of the pieces you have for sale. I will also trade my extras for Fire-King items that I need.

Lantern Hill
Florence Hoijer
Star Rt., Box 8A
Stephenson, MI 49887

Jane Ray   **We Pay**

Plate, salad	2.00
Plate, dinner	3.00
Platter	4.00
Bowl, dessert	1.50
Bowl, cereal	2.00
Bowl, chili	1.50
Bowl, soup	3.00
Bowl, vegetable	4.00
Sugar Bowl w/Lid	3.00
Creamer	2.50
Cup, demitasse	5.00
Saucer, demitasse	3.00
Mug, plain	1.50
Pitcher, milk, 20-oz, plain	6.00
Egg Cup, double	4.00

FISHING TACKLE

Little did James Heddon know when he carved the first wooden lure many years ago that he would not only change the way fishing would be done from then on but would also unknowingly initiate one of the most interesting categories of collectibles today.

Collecting old fishing tackle has really caught on in the last few years and still hasn't reached its peak. Old wooden lures are still the most popular items, but many other fishing-related items are also of interest to collectors.

I've tried to list a few of the items I will buy, but there are many more too numerous to mention. Please feel free to call any time. Prices listed are for items in excellent condition. I am also interested in many **old fishing and hunting advertising items.** Also wanted are **old duck calls.** I refuse to get into bidding wars with fellow collectors; but I want you to know, if it's top dollar you are wanting, give me a call.

Randy Hilst
1221 Florence, Apt. 4
Pekin, IL 61554; 309-346-2710

Lure	We Pay
Winchester	100.00
Creek Chub Pikie	3.00
Shakespeare Revolution	65.00
Gee-Wiz Frog	25.00
Heddon 5-Hook Minnow	35.00
Heddon Slope Nose	125.00
Charmer Minnow	125.00
South Bend Whirl Oreno	45.00
Michigan Life Like	225.00
Shakespeare Mouse	3.00
Chippewa Lure	40.00
Pflueger Kent Frog	75.00
Pflueger Palomine	3.00
Garland Cork Head Minnow	45.00

Related Items	We Pay
Winchester Reel	50.00
Meek Reel	60.00
Heddon Fly Rod	45.00
Orvis Fly Rod	45.00
Shakespeare Minnow Trap	35.00
Creek Chub Catalog, pre-1950s	35.00
Heddon Catalog, pre-1950s	45.00
Perdew Duck Call	75.00

Collector looking for old Rapala fishing lures: freshwater and saltwater types in all sizes and colors. I prefer lures with no major damage (missing lip, cracked or peeling finish, etc.) – broken or missing hooks are acceptable. Also wanted are any old fishing catalogs from 1940 through the 1970s with advertising for Rapala lures. Below are some of the lures I am seeking and prices I am willing to pay for lures with no damage. Please send a list of what you have and/or pictues.

T.C. Wills
103 Virginia St.
Dyess AFB, TX 79607

We Pay

Minnow, Original Rapala, black writing on lip...**6.00+**
Minnow, Made in Finland on belly, Finlandia Vistin on lip ....**5.00+**
Minnow, jointed w/above markings ....**5.00+**
Fishing catalogs, depending on condition/advertising, minimum.............**1.00+**

Always buying old fishing tackle: wooden lures, quality old reels, fine rods, tackle boxes and their contents, catalogs, etc. I'm a private collector paying retail prices for the above items. Call or write; I will respond within twenty-four hours.

Rick Edmisten
3736 Sunswept Dr.
Studio City, CA 91604; 818-763-9406

I am buying all types of fishing tackle. Especially wanted are old bait-casting reels and unusual fishing reels as well as anything relating to fishing circa pre-1960.

Robert Lappin
Box 1006
Decatur, IL 62523; 217-428-2973

We Pay

Bait-Casting Reels, metal only...**5.00-500.00**
Wooden Lures ....**3.00+**
Winchester Items ....**20.00+**
Reels, before 1900 ....**40.00+**
Advertising Signs...**10.00+**

Wooden Fishing Creels...**20.00+**
Fishing Lures, old only...**20.00+**
Any Old, Unusual Related Item...**Call or Write**

FOUNTAIN PENS

    Fountain pens produced between 1880 and 1945 are very collectible, as well as some produced later (such as Parker's Spanish Treasure pen). The most valuable pens represent major brands like Parker, Sheaffer, Waterman, Wahl-Eversharp, Conklin, and Swan. Pens commanding the best prices are those that are either very large, very fancy, or very rare.

    I prefer very fancy and rare pens but will consider purchasing any high-quality pen that is in excellent condition and free defects such as cracks, damage, or missing parts.

    The following list reflects the current pay for fountain pens. Some of these pens have identifying numbers stamped on the end of the holders. Prices are for pens in excellent condition. I have published a book on collectible fountain pens. Write for further information on the book or if you have fountain pens to sell. Please send a photocopy of pens you wish to sell.

Glen Bowen
2240 N Park Dr.
Kingwood, TX 77339

We Pay

Parker #41 or #31 Sterling or Gold-Filled Filigree **800.00**
Parker #47 Pearl Sided w/Floral Design Gold-Filled Cap **1,000.00**
Parker #15 Pearl Sided w/Gold-Filled Filigree Cap **600.00**
Parker #45 Pearl Sided w/Gold Filled Filigree Cap................................**600.00**
Parker #37 or #38 Gold-Filled or Sterling Snakes.....................................**Call**
Parker #59 or #60 Gold-Filled or Sterling Indian Aztec Design...................**Call**
Parker #58 Gold-Filled Partial Indian Aztec Deisgn............................**1,000.00**
Parker #35 or #36 Gold-Filled or Sterling Floral Pattern **1,000.00**

Parker #52 or #53 Gold-Filled or Sterling Swastika Design **1,500.00**
Parker #39 or #54 Gold-Filled or Sterling Floral Design **800.00**
Parker #40 Gold-Filled or Solid Gold Floral Design................................**500.00**
Parker #43 or #44 Gold-Filled or Sterling Floral Design **500.00**
Parker #14 or #16 Gold-Filled or Sterling Filigree Design **300.00**
Parker #33 or #34 Gold-Filled or Sterling Overlay..................................**400.00**
Parker #62 Gold-Filled Floral Engraved Pattern......................................**600.00**
Waterman #452, #454, #0552, or #0554 Gold-Filled or Sterling **150.00**
Waterman #456, #458, #0556, or #0558 Gold-Filled or Sterling **600.00**
Waterman #552, #554, #555, or #556 Gold Overlay..................**250.00-1,000.00**
Waterman Ripple Pattern #7, #56, or #58 ....**100.00-500.00**
Waterman Ripple Pattern #52, #54, or #55 ....**50.00-200.00**
Waterman 100-Year Brown, Black, or Burgundy **50.00-200.00**
Waterman 100-Year Blue, Yellow, Red, or Green Transparent.................**200.00**
Waterman #20 Black, Red, or Red & Black pattern **500.00-1,000.00**
Waterman Patrician, Multicolored..**100.00-250.00**
Wahl-Eversharp Gold-Filled or Sterling #2, #3, #4, #5, or #6 ....**100.00**
Wahl-Eversharp Oversize in Various Colors, Roller Ball Clips **100.00-200.00**
Wahl-Eversharp Oversize Doric (fluted sides) in Various Colors.**100.00-200.00**
A.A. Waterman Gold-Filled or Sterling Overlay **100.00-500.00**
Aiken-Lambert Gold-Filled or Sterling Overlay **50.00-200.00**
Conklin Crescent Filled, Gold-Filled or Sterling...........................**50.00-300.00**
John Holland Gold-Filled or Sterling Filigree **50.00-300.00**
Paul Wirt Gold-Filled, Sterling Overlay or Filigree **50.00-300.00**
Parker Duofold Sr., Blue or Yellow...**100.00-400.00**
Parker Duofold Sr., Red, Green, Black & Pearl, or Black................**25.00-100.00**

FURNITURE

I buy sofas, couches, and chairs including dining chairs in damaged condition that have finished wood exposed. I pay more for pieces that have carving and for sets of furniture such as a sofa and one or two matching chairs. I also buy dining chairs individually or in sets of four or more if they have upholstered bottoms. I will buy current reproduction pieces as well as pieces made before 1950. I usually will not purchase modern pieces unless they are unique. You must contact me first before sending any item. All letters will be answered. Photos helpful.

Leon Mahan
Route 1, Box 1000
Heiskell, TN 37754

We Pay

Dining Chairs, ea	**5.00+**
Upholstered Chairs, w/exposed wood trim, ea	**10.00+**
Upholstered Chairs, w/carving, ea	**15.00+**
Upholstered Couches or Sofas, w/exposed wood trim, ea	**10.00+**
Upholstered Couches or Sofas, w/carving, ea	**15.00+**
Upholstered Living Room Sets, w/exposed wood, per set	**20.00+**
Upholstered Living Room Sets, w/carving, per set	**30.00+**
Footstools or Ottomans, w/carving, ea	**5.00+**
Parts of Upholstered Pieces	**Write**

FRUIT JARS

I'm always buying old fruit jars and would like to hear from you, whether you have just one jar or a complete collection. I like strong colors such as amber, cobalt blue, and black and all midget jars as well as most half-pints.

John Hathway
Rt. 2, Box 220
Bryant Pond, ME 04219; 207-665-2124

Jars Marked	We Pay
ABC	200.00+
Advance	200.00+
Air Tight Fruit	400.00+
Alston	150.00+
Atterbury	700.00+
Beaver, amber	400.00+
Beehive	100.00+
Commodore	900.00+
Gessner's Patent	200.00+
Indicator	900.00+
Millville, amber or cobalt	2,000.00+
N Osborn	300.00+
Doctor Ramsay's	1,000.00+
Ravenna Glassworks	1,000.00+
Reservoir	200.00+
The Salem Jar	400.00+
J.J. Squire	700.00+
A. Stone	300.00+
Sure	300.00+
Thompson	300.00+
Van Vliet	400.00+
Websters	600.00+
Woods Fruit	150.00+

GAMBLING

I buy early gambling devices. I am especially interested in cheating devices such as card holdouts and anything used to perpetuate a crooked card or dice game. Pre-1900 items are preferred. See list! Send photos if possible!

Ron White
6924 Teller Ct.
Arvada, CO 80003

We Pay

Dealing Boxes	300.00-700.00
Card Trimmers	500.00-800.00
Corner Rounders	500.00-800.00
Holdouts	50.00-1,000.00
Decks of Cards, pre-1900, complete	25.00-100.00
Faro Case Keepers	200.00-500.00
Faro Layouts	200.00-400.00

GAMES

I am buying board games from the 1950s through the 1970s, especially TV show and movie titles. I'm also interested in older games with wood or metal playing pieces. No trivia or game shows wanted. Boxes must be in excellent to mint condition; extra premium prices paid for sealed games. Some examples are listed below.

Mary Kay Stone
2640 Beekman St.
Cincinnati, OH 45225; 513-471-0320

We Pay

Alien	20.00+
Barbie	15.00+
Baretta	5.00+
James Bond	20.00+
Charlie's Angels	5.00+
Cheyenne	40.00+
Clue	5.00+
Columbo	5.00+
The Fugitive	60.00+
Gilligan	30.00+
The Godfather	20.00+
Gunsmoke	40.00+

Hogan's Heroes .... **30.00+**
Hopalong Cassidy .... **40.00+**
I Spy .... **30.00+**
Lie Detector .... **15.00+**
Lost in Space .... **60.00+**
Mission Impossible .... **60.00+**
Mr. Ed .... **30.00+**
Mystery Date .... **15.00+**
Outer Limits .... **75.00+**
Rifleman .... **40.00+**
Risk .... **5.00+**
Star Wars .... **5.00+**
Stratego (wood pieces) .... **5.00+**
Time Tunnel .... **75.00+**
Twilight Zone .... **75.00+**

GASOLINE GLOBES

Private collector buying **gasoline globes, auto-related globes, and various advertising globes** (i.e., shoe repair, beauty shop, etc.). All brands and logos considered. Seriously seeking Stoll Oil, Wespeco Oil, numerous picture globes as well as one-piece etched and raised-letter globes. I buy single lens, glass bodies, and metal band bodies. Sample prices for quality pieces are listed here. Prices will vary depending on quality and rarity of piece, but I always pay fair price – I am not a reseller. I also buy unique gas pumps, clock face, Art Deco, and Wayne pumps.

Wayne Priddy
315 Mayfield-Metropolis Rd.
Paducah, KY 42001
502-554-5619 or 402-444-5915
Digital Page 1-800-841-7243-20742

We Pay

Wespeco ....**500.00-1,000.00+**
Stoll Oil...**300.00-500.00+**
Golden-Tip...**300.00-500.00+**
Silver-Tip ....**300.00-500.00+**
Gulf No-Nox (raised letters) ....**400.00-500.00+**
Good Gulf (etched letters) ....**400.00-500.00+**
Magnolia Gasolene (single lens)..**175.00**

Gas pump globes were first introduced in the early 1910s; they were used to advertise the brand of gas being sold at the gas stations. Some globes simply had brand names on both sides. The most desirable globes had pictures on them such as Indians, lions, old cars, flowers, birds, etc. There are four basic types of gas pump globes. The earliest globes were one-piece milk glass with advertising on both sides. Then there were metal-rimmed globes with glass lens inserts held in place with metal snap rings. Next there were the glass bodies with two glass advertising lenses held on by two or three tiny bolts on each lens. Last were the plastic globe bodies with two glass lenses, and these were the most common. I will pay the following prices for original gas pump globes in nice condition (not cracked or faded).

Walt's Antiques
2513 Nelson Rd.
Traverse City, MI 49684; 616-223-7386

We Pay

One-Piece Glass Globes ....**200.00+**
Metal-Rimmed Bodies w/Two Glass Lenses............................**185.00+**
Glass Bodies w/Two Glass Lenses ....**125.00+**
Plastic Bodies w/Two Glass Lenses ....**65.00+**

GLASS HATS

I am seeking glass hats of all shapes and sizes. I prefer older glass, and all items must be in mint condition with no cracks or chips. Photos are preferred but offers will be accepted, too. Most glass hats were used for toothpick holders or advertising. Prices paid vary on rarity and need for my collection. Contact me giving a full description of your item. I pay fair prices.

B. McCurry
c/o Terrye Stevens
Rt. 3, Box 97
Plainview, TX 79072

We Pay

Depending on Rarity & Desirability **4.00-30.00**

GLASS KNIVES

I am a friendly and enthusiastic collector of glass knives and am editor of the newsletter, *The Cutting Edge*, the publication of the Glass Knife Collectors Club. There are a few glass knives that I don't yet have, and these are very hard to find; but I will pay top prices for them. (I already have lots of crystal glass knives with patterns of three stars, three pinwheels, or daisy-like flowers.) A rubbing, zerographic copy, or photo is much appreciated. Size and color are important, because some glass knives are common in some sizes and colors and rare in others. Small nicks on the blade are acceptable, particularly if the knife is very rare. Please write or call. The following prices are approximate, and other glass knives are also wanted.

Adrienne Escoe
P.O. Box 342
Los Alamitos, CA 90720; 310-430-6479

We Pay

Forest Green or Amber Grid (Aer-Flo)	**200.00**
Crystal thumbguard, 8½" w/ribbed handle	**150.00**
Crystal Plain Handle (curvy handle)	**125.00**
Pink Plain Handle, 8" or 8½" only	**150.00**
Crystal Mini-Thumbguard, 6" or 6½" only	**125.00**
Pink E.S.P. or B.K.	**150.00**

GLASS

SCOOPS

I am buying glass scoops. They were produced between 1890 to about 1940 as novelty or giveaway promotional items. I particularly want colored glass scoops or crystal scoops with embossed advertising (usually a business name with city and state), but I will also buy plain crystal scoops. Nearly all scoops have some chips and flakes from years of usage. I collect **glass knives** as well.

Al Morin
668 Robbins Ave. #23
Dracut, MA 01826; 508-454-7907

We Pay

Crystal, plain	**10.00**
Crystal, w/embossed advertising	**20.00**
Colored, plain	**20.00**
Colored, w/embossed advertising	**30.00**
Milk Glass or Opaque Colored, ea	**35.00**

GLASSWARE

I'm interested in buying nice pieces of **Moon and Star** glassware made by L.E. Smith and L.G. Wright since the 1960s. I prefer red, amberina, light blue, sapphire blue, and some of the nicer amber pieces. Prices depend on size and color, so it's difficult to evaluate specific items; but these are some that I'm particularly interested in:

Water Pitchers	Candlesticks
Water Goblets	Epernes
Wine Goblets	Banana Boats
Decanters	Cake Plates
Miniature Lamps	Spooners
Fairy Lamps	Cheese Dishes
Other Lamps	Butter Dishes
Plates	Sugar Shakers
Tumblers	Syrup Dispensers
Compotes	

Please write or call with information about your Moon and Star items. Other wants needed to complete some collections are listed below.

Linda Holycross
Rt. 3, Box 21
Veedersburg, IN 47987; 800-292-3703

Other Wants   **We Pay**

Jadite Measuring Cup, 2-cup size...**10.00**
Jadite Milk Pitcher, 20-oz, plain..**10.00**
Jadite Egg Cup **3.00**
Jadite Philbe Items (with embossed design).......................**5.00-15.00+**
Jane Ray Demitasse Cup & Saucer..**4.00**
Jane Ray Bowls, many sizes...**2.00+**
Boopie Stemware, any size in ruby, ea..................................**up to 10.00**
Spiral Salt & Pepper Shakers, green, pr **20.00**
Fire-King Turquoise or Azurite Items...**Write**
Cherry Blossom Berry Bowl, green, 4 3/4".....................................**7.00**
Cherry Blossom Cereal Bowl, green, 5 3/4" **12.00**
Cherry Blossom Soup Bowl, green, 7 3/4" **20.00**
Cherry Blossom Salad Plate, green, 7" **8.00**
Cherry Blossom Dinner Plate, green, 9" **10.00**
Cherry Blossom Sugar Bowl Lid, green **10.00**
Cherry Blossom Tumbler, footed (beware of reproductions).....................**14.00**

I am buying **miscellaneous Depression glass as well as collectible glassware from the 1940s-60s.** I prefer less expensive patterns and these colors: blue, turquoise, pink, crystal, amethyst, white, pale green, and pale yellow. All items must be in excellent condition. I have listed some sample items I may be interested in. Please send inquiries.

Vintage Charm
P.O. Box 26241
Austin, TX 78755

We Pay

Columbia, cup & saucer set **2.50**
Bubble, cup & saucer set...**2.50**
Lu Ray, creamer **3.00**
Swanky Swigs **2.00**

Wanted: **Coudersport glass tableware pieces and vases** made at the Bastow Glass Company in Coudersport, Pennsylvania, between 1900 and 1904. The company made berry sets, creamers, spooners, large covered sugar bowls, covered butter dishes, etc. Some items were painted in gold or colors. The basic molds were used to make novelty candy-type dishes in opalescent glass.

I am looking for the Trailing Vine pattern, Three-Fingers and Panel pattern, and 12" tall tri-cornered tulip-type vases. These patterns were made in milk glass, blue opaque, custard, pink clear and opaque, emerald green clear, and clear and amber.

The values of these items range from $30.00 to $400.00. Please send a photo of your item for an offer. Any collector or dealer interested in more information on these items please send SASE.

Tulla Majot
P.O. Box 230
Coudersport, PA 16915

We are interested in all types of old, colored, and unusual glass items including **carnival glass, art glass, opalescent glass, and Depression glass** – to name a few. We want glass produced in the 1950s and before. If you have any item for sale, call or write with description and price. (A photo would be great.)

Specific items sought include:
- Depression glass, but no marigold wanted
- Carnival glass, all colors wanted except marigold (unless piece is large or unusual)
- Art glass, all colors wanted
- Opalescent glass, all colors wanted

Bob & Becky Papagno
560 N Main St.
Caribou, ME 04736; 207-498-8298

Wanted **pink milk glass made by Jeannette Glass Company in 1958 and 1959**. Specific wants are listed below.

Janie Evitts
265 Colonial Oaks
Dayton, TX 77535
409-258-7700 (after 6pm or weekends)

We Pay

Pheasant Candle Holders, pr	**75.00+**
Wall Pockets, pr	**75.00+**
Vase, heavy bottom, 9"	**25.00+**

GLOW LIGHTS

I am buying glow lights. These are clear glass light bulbs with heavy metal filaments inside in the shape of familiar objects. They were made in the United States between the 1920s and '60s. I will buy any, but I am especially looking for the following. I am also looking for catalogs or other advertising and sales helps on these.

Cindy Chipps
4027 Brooks Hill Rd.
Brooks, KY 40109; 502-955-9238

We Pay

Star of David w/Wreath	**50.00**
Star of David w/Menorah	**50.00**
'Keep on Truckin'	**40.00**
Horse's Head w/Pedestal	**60.00**
'Jesus Saves'	**50.00**
Liberty Bell	**45.00**
Smile Face	**50.00**
Bucking Bronco	**60.00**
'U Turn Me On'	**50.00**
Playboy Rabbit	**100.00**
Mickey Mouse	**400.00**
'God Loves You'	**50.00**
'God Loves Me'	**50.00**
Zodiac Signs (Gemini, Cancer, Scorpio, & Sagittarius), ea.	**50.00**
Iris (group of three), tube-shaped bulb	**45.00**
Tulips (group of three), tube-shaped bulb	**45.00**
Any Letter or Number	**15.00-40.00**
Others	**15.00-400.00**

GOEBEL CATS

I collect Goebel cat figurines and have over three hundred of them in my collection. I want to add to my collection any that I don't already have (from crown mark to current mark). At this time, there are no books available on Goebel figurines (other than Hummels), so I have no idea what is out there waiting for me. Some items included on my want list are:

Ashtrays	Lamps
Banks	Match Safes
Bookends	Pin Trays
Candle Holders	Pretzel Holders
Creamers	Salt & Pepper Shakers
Disney	Teapots

If you have any Goebel cats or cat-related figurines, a photo with description of size, color, pose, and any incised number on the bottom would be most helpful.

Linda Nothnagel
Rt. 3, Box 30
Shelbina, MO 63468; 314-588-4958

We Pay

Depending on Trademark, Size, Etc..**20.00-250.00**

GOLF

Wanted: all old golf-related items such as clubs, balls, equipment, etc. Single items as well as collections are sought.

Virginia Young
P.O. Box 42
Amherst, NH 03031; 603-673-3717

We Pay

Club Sets, usable	**25.00-100.00**
Clubs, ea	**Write**
Balls (collectible), ea	**5.00+**
Golf Trophies, pre-1930	**10.00+**
Golf Ephemera (prints, photos of players, etc.)	**Write**

Every golfer has a marker he or she uses whenever they want to pick their ball up off of the green.While many use pennies, dimes, and in rare cases silver dollars, others use items made for just that purpose. Markers come in just about every durable substance known to man from plastic to gold. Value is determined by substance, who may have used it, and where it was used. Please list all these factors when writing, and I will make you an offer accordingly, usually by return mail. Other golfing memorabilia is also desired.

Norm Boughton
1356 Buffalo Rd.
Rochester, NY 14623

I am a collector interested in buying **wooden-shafted golf clubs.** I will buy one or an entire collection. The amount I will pay depends on age, condition, and maker. Send either photos or a complete description including club type, condition, and any markings. Also, please state your asking price. All correspondence will be answered.

Dennis K. Burkhart
2720 Ridge Boulevard
Erie, PA 16506

GRANITEWARE

I am always looking for quality swirl graniteware in all colors (blue, cobalt blue, green, brown, and red). Also wanted are unusual gray pieces or common gray pieces with original paper or stamped labels. Listed are just a few pieces I want with prices I pay for items in excellent condition. Please call or send a photo.

Daryl
P.O. Box 2621
Cedar Rapids, IA 52406; 319-365-3857

Items in Swirl Colors	We Pay
Butter Churn, green, up to	1,000.00
Butter Churn, blue, up to	850.00
Cream Can, colors other than old red, ea, up to	250.00+
Cream Can, old red, up to	1,000.00+
Sugar Bowl, colors other than old red, ea, up to	400.00
Coffeepot, old red, up to	750.00+
Muffin Pan, all colors, ea, up to	400.00+
Measurer, all colors, ea, up to	400.00+
Water Pitcher, all colors, ea, up to	250.00+
Funnel, colors except old red, ea, up to	250.00+
Funnel, old red, up to	500.00

Items in Gray	We Pay
Biscuit Cutter, up to	300.00
Match Safe, up to	200.00
Butter Churn, floor model, up to	1,000.00
Comb Case, up to	250.00+
Shaker Set, up to	250.00+
Castor Set, up to	1,000.00+

GRAPETTE

We will buy almost anything pertaining to Grapette. We are interested in the history of the company, most printed matter, and product advertising. We might purchase Nugrape items, since Grapette later became Nugrape. Grapette concentrate came in glass bottles in the shapes of clowns, elephants, cats, and bears. The clown and elephant bottles say 'Grapette' and 'Camden,

Ark' on the bottom. The cat and bear are only marked on the lid. (There is a Snowcrest bear that some people mistake for the Grapette one, but it is much smaller.) When the concentrate was gone, the cardboard was removed from the lid, and you had a piggy bank. We will also buy bank lids. They are green and white or purple and white and have a slit cut in the top. There was also Lemonette and Orangette in small bottles and concentrate, which would be of interest to us also. If you know of other items, we would like to hear from you.

Hicker' Nut Hill Antiques
Genie & Robert Prather
Rt. 2, Box 532-Y
Tyler, TX 75704

We Pay

Bank Lids	**35¢-75¢**
Bank, bear w/lid	**15.00**
Bank, cat w/lid	**10.00**
Bank, clown w/lid	**3.00**
Bank, elephant w/lid	**6.00**
Brass School Crossing Markers	**5.00**
Clocks	**Write**
Printed Matter	**Write**
Soda Bottle, Grapette	**2.00**
Soda Bottle, Lemonette	**3.00**
Soda Bottle, Orangette	**3.00**
Wooden Soda Crates	**3.00+**
Any Miscellaneous Items	**Write**

I am an active collector of Grapette memorabilia and buy advertising signs, clocks, store displays, cardboard signs, bottle carriers, Grapette cat and elephant banks, extra bank lids, unused pop bottle caps, thermometers, bottle openers, calendars, stadium cushions, coolers, etc. If an item has Grapette, Orangette, Lymette, Lemonette, or Cherryette on it, I am interested. I buy mint to near-mint condition items and will pay fair prices for items that interest me. Condition is very important to me, so please describe any flaws the item has when you write. If possible, send a photo of the item along with your price.

Connie Sword
P.O. Box 23
McCook, NE 69001-0023

HALLOWEEN

We want to buy all types of old Halloween items from the 1880s through the 1950s! We especially like German papier-mache candy holders such as witches, black cats, pumpkin characters, and vegetable people. We also want papier-mache Halloween lanterns (cat heads, pumpkins, etc.) with tissue-paper faces as well as celluloid Halloween toys. Other items we want are hard plastic Halloween toys from the 1940s-50s, wooden-handled tin noise-makers with Halloween scenes, tin 'clickers' with Halloween themes, early composition pumpkin people, 'Dennison' catalogs advertising Halloween decorations, pre-1920 Halloween post cards, 'Jack Pumpkinhead' material from the *Wizard of Oz* stories, and other unusual old Halloween items. Sample prices are below. We will answer all letters!

Bob & Diane Kubicki
P.O. Box 33059
W.P.A.F.B., OH 45433; 513-698-3650

We Pay

Book, *Jack Pumpkinhead of Oz*, old version	**30.00+**
Candy Holder, black composition cat, removable head, glass eyes, 4"	**65.00+**
Candy Holder, black composition cat in dress, removable head German	**225.00**
Candy Holder, papier-mache witch, German	**175.00**

Candy Holder, composition vegetable man, 8"...**100.00+**
Catalog, 'Dennison's' (Halloween decorations) ....**12.00+**
Clicker, tin w/Halloween scene ....**2.00+**
Lantern, papier-mache black cat head w/paper face................................**45.00+**
Lantern, pumpkin head w/tissue face, 6"...**45.00+**
Lantern, papier-mache pumpkin, German, 4" ....**65.00+**
Noisemaker, ratchet type w/composition pumpkin man........................**75.00+**
Post Card, Halloween vegetable people, dated 1911.................................**5.00+**
Pumpkin Man, composition, wearing black hat, 4" ....**45.00+**
Pumpkin, composition, w/vegetable people, German, large ....**285.00+**
Tambourine, paper & wood w/pumpkin face, German............................**55.00+**
Toy, clown on wheels, orange hard plastic ....**12.00+**
Toy, witch on motorcycle, hard plastic ....**25.00+**
Toy, black cat on pumpkin, celluloid, 5"...**55.00+**
Toy, pumpkin car w/witch & black cat, celluloid, 4" long ....**100.00+**

HEAD VASES

I will buy any head vase that you have to sell – ladies, men, children, or animals! These vases must be a head form with a hole in the top for flowers, etc. Price paid will depend on condition and style of head. Please send picture if available or detailed description. I will buy one or thousands!

Jean Griswold
1371 Merry Lane
Atlanta, GA 30329; 404-321-4033

HEISEY

I am looking for items in the **Twist pattern in Moongleam (green)**. Especially wanted are stemware items and footed tumblers, but all pieces are desired. Below are some of my needs. All items must be mint.

Tom Mattingly
P.O. Box 278
Churchton, MD 20733; 301-261-9522

We Pay

Stemware	**40.00+**
Jug, 3-pt	**160.00+**
Candlesticks, pr.	**50.00+**
Kraft Cheese Plate	**40.00+**
Creamer, zigzag handles	**45.00+**
Oil Bottle	**90.00+**
Cocktail Shaker	**450.00+**
French Dressing Bottle	**100.00+**

———

I am extremely interested in **Alexandrite (lavender) and Heisey Chintz in Sahara (yellow)**. I am also buying **Fostoria's Versailles in green, Fostoria's Romance, and Moderntone in cobalt**.

Susan Correa
12636 Shirley St.
Omaha, NE 68144
402-731-8226 or FAX 402-731-2313

Alexandrite   **We Pay**

Mayonnaise, w/dolphin feet & ladle	**200.00**
Individual Nut Dish, w/dolphin feet	**100.00**
Plate, 6" sq	**25.00**
Cup & Saucer, set	**90.00**
Stem Pieces	**Call or Write**

Chintz Pattern in Sahara   **We Pay**

Mayonnaise, w/dolphin feet, 5½"..**50.00**
Sugar Bowl, three dolphin feet..**35.00**
Finger Bowl **15.00**
All Stem Pieces..**Write or Call**

I am buying old elegant glassware: **Heisey, Tiffin, Cambridge, Lancaster, etc.** Prices paid depend on pattern, color, manufacturer, etc. Wheel-cut patterns are preferred.

Peg 'O' My Heart
4831 81st Place, SW
Mukilteo, WA 98275

HULL

I am looking for all pieces of Hull in matte finish in the patterns listed below. Items with cracks or chips are not wanted. Please call or send photo of your item(s).

Daryl
P.O. Box 2621
Cedar Rapids, IA 52406; 319-365-3857

Advertising Plaques	Open Rose
Bow Knot	Orchid
Calla Lily	Poppy
Crab Apple	Thistle
Dogwood	Tulip
Iris	Water Lily
Little Red Riding Hood	Wildflower
Magnolia	Woodland
Morning-Glory	

Hull Pottery of Crooksville, Ohio, produced many varied designs and patterns. I collect only one of their patterns, House 'N Garden in mirror brown with white foam trim. I want to expand my service of four to service for twelve or more. I am interested in dinnerware along with serving pices and special pieces such as various casseroles, leaf dishes, gingerbread men plates, etc. I'm not too interested in other pieces except those shaped like pigs. Marked items are preferred but unmarked ones will be considered. As I am extremely hard to catch by phone, writing would be better. All replies with SASE will be answered. Please don't ask me to make offers. Pricing is open and depends on the item and its condition.

The Trunk Shop
C.W. Gray
123 W 3rd St.
Hermann, MO 65041; 314-486-2804

I wish to purchase the following items:

#1 Bandana Duck, #76, 3½x3½"
#2 Bandana Duck, #75, 5x7"
#3 Bandana Duck, #74, 7x9"

Also I am interested in other unusual items of Hull, especially the Corky Pig banks and Magnolia matte items of the 1940s.

Marion Parsons
Box 492
Ashland, AL 36251; 205-354-3743

HUMMELS

We wish to buy Hummel figurines and prefer those with an early mark: Crown Mark (1934-50); Full Bee (1940-56); Stylized Bee (1955-72); 3-Line Mark (1964-72); and Goebel Bee (1970-79). Each Hummel will bear a facsimile of Sister M.I. Hummel's Signature, 'M.I. Hummel,' with rare exceptions.

As with other fine antiques and collectibles, condition is of prime importance. Additionally, since many Hummels come in more than one size and were produced over a period of time encompassing more than one 'mark,' it is necessary to know size and mark to establish 'fair' value. (Please note that there may be a slight variation of as much as ¼" in size between two examples of the same item or figure.) The listing here represents only a sampling of items we wish to buy. We respond to all offerings by telephone or letter.

Fred & Lila Shrader
2025 Hwy. 199 (Hiouchi)
Crescent City, CA 95531; 707-458-3525

We Pay

Apple Tree Boy, #142, 4", Stylized Bee Mark...65.00
Baker, #128, 5", Stylized Bee Mark 85.00
Boy w/Toothache, #217, 5½", 3-Line Mark...85.00
Carnival, #328, 6", 3-Line Mark...90.00
Goose Girl, #47, 4", Stylized Bee Mark 95.00
Goose Girl, #47, 4", Crown Mark..185.00
Little Bookkeeper, #306, 5", 3-Line Mark..110.00
Little Pharmacist, #322, 6", Goebel Bee Mark...75.00

Madonna Plaque, #48, 3x4", Goebel Mark **35.00**
Photographer, #178, 5", Goebel Mark...**100.00**
Prayer Before Battle, #20, 4¼", 3-Line Mark **70.00**
Ride Into Christmas, #396, 5¾", Goebel Bee Mark **145.00**
Sensitive Hunter, #6, 5", 3-Line Mark...**75.00**
Signs of Spring, #203, Goebel Bee Mark **70.00**
Star Gazer, #132, 5", Stylized Bee Mark..**80.00**
Telling Her Secret, #196, 7", Stylized Bee Mark....................................**175.00**
Tuneful Goodnight, #180, 4x4¾", Full Bee Mark **225.00**
Valentine Gift, #387, 5¾", Goebel Bee Mark..............................**250.00**
Wash Day, #321, 6", 3-Line Mark **110.00**
Wayside Devotion, #28, 7½", Full Bee Mark...............................**220.00**

ICE CREAM SCOOPS

Ice cream scoops are wanted for my collection. I am seeking the older and more unusual ice cream scoops. Please, none marked Gilchrist or Hamilton Beach. Listed below are some examples. Prices will depend on condition.

Lillian M. Cole
14 Harmony School Rd.
Flemington, NJ 08822; 908-782-3198

Manufacturer	We Pay
Pi-Alamoder, Inc.	**300.00+**
Modern Specialty Co.	**300.00+**
Dan Dee Dipper Co.	**300.00+**
Mosteller Mfg.	**300.00+**
J. Schloemer	**300.00+**
Sanitary Mould Co.	**300.00+**
Bohlig Mfg.	**300.00+**

ILLUSTRATOR ART

I am an avid Maxfield Parrish collector interested in prints, books, magazines, ads, and calendars. Please send a detailed description and a photo of your Parrish items along with your asking price. I will respond immediately to all offers.

Lisa Stroup
P.O. Box 3009
Paducah, KY 42002-3009

I am a private collector interested in purchasing framed and unframed prints, posters, and photographs. Below is just a partial listing of items I am looking for. Please write or call with your information. I pay top dollar and guarantee a fast response to your correspondence. I also pay finder's fees for assistance in locating these items.

John S. Zuk
666 Plainfield Ave.
Berkeley Heights, NJ 07922; 908-464-8252

	We Pay
Maxfield Parrish Prints	100.00+
Wallace Nutting Prints	100.00+
R.A. Fox Prints	50.00+
Erte	250.00+
Louis Icart	100.00+
Stieglitz Photos, black & white	100.00+
Ansel Adams Photos, black & white	100.00+
Man Ray Photos, black & white	100.00+
Jules Cheret Posters	100.00+
Rene Penea Posters	100.00+
Cassandre Posters	100.00+
Capiello Posters	100.00+

We buy a wide range of illustrator items (including prints, framed pictures, magazines, calendars, posters, books, etc.) by the following:

Philip Boileau	Maxfield Parrish
A.B. Frost	Frederic Remington
Philip Goodwin	Jessie Wilcox Smith
Bessie Pease Gutmann	N.C. Wyeth
Zula Kenyon	Early Photographers
Wallace Nutting	

We also purchase early golf prints, unusual cupid prints, as well as Black cupids and items. We pay $2.00 each for color 'Cream of Wheat' ad in a complete issue of *Needlecraft* or *Etude* ($3.00 each from other complete magazines). We pay $15.00 each for Buzza Mottos. These were framed picture poems from the 1920s, 7" x 10" print size, usually with a special hanger labeled 'Buzza.'

We pay shipping. Please describe clearly, stating print size, condition, and price.

Antiques by the Beatties
3374 Ver Buker Ave.
Port Edwards, WI 54469; 715-887-3497

I am buying etchings by the French artist, Louis Icart, and the American illustrator, Maxfield Parrish. Most of Louis Icart's works were done in the 1920s and '30s and are pencil signed. If you call me with a description, I can identify the etching's title for you, or you can reference my book, *Louis Icart: The Complete Etchings*, which is fully illustrated. The etchings need not be in perfect condition, although if they're not, prices will be lower than those listed below.

I am buying prints and calendars by Maxfield Parrish, who worked from the 1890s through the 1960s. His most popular works are from the 1920s and '30s. I especially like to buy the Edison-Mazda calendars from 1918 through 1934 and the larger art prints. Color, condition, and framing are very important in determining prices. Faded or foxed pictures are worth less. Some prints come in more than one size – bigger is always better.

William Holland Fine Arts
1708 E Lancaster Ave.
Paoli, PA 19301; 215-648-0369

Louis Icart Etching	**We Pay**
Don Juan	750.00
Milkmaid	825.00

Recollections	**1,200.00**
Duet	**1,400.00**
Best Friends	**1,500.00**
Untied Ribbon	**2,000.00**

Maxfield Parrish Print	**We Pay**
Cleopatra	**up to 1,200.00**
Moonlight (1934)	**up to 500.00**
Hilltop	**up to 500.00**
Aucassin	**up to 350.00**
Dinkey Bird	**up to 100.00**

INDIAN ARTIFACTS

We are always buying any Indian or prehistoric art or antiquities. We are the editors of *Who's Who in Indian Relics* and the founders of *Prehistoric Antiquities*, the only buy-sell-trade publication in this collecting field. We are interested in all flint, stone, pottery or bone artifacts and/or beadwork, baskets, blankets, historic pottery or rugs. We also buy artifacts from around the world, European flint, pre-Columbian pottery, or Mexican stone.

Due to the nature of artifacts, no two are exactly alike; there are variables such as size, color, workmanship, and age. Due to these variables, it is difficult to give approximate values; each artifact must be appraised on its own merits. We have attempted to give the approximate prices of some authentic artifacts and the approximate values that we would be willing to pay. Please contact us if you have artifacts to sell, as we will pay more than anyone in the USA.

Len & Janie Weidner
13706 Robins Rd.
Westerville, OH 43081; 614-965-2868
800-444-1280
305-745-2971 (January through March)

We Pay

Birdstones **200.00-5,000.00**
Flint Spears **20.00-2,000.00**
Pipes **20.00-5,000.00**
Pottery **20.00-5,000.00**
Beadwork **50.00-5,000.00**
Axes **20.00-2,500.00**
Baskets...**30.00-10,000.00**
Bannerstones...**40.00-5,000.00**
Books **1.00-1,000.00**

We are both collectors of Native American material as well as being dealers with extensive collector connections. We are interested in purchasing Native American and Western material. Entire collections or single items wanted.

Sam Kennedy III
P.O. Box 168
Clear Lake, IA 50428
515-357-7151 or 515-357-8550

We Pay

Southwest & Western Baskets, ea..**75.00-10,000.00**
Northwest Baskets, ea **50.00-500.00**
Stone Axe Heads, ea **25.00-300.00**
Arrowheads, ea **1.00-200.00**
Historic Pueblo Pottery...**25.00-2,000.00**
Photographs, Paintings, or Etchings of Indians, ea **10.00-500.00**
Navajo Rugs or Saddle Blankets, ea **30.00-15,000.00**
Bows or Arrows **30.00-500.00**
Beadwork Items..**Varies**
Hopi Kachinas...**100.00-500.00**

INSULATORS

Glass insulators were first used around the middle of the 1800s, and they have been in continuous use throughout all of this century. They were used to separate a charged electrical wire from the ground. Insulators are found in a very large assortment of patterns and colors, the smallest one being the size of a baseball and the largest ones being over a foot in diameter and weighing thirty pounds.

The earliest insulators were fastened to a straight pin. Later on, straight pins were replaced by threaded pins. Many had small projecting points at the bottom. These are known as 'drip points.' Colors will be mostly aqua and clear, but almost any color except red can be found. The following are a few I'm looking for.

Michael Bruner
6980 Walnut Lake Rd.
West Bloomfield, MI 48323

We Pay

American, embossed base, amber	**125.00**
Dominion 42, clear	**10.00**
Dominion 42, cornflower blue	**85.00**
Duquesne, cornflower blue	**20.00**
Emmingers, embossed base	**700.00**
E.R.W.	**175.00**
Fall River Police Signal	**30.00**
Fluid Insulator	**600.00**
H.G. Co. (front) Petticoat (back), smooth base, amber	**60.00**

Hemingray 19, w/drip points in cobalt glass...**50.00**
Locke Insulator Co., amber **150.00**
McMicking, aqua...**25.00**
Mulford & Biddle, amber **150.00**
Tillotson, aqua **100.00**

JEWEL TEA

The Jewel Tea Company in Illinois had door-to-door salesmen who sold basic grocery items to America's housewives such as sugar, oatmeal, butter, coffee, tea, spices, soap powders, cleansers – a multitude of 'Home-Sweet-Home' needs. We buy the tins, boxes, and containers these products came in. The metal containers must lack rust, and the paper items must be very clean. Almost all of these products came in several sizes, and we buy them all. Look for the 'circle Jewel T' logo, and let us pay you cash! All letters answered.

Memory Tree
P.O. Box 9462
Madison, WI 53715
414-261-6641 or FAX 414-261-9461

JEWELRY

Rhinestone jewelry and any signed jewelry by designers listed below are wanted. Colored stones and sets are preferred, but individual pieces are acceptable. Jewelry in the form of butterflies, bugs, dragonflies, flowers, and tiaras are especially sought. I will buy one piece or a hundred.

Nancy Beall
1043 Greta
El Cajon, CA 92021; 619-588-1488

We Pay

Schiaparelli, ea ....**20.00-120.00+**
Coco Chanel, ea ....**30.00-300.00+**
Christian Dior, ea...**10.00-150.00+**
Yves St. Laurent (YSL) ....**10.00-150.00+**
Givenchy ....**10.00-75.00+**
Joseff..**25.00-150.00+**
Eisenberg...**10.00-150.00+**
Miriam Haskell ....**10.00-125.00+**
Pierre Cardin...**10.00-25.00+**

    I buy vintage costume jewelry by the piece, a boxful, or an estate. The jewelry I buy is from the Victorian era to the 1940s, sometimes up to the 1950s & '60s. I especially like nice things from the 1930s and '40s. I like large brooches but also buy sets. I have settled many an estate of costume jewelry by buying the entire amount. I pay very fair market prices. Condition should be good, but I also buy pieces that need stones, pin-backs, and sometimes plating. I pay according to condition. I like signed pieces but purchase unsigned as well.

The Curiosity Shop
Lynell Schwartz
P.O. Box 964
Cheshire, CT 06410; 203-271-0643

We Pay

Haskell Necklaces w/Pearls...**75.00+**
Haskell Earrings w/Pearls..**25.00+**
Haskell Pins w/Pearls ....**50.00+**
Schiaparelli ....**75.00+**
Trifari Clips or Brooches, 4" or longer ....**150.00+**
Trifari Pearls...**10.00+**
Trifari Crowns ....**75.00+**
Trifari Pieces (w/red, blue & green stones)...**65.00+**
Unsigned Brooches, Earrings, Etc., large..................................**Market Price**
HAR Genies...**90.00+**
Bakelite Pins or Bracelets, carved, wide, good color..............................**75.00+**
Bakelite Geometric Bangles, w/dots, stripes, zigzags, etc. ....**150.00+**
Bakelite Figural Pins...**75.00+**
Box Lots or Estate Settlements...**Negotiable**

As a collector/dealer of all types of costume jewelry, I am always looking for interesting things to purchase. This includes signed or unsigned costume jewelry from the 1800s through the 1960s; figural charms and charm bracelets made of gold, gold-filled or silver; and early plastic jewelry. Ladies' items such as compacts, makeup items, pill boxes, and virtually anything decorated with rhinestones will also be considered. I also purchase broken jewelry and pieces missing stones to use for repairs. I would prefer items be pre-priced but will make offers if necessary.

Pamela Wiggins
Depression Delights
6025 Sunnycrest St.
Houston, TX 77087

We Pay

Signed Jewelry (Eisenberg, Haskell, etc.) ....**up to 75.00**
Unsigned Jewelry ....**up to 25.00**
Compacts, Pill Boxes, Etc...**up to 25.00**
Repair Jewelry...**Variable**

I am a dealer who carries an extensive line of gold, sterling, signed and unsigned costume, Bakelite, and unusual jewelry of all materials. I especially want to buy white gold pieces from the 1920s and '30s; sterling animals, figurals, faces – Art Nouveau or the unusual; Mexican and Indian pieces; signed or unsigned costume jewelry; and Bakelite people, faces, animals and fruits.

It is impossible to quote a price sight unseen, because even pieces made by the same company are not equally valuable. Price is determined on the merit of each piece. I have a big turnover in my shop and can afford to pay the highest prices for good pieces. Please let me hear from you. I am interested in most items made before 1975. I will answer all replies with SASE enclosed. Send photocopy, if possible, or describe noting any marks, condition, etc., and asking price. I will pay all postage on items purchased.

Diane Wilson
P.O. Box 561
Wexford, PA 15090

Pre-1970s **Mexican silver items** such as perfume bottles and small boxes are wanted. I like large pins in the shape of birds, flowers, animals and freeforms. These same motifs are wanted in bracelets, necklaces, earrings, and rings with colored stones or made of heavy sterling. Please write and send me a photocopy of your piece or pieces, and I'll get back to you as soon as possible. Buying one or one hundred pieces, if the price is right.

Jewell Evans
4215 Cork Lane
Bakersfield, CA 93309
805-833-3775 or FAX 805-325-8300

JUKEBOXES

I am buying jukeboxes of all kinds. This includes Wurlitzer, Seeburg, Rockola, AMI, and others. I specialize in AMI jukeboxes and deal in restoration and am a supplier of parts. I will buy these in any condition, whole or in parts. I prefer jukeboxes from the '30s to the '60s. Prices below are for complete machines in restorable condition.

Jim Dunham
4514 Maher Ave.
Madison, WI 53716-1735; 608-222-6529

We Pay

AMI Streamliner ....**600.00+**
AMI Singing Towers ....**650.00+**
AMI Singing Towers Deluxe ....**1,000.00+**
AMI-A...**600.00+**
AMI-B ....**450.00+**
AMI-C ....**400.00+**
AMI-D ....**300.00+**
AMI-E ....**200.00+**
AMI-F ....**150.00+**
AMI-G ....**150.00+**
AMI-G 200...**300.00+**
AMI-H..**375.00+**
AMI-I ....**350.00+**
AMI-J ....**300.00+**
AMI-K ....**300.00+**
AMI Lyric ....**200.00+**
AMI Continental II...**500.00+**

KALEIDOSCOPES

I collect toy kaleidoscopes. Any and all types are appreciated, ranging from the dimestore cardboard variety to wooden models from the early 1900s. A primary manufacturer is the Stevens Toy Co. of St. Louis, Missouri. Other scopes may come from Japan, Germany, or England. Some types were used as advertisements or as giveaways during promotions. They should be in near-mint condition. Listed below are some of the scopes I am seeking, but I would be interested in hearing of any and all types.

Joan Walsh
520 Oak Run Dr. #9
Bourbonnais, IL 60914

We Pay

Advertising	**10.00+**
Campbell's Soup Can Kids	**15.00+**
Clown Cop	**10.00+**
Corning Ware	**10.00+**
Glass Model	**10.00+**
Mickey Mouse	**34.00+**
Pixie Deluxe Model	**10.00+**
Porcelain Model	**10.00**
Raggedy Ann & Andy	**24.00+**
Wooden Model	**10.00+**
Any Musical Variety	**10.00+**
Any Character Variety	**10.00+**

KANSAS

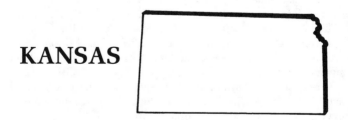

For a short time from the late 1800s to around 1912, there were many glass and pottery plants in the area of southeast Kansas. Abundant natural gas (which began to run out by 1912) attracted two well-known fruit jar producers (Mason and Ball) to the Coffeyville area. Other glass plants (whose products are unknown today) also located there as well as several window-glass plants. A few of the products known to have been produced in the area are listed below. Also listed are sample miniature bricks which were put out by as many as a dozen or so different brick and tile plants.

Here, as everywhere else in the early days of the United States, a popular way for a merchant to advertise was to sell or give away a ceramic or glass souvenir featuring a view of a local park, a building, or a special event to visitors and local customers as well. Most of these plates, vases, jugs, etc. were made in Germany and England, as were view post cards and other items. Some souvenirs carried the message 'souvenir of (name of town, state).' We buy these as well as similar items with street names, buildings, etc. found on them. We also want post cards, calendars, or any advertising material.

Listed below are glass, pottery, souvenir, advertising, and related items we buy. We will buy other items and even some damaged pieces if contacted for prices. Please note that my hometown, Dearing, may also be spelled Deering.

Billy & Jeane Jones.
P.O. Box 82
Dearing, KS 67340; 316-948-6389

We Pay

Premium Glass Fruit Jar, Coffeyville, KS, pt or qt	**10.00**
Premium Glass Fruit Jar, Coffeyville, KS, ½-gal	**12.00**
Premium Glass Fruit Jar, Coffeyville, KS, 1-gal	**35.00**
Premium (Plain) Fruit Jar, sizes as above	**8.00**
Premium 'Improved' Jar	**15.00**
Premium Lid w/Coffeyville	**3.00**
Premium Wire Clip	**4.00**
Premium Magazine Ads, Etc.	**3.00**
Lace Edge Glass Plate, w/'Premium Jar,' Coffeyville, 7"	**50.00**
Lace Edge Glass Plate, w/'Ball Jar,' Coffeyville, 7"	**75.00**
Lace Edge Glass Plate, w/'Pioneer Glass,' Coffeyville, 7"	**40.00**
Ball, The Mason, or Premium Wooden Boxes, Coffeyville	**15.00**
Coffeyville, Independence, Cherryvale, Buffalo, Etc., Miniature Bricks	**15.00**
Any Tin or Cardboard Advertising Sign, Etc., any marked as above	**Write**
Stoneware Jug, bottom incised 'Made in Coffeyville,' brown	**25.00**
Stoneware Crock or Churn, bottom incised 'Made in Coffeyville,' brown.	**30.00**
Terraco O.&H. Coffeyville, KS; Pitcher, terra cotta, brown pottery	**30.00**
Coffeyville Pottery & Clay Co. Miniature Jug	**40.00**
Coffeyville Pottery & Clay Co. Crock, Churn, or Jug, smaller than 4-gal	**30.00**
Coffeyville Pottery & Clay Co. Crock, Churn, or Jug, 4-gal or larger	**20.00**
Coffeyville Stoneware Co. Miniature Jug	**35.00**
Coffeyville Stoneware Co. Crock, Churn, or Jug, smaller than 3-gal	**25.00**
Coffeyville Stoneware Co. Crock, Churn, or Jug, 3-gal or larger	**20.00**

Any Stoneware w/Sponge, Advertising, marked as above, etc. ....**Write**
Magazine Ad, Etc., relative to above **2.00**
Magazine Ad, Rea-Patterson Milling Co. **2.00**
Advertising Signs (including Rea-Patterson), tin, cardboard, paper.........**Write**
Advertising Items, Page Milk, Sweetheart Flour, Dearing, Millers Cash Stove,
    Etc. **10.00**
Picture or Post Card, any company listed..**Write**
Calendar Plate, Dearing or Deering, early 1900s **30.00**
Calendar Plate, Coffeyville, Independence, early 1900s **20.00**
Calendar Plate, Jefferson, Tyro, Chanute, early 1900s **25.00**
Calendar Plate, Caney, Wayside, early 1900s...**12.00**
Calendar Plate, Parsons, Oswego, Altamont, early 1900s **12.00**
Plate, Dearing or Deering, china, scenic view, early 1900s.......................**20.00**
Plate, towns as listed above, china, scenic view, early 1900s....................**10.00**
Vase, Jug, Etc., Dearing, china, scenic view..**15.00**
Vase, Jug, Etc., other southeast KS cities, china, scenic view......................**8.00**
Souvenir Item, Dearing, Heisey Custard or other glass companies **35.00**
Ashtray, Dearing, marked Smelter, early 1900s **20.00**
Picture, Dearing, marked Smelter **10.00**
Plate, Dearing, marked White's Amusement Park.......................................**25.00**
Spoon, Dearing, sterling **20.00**
Spoon, other southeast KS cities, sterling ....**Write**
Other Items (tokens, etc.), Dearing, marked ....**Write**
View Post Card, Dearing, early 1900s **10.00**
View Post Card, Coffeyville, Chanute **2.00**
View Post Card, other southeast KS towns...**1.00+**
Calendar, Dearing, early 1890-1930 ....**15.00**
Calendar, Coffeyville, Chanute or Other Southeast KS Towns..................**3.00+**
Bottle Cap, Carlton Hall, ca 1950s..**25¢**

KENTUCKY DERBY AND RACING
COLLECTIBLES

I am buying tumblers from the three thoroughbred Triple Crown races: Kentucky Derby, Preakness, and Belmont. One glass wanted or an entire collection. Write for the latest prices.

Ron Kramer
P.O. Box 91431
Louisville, KY 40291

Kentucky Derby Glasses   We Pay

1973, '72, or '71	12.00-14.00+
1970, '69, '68, '67, '66, '64, or '63	15.00-22.00+
1965, '62, '60, or '59	27.70-31.00+
1961, '57	45.00+
1958, '56, '55, '54, '53, '52, '49, or '48	55.00-85.00+
1951	195.00+
1950	138.00+
1945, '41, '40 aluminium, or Beetleware	Write

I am interested in buying horse racing collectibles. A few items of interest with prices I pay are given below.

Jerry Newfield
1236 Wilbur Ave.
San Diego, CA 92109; 619-488-7332

We Pay

Racing Programs	50¢+
Kentucky Derby Glasses	3.00+
Racing Pins	1.00+

KEWPIES

Rose O'Neill was one of our early illustrators and cartoonists. Often referred to as the 'mother of the Kewpies,' she was also a serious artist, sculptor, and writer. I am a collector and dealer of her works and wish to buy German bisque Kewpies and Scootles, any original drawings and watercolors, and letters. Especially wanted are Kewpie Doodle dogs, either alone or attached to a basket, bowl, etc. Authentic Kewpies are incised (usually on the bottom) with her signature or sometimes marked with a C in a circle. Some very tiny Kewpies were not signed.

There were so many Kewpie items made as figurines, favors, dolls, etc. that it would be impossible to list everything. Not all are yet known. I want all O'Neilliana and will pay fair prices, so let me know what you have. Price it, and send a photo or sketch, if possible.

Lillian D. Rosen
One Strawberry Hill Ave., Apt. 1F
Stamford, CT 06902

We Pay

Straight Bisque Kewpies, all sizes, ea ....**75.00+**
Action Kewpie, various poses, ea ....**300.00+**
Clothed Kewpie, w/bisque hats (firemen, cowboys, Indians, clowns, soldiers, etc.), ea ....**400.00+**
Kewpie w/Musical Instrument..**300.oo-500.00+**
Glass-Eyed Bisque Kewpie, sm ....**200.00+**
Glass-Eyed Bisque Kewpie, lg...**up to 2,000.00**
Twin Kewpies w/Books, Cannonballs, Clown Hats, Etc.............**300.00-500.00+**
Kewpie w/Crepe Paper or Felt Clothing & Hat..........................**250.00-350.00+**
Kewpie w/Animal (rabbit, chick, etc.)..**150.00-200.00+**
Kewpie Dogs or Other Unusual Kewpie in or on Basket, Vase, Etc. ......**400.00+**
O'Neill Illustrations (especially watercolors & paintings) ....**1,000.00+**
Letters from Rose O'Neill ....**40.00-50.00+**

KNIVES

I am buying **all types of pocketknives and non-folding knives**. I prefer U.S. pocket knives made before 1940 but will consider any others as well. Generally knives longer than 3½" (closed blades) are more valuable than smaller ones.

I'm interested in all kinds of non-folding knives but prefer larger (over 9" total length) hunting styles with original sheaths. All correspondence will be answered but please give detailed description in first letter. A photo, photocopy, or traced drawing showing all blades open will be appreciated.

Denny Stapp
7037 Hynes Rd.
Georgetown, IN 47122; 812-923-3483

We Pay

Wabash Cutlery Co., 1-blade, colorful handle, 5".....................................**150.00**
Keen Kutter #26004, 2-blade, pearl handle, 3⅞" **150.00**
Case Tested XX 62086, 2-blade, bone handle, 3¼"...................................**250.00**

Case Tested XX 6225 ½, 2-blade, bone handle, 3".....................................**125.00**
Case Brothers #2551, 2-blade, ebony handle, 4½"...................................**500.00**
Remington #R1123, 2-blade, bone handle, 4½" **850.00**
Remington #R1263, 2-blade, bone handle, 5⅜" **900.00**
Winchester #4961, 4-blade, bone handle, 4"...**150.00**
Winchester #1950, 1-blade, stag handle, 5¼" **450.00**
Winchester #1920, 1-blade, bone handle, 5"..**500.00**
George Wostenholm Hunting Knife, bone handle, 10" overall **300.00**
Marble's Gladstone Mich (Michigan) Hunting Knife, stag handle, 11" **175.00**

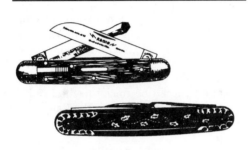

I am buying **all old hunting knives, daggers, and swords**. I prefer knives made before 1960 and especially love knives made prior to 1900. I will buy one piece or entire collections. Big premiums paid for complete collections or truly unusual items.

Robert Lappin
Box 1006
Decatur, IL 62523-217-428-2973

Knives   **We Pay**

Doctor ....**20.00+**
Elephant Toe or Sunfish...**50.00+**
Hunting...**5.00+**
Keen Kutter ....**10.00+**
Marble ....**20.00+**
Randall **75.00-500.00**
Scagel ....**200.00+**
Winchester ....**30.00+**
Any Custom-Made Knife...**Call or Write**
Any Large Folding Knife ....**25.00+**
Any Unusual Shape or Advertiser ....**5.00+**
Any Knife-Related Item ....**2.00+**
Hardware Cutlery Catalogs...**15.00+**

Swords or Daggers   We Pay

Lodge Swords..**20.00+**
Black Forest Daggers & Hunters ....**125.00+**
Any Old Sword ....**50.00+**

I am interested in **all types of Bowie knives**; I prefer Bowies with bone or stag handles. I am especially interested in any knife with engraving on the blade. I prefer knives that were made before 1900 but will accept some later ones if they are unusual. I will pay top prices for knives in excellent condition with original scabbards. Prices given below are for knives in excellent condition, but I will buy Bowie knives in lesser condition as well. It is best to send a photo or drawing of the knife you have for sale. I am especially interested in any Bowie knife that can be traced to the Civil War or Indian War periods. I am a collector, so I will pay more than any dealer; please contact me first. I will answer all inquiries.

David L. Hartline
P.O. Box 775
Worthington, OH 43085

We Pay

Bowie, stag handle, no maker's name, 12".......................................**50.00-200.00**
Bowie, maker's name w/scabbard, 15"...**100.00-300.00**
Bowie, engraving or motto on blade, 15"...**125.00-400.00**
Bowie, presentation blade w/scabbard, lg **200.00-500.00**

LAMPS

As a new collector of motion lamps, I find this style of lamps from the '40s and '50s to be particularly interesting. They should be in good working order – no warping from the heat of the bulb. Nature scenes, campfires, waterfalls, forest fires, and Smokey Bear lamps are examples of some I am currently seeking. I will pay from $15.00 to $35.00 for these moving lamps depending on their age and condition.

Deborah Summers
3258 Harrison St.
Paducah, KY 42001

LAW ENFORCEMENT

We are interested in antique law enforcement badges and other items related to crime and law enforcement. Some items include reward posters, photographs of early lawmen and outlaws, weapons of officers and criminals, and things that relate to criminals of the 1920s-30s (i.e., Charles 'Pretty Boy' Floyd, the Barrows Gang, the Barker Gang, Alvin Karpis) or criminal acts such as the Kansas City Massacre. Special interests include Old West badges and those from Arkansas, Oklahoma, Texas, and other western states.

H.A. Tony Perrin & J. Larry Croom
Antiques of Law & Order
H.C. 7, Box 53 A
Mena, AR 71953
501-394-2863 after 5 PM

We Pay

Badges	**25.00-150.00**
Badges, sterling silver	**50.00+**
Badges, solid gold	**100.00+**
Reward Posters	**10.00+**

Photos ....**10.00+**
Crime Items ....**10.00+**

LEVI STRAUSS

Levi Strauss started manufacturing canvas work pants around 1853 during the California Gold Rush. This product evolved over the next century to become one of the most popular items of clothing in the United States.

Vintage and collectible items of denim manufactured by Levi have a capital 'E' on a red tab or back pocket. Jackets would have this red tab sewn adjacent to the breast pocket. This capital 'E' denotes that the product was made prior to 1971. The lower case 'e' was used thereafter. Other characteristics to look for in vintage Levis are visible rivets inside the jeans and single pockets and silver-colored buttons on jackets with vertical pleats.

I buy a variety of Levi products. Prices paid depend on size, condition, and rarity. I also buy vintage denim jeans and jackets by Lee, Wrangler, Bluebell, J.C. Penney, Oxhide, Big Yanks, James Dean, Doublewear, and Big Smith. Other interests include vintage fabrics and linens such as state map souvenir tablecloths, 1940s-50s drapery or bark cloth yardage, and items with any Western or Southwestern motif.

Dan Kelley
P.O. Box 239
Fayetteville, AR 72702; 501-444-7541

We Pay

Levi 'Big E' Jeans, good condition...**25.00+**
Levi 'Big E' Jeans, w/visible rivets ....**50.00+**
Levi 'Big E' Jackets, w/single pockets & pleats ....**75.00+**
Levi 501 Jeans, blue, 28-36 waist, good condition **10.00**
Levi Jackets, denim, non-vintage **10.00-12.00**
Levi, Lee, Wrangler, or Other Western Shirts, denim w/snaps **4.00-5.00**

LICENSE PLATE ATTACHMENTS

I collect cast aluminum license plate attachments also known as crests, piggybacks, and add-ons. These attachments were made of heavy sand-cast aluminum. The purpose of these crests was largely promotional. They were sold for about fifty-nine cents in all tourist meccas. Florida must have been like heaven for the traveling salesman who wrote orders for these crests. It seems every city and beach in Florida had a crest boasting its name and slogan. Examples would be: 'Miami Beach,' 'Land of Sunshine,' or 'World's Playground.' They all seemed to have adornments flanking both sides of the name – for instance, 'Florida' with a palm tree on one side and a sailfish on the other.

I have sufficient 'Miami,' 'Miami Beach,' and 'Florida.' I want attachments from other Florida cities, towns, and beaches, as well as cities and towns from other states. I am paying $15.00 to $35.00 depending on rarity and condition. I will also consider broken ones if repairable. Please contact me for prices.

Edward Foley
227 Union Ave.
Pittsburgh, PA 15202; 412-761-0685

LICENSE PLATES

One of the most collectible types of **Michigan license plates** are those that were issued for motorcycles. The state of Michigan started making motorcycle plates in 1910, the same year as car plates. Those from 1910 through 1914 were made of porcelain or steel. Plates from 1915 through 1919 were of stamped steel and had an aluminum 'state seal' affixed to the upper left-hand corner. Those from the following years were of stamped steel embossed with 'Mich,' the year, and the number. The word 'cycle' wasn't put on motorcycle plates until the 1970s. In general, motorcycle plates are about one-fourth the size of car plates and were even smaller in the 1940s and 1950s. The only cycle plate that was vertical instead of horizontal was the 1924 plate. I will pay the following prices for Michigan motorcycle plates in nice condition. I also pay top prices for all other types of old and unusual Michigan license plates in nice condition.

Walt's Antiques
2513 Nelson Rd.
Traverse City, MI 49684; 616-223-7386

Porcelain Plates (w/only minor rim chips)   **We Pay**

1910	500.00
1911	400.00
1912	300.00
1913	200.00
1914	150.00

Steel Plates   **We Pay**

1915-19 w/Aluminum 'State Seal' Attached	125.00-150.00
1920-29	85.00-125.00
1930-42	50.00-85.00
1943-49	20.00-50.00

LIGHTNING ROD BALLS

These beautiful ornaments are found in a variety of shapes and sizes. Most are approximately 4½" in diameter, but some are as small as 3" and others may be as large as 5½" in diameter. The production of lightning rod balls began in the mid-1800s and still continues (although in very limited terms) today. The heyday of their production was during the first part of this century. As many as thirty different patterns were produced.

Most were made of white opaque glass, but many other colors such as ambers, cobalts, greens, reds, etc. were used as well. Some will have a 'mirror-like' coating on the inside. These are found in a limited variety of patterns and colors. Condition of the collars can be less than perfect, but the ball itself should be free from cracks, chips, or other problems. These are some of my wants along with prices I will pay.

Michael Bruner
6980 Walnut Lake Rd.
West Bloomfield, MI 48323

We Pay

4½" round in green mercury	**150.00**
3" round in orange	**160.00**
5½" pleated in red	**300.00**
4½" moon & star pattern in cobalt	**350.00**
5" R.H.F. in amber	**100.00**
3" in gold mercury	**170.00**
4½" round pleated in amber	**150.00**
5" swirl pattern in cobalt	**325.00**
5" dot & dash pattern in amber or cobalt, ea	**375.00**
5" quilted pattern in cobalt	**75.00**
4½" round in yellow	**600.00**
4½" Maher in red	**100.00**
3" round in red	**50.00**
5½" sharp pleated in amber	**90.00**
4½" round in pink	**125.00**
3" round in silver mercury	**100.00**
4½" round, sharp pleated in green	**125.00**
Electra, cone shaped in red	**175.00**
D&S, 6-sided in red	**45.00**
J.F.G. in cobalt	**15.00**
Onion pattern in cobalt	**600.00**
5" quilt pattern in gold mercury	**190.00**
Shinn system belted pattern in amber	**45.00**
4½" round in lime green opaque	**35.00**

LUNCH BOXES

I am collecting and would like to purchase lunch boxes and thermoses for children. My favorites are the ones from 1950 to 1989. Below is a listing of some that I want and prices I will pay for them in excellent condition. Price will be lower for items in lesser condition.

Terri Mardis-Ivers
1104 Shirlee Ave.
Ponca City, OK 74601
405-762-5174 or 405-762-8697

We Pay

Casey Jones, dome lunch box, metal	**80.00**
Casey Jones, thermos	**40.00**
Gene Autry, lunch box, 1950s	**65.00+**
Gene Autry, thermos	**35.00**
Jetsons, dome lunch box, 1963	**175.00**
Jetsons, thermos, 1963	**40.00**
Lone Ranger, lunch box, 1950s	**65.00+**
Lone Ranger, thermos	**35.00**
Lost in Space, dome lunch box, 1966	**125.00**
Supercar, lunch box, metal	**65.00**
Supercar, thermos	**35.00**
Star Trek, dome lunch box	**135.00**
Star Trek, thermos	**40.00**
Toppie the Elephant, lunch box	**200.00**
Toppie the Elephant, thermos	**60.00**
Volkswagon Bus, dome lunch box, metal	**85.00**

I also want the following boxes or thermoses, and I will pay $20.00 or more for these:

Alvin & the Chipmunks
Atom Ant
Annie Oakley
Americana
Banana Splits
Batman
Beany & Cecil
Beatles
Beverly Hillbillies
Blondie
Boating
Bond XX
Bobby Soxer, vinyl
Boston Bruins
Brady Bunch
Brave Eagle
Bread Loaf
Buccaneer
Bullwinkle
Cable Car
Campbell Kids
Captain Astro
Carnival
Cartoon Zoo
Casper
Chuck Wagon
Circus Wagon
Cowboy in Africa
Deputy Dawg, vinyl
Dick Tracy
Dr. Seuss
Dudley Do-Right
Dutch Cottage, dome
El Chavo
Emergency, dome
Fireball XL5
Fire House, dome
Flintstones
Frontier Days
Gentle Ben
Gigi
Globetrotter, dome
    (sticker-covered suitcase)

Gomer Pyle
Go-Go's
Great Wild West
Green Hornet
Gunsmoke
Hector Heathcote
Hogan's Heroes
Hometown Airport
Hopalong Cassidy
Howdy Doody
It's About Time
James Bond
Junior Nurse
Kellogg's Frosted Flakes
Knight in Armor
Liddle Kiddles
Linus the Lion Hearted, vinyl
Loonie Tunes TV Set
Ludwig Von Drake
Man from UNCLE
Mod Floral
Monkees
Munsters
Paladin
Pink Panther
Porky's Lunch Wagon
Psychedelic, dome
Rifleman
Ringling Brothers Circus
Sabrina
Soupy Sales
Smokey Bear
Snack Sack, vinyl
Steve Canyon
Tinker Bell
Treasure Chest
Twiggy
Underdog
U.S. Space Corps
Voyage to the Bottom of the Sea
Wild, Wild West
Woody Woodpecker
Yosemite Sam

Hundreds more lunch boxes and thermoses are wanted. Photos would help me judge condition. Please send SASE with inquiries.

LIMITED EDITION COLLECTIBLES

I'm interested in buying **Kitty Cucumber items**. These are cat figurines stamped Kitty Cucumber that have a sticker saying Schmid on the bottom.

Jean Brown
824 N Main
Independence, MO 64050

We Pay

Figurines	**5.00+**
Thimbles	**3.00+**
Ornaments	**3.00+**
Music Boxes	**10.00+**

MAGAZINES

I am interested in all harmless collectibles. That would include magazines, baseball and other sports memorabilia, post cards, comic books, books, advertising, and fishing items – to name a few. I also clean attics. I am interested in just about everything collectible. Give me a jingle or drop a line. Below are some samples prices of what I can pay.

Countryside Collectibles
P.O. Box 1147
Midland, MI 48640; 517-687-5626

Magazines   **We Pay**

Ladies' Home Journal ....**up to 50.00**
Sports or *Sports Illustrated* ....**up to 50.00**
Pictorial Review ....**up to 35.00**
Life ....**up to 25.00**
McCalls ....**up to 15.00**
Time ....**Write**
Newsweek ....**Write**
Field & Stream ....**Write**

I am looking for the following issues of *Spinning Wheel Magazine* to complete my collection. I will reimburse shipping costs. All magazines must be in mint condition with the covers intact, no writing in or on the magazines, and no articles cut out.

Diana McConnell
14 Sassafras Lane
Swedesboro, NJ 08085; 609-467-0685

Spinning Wheel Magazine   **We Pay**

1970, January through December (except July & August), ea ....**75¢**
1971, January through December (except May, June, October, & November), ea ....**75¢**
1972, March, May through December (other months not needed), ea ....**75¢**
1973, any issue, ea **1.00**
1974, any issue, ea **1.00**
1975, January through March, May, June, & September (other months not needed), ea **1.00**
1976-79, any issue, ea **1.00**
1980 to present, any issue, ea **1.25**

I am actively looking to buy *Life* and *Judge* magazines published between 1900-20 for research material. Magazines need to be intact and readable.

Some minor damage is acceptable, providing the price is reasonable. Call with what you have!

George & Pamela Curran
P.O. Box 713
New Smyrna Beach, FL 32170-0713; 904-345-0150

We Pay

Life, 1900-20, ea ....**10.00+**
Judge, 1900-20, ea ....**10.00+**

MARBLES

    I am buying handmade marbles from 1870 through the 1930s and am also interested in finding machine-made marbles from the 1930s through the 1950s. I also buy packaged sets of marbles in the original bags or boxes. I will buy one marble or an entire collection. Listed below are some of my wants – the more unusual the better!

David A. Smith
1142 S Spring St.
Springfield, IL 62704; 217-523-3391

We Pay

Handmade (Popeyes, corkscrews, oxbloods, etc.) ....**3.00+**
Beaded Lutz, any color ....**10.00+**
Onionskins, any kind..**5.00+**
Indians, any kind ....**10.00+**
Divided or Solid-Core Swirls, any size..**5.00+**
Sulphide Figure Marbles, any figure inside ....**10.00+**
Handmade Agates, any size...**3.00+**
Sets (original bags of marbles)..**5.00+**

I am a marble collector who needs your help in finding marbles made from the 1850s through the 1940s. These little works of art represent one of the oldest games in the world dating back to B.C. Photos helpful; send, write, or call. I will consider any and all marbles.

Anthony Niccoli
823 E 25th Ave.
N Kansas City, MO 64116; 816-471-1370

We Pay

Handmade, ea **1.00-1,000.00**
Comic Face, ea **30.00-200.00**
Machine-Made, ea...**50¢-100.00**
Contemporary, ea...**25¢-25.00**
Hand-Painted, ea..**10.00-1,000.00**
Boxes, ea...**10.00+**
Bags, ea...**3.00+**
Games, ea ....**5.00+**
Advertisements, ea...**5.00+**
Books, ea ....**5.00+**
Paperweights, ea **10.00-200.00**
Other Memorabilia...**10.00+**

Machine-made and man-made marbles in mint, unpolished condition are wanted – no game marbles, cat's eyes, or Benningtons. We like swirls, lutz, clambroth, onionskins, sulphides, agates, micas, carnelians, cyclones, turkeys, flames, corkscrews, Popeyes, and pee wees. I will also buy marbles by the box lot. Old marble boxes and containers as well as prints of marble players are wanted. Prices paid are according to quantity and type. Photos are helpful.

Gram & Me, Marbles
908 E Maywood Ave.
Peoria, IL 61603

Private collector looking to augment paperweight collection with large hand-made marbles (the larger the better): swirls, latticinio, onionskins, lutz, clambroths, and paperweight millefiori types in mint or near-mint condition. One or two pontil marks should be clearly visible at opposite poles of the marble. Please write or call first with description or photo together with your asking price.

Andrew Dohan
49 E Lancaster Ave.
Frazer, PA 19355; 215-647-3310

MATCH SAFES

I am an advanced collector interested in purchasing quality pocket match safes. I collect all categories but am especially interested in figural, enameled, fancy and unusual match safes. I am interested in one item or an entire collection. Please send picture and/or description along with price desired. I respond to all inquiries. Listed below are some of the items I am interested in buying.

George Sparacio
P.O. Box 791
Malaga, NJ 08328

We Pay

Baden Powell, figural	**225.00+**
Billiken, figural, sterling	**350.00+**
Cigar, figural, enamel band	**450.00+**
Domino, figural, vulcanite	**50.00+**
Enameled, on brass, French type	**125.00+**
Enameled, on sterling	**135.00+**
Fire or Firemen Motif	**110.00+**
Figural, most types	**125.00+**
Niello, Russian, silver	**150.00+**
Oriental, figurals, brass	**175.00+**
Pants, figural, pewter	**65.00+**
President Cleveland, figural, plated brass	**175.00+**
President Grant, figural, plated brass	**225.00+**
Running Pig, figural, brass	**155.00+**
Tartan, go-to-bed	**125.00+**

MILITARIA

I am buying **military items that date prior to and through WWII**. Free appraisals given for any military item accompanied by photo and SASE. Listed below are some of the items I seek with prices I will pay.

Tom Winter
817 Patton
Springfield, IL 62702; 217-523-8729

We Pay

Awards	**up to 200.00**
Badges	**up to 200.00**
German Helmets	**50.00+**
German Patches	**5.00+**
German S.S. Daggers	**up to 1,000.00**
Japanese Medals	**25.00+**

Japanese Samurai Swords	**up to 2,500.00**
Medals	**up to 200.00**
Regimental Flags	**up to 600.00**
U.S. Leather Flight Jackets, A2	**up to 350.00**
U.S. Fighting Knives	**25.00-200.00**
WWI Marine Corp Items	**up to 100.00**

I am interested in **all types of edged German weapons, bayonets, swords, fighting knives, etc.** I am mainly interested in WWI German bayonets and daggers. I will buy WWII German daggers but only original ones. (80% of all WWII German daggers in the United States are reproductions.) I am interested in all unusual German knives, Bowie knives, sawtooth bayonets, fighting knives, swords with engravings or owner's name, etc. I am also interested in German medals and uniforms from WWI. Photos and description will be helpful when you answer this ad. I am a collector and will pay more than a dealer. Please contact me first. I will answer all inquires regarding listing below.

David L. Hartline
P.O. Box 775
Worthington, OH 43085

We Pay

German WWI Model 05 Butcher Bayonet **25.00-50.00**
German WWI Sawtooth Bayonet w/Scabbard **40.00-100.00**
German WWI Sawtooth Bayonet w/Engraved Blade **50.00-150.00**
German Trench Knife w/Scabbard..**25.00-75.00**
German Bowie Knife w/Stag Handle **50.00-150.00**
German WWI Dress Sword w/Scabbard **75.00-150.00**
German WWII Dress Dagger, EX **100.00-500.00**

We buy **German and Japanese items of WWI and WWII.**

D. Lerch Co. Promotions
P.O. Box 586
N White Plains, NY 10603; 914-739-4931

We Pay

Daggers...**up to 1,000.00**
Documents ....**up to 200.00**
Helmets ....**up to 300.00**
Holsters ....**up to 50.00**
Lugers..**up to 600.00**
Swords ....**up to 600.00**

I am buying **WWI military items from the 1914 through 1918 war.** I am particularly interested in items from the **American Ambulance Field Service and the French Foreign Legion.** The types of items I am looking for are uniforms, helmets, insignia, documents, medals, ambulance plates, etc. – practically anything which would be related to these two volunteer groups. Please let me know if you have anything in this area. I will pay generous prices for such items.

Dennis Gordon
1246 N Ave.
Missoula, MT 59801; 406-549-6280

MISCELLANEOUS

I collect, buy, sell, and trade all older flea market-type items.

Tammy Rodrick
Rt. #2, Box 163
Sumner, IL 62466

We Pay

Beer Steins	up to 10.00
Blue Willow & Locs of Scotland Pieces	up to 5.00
Cereal Rings	up to 5.00
Character Dolls	up to 25.00
Clocks	up to 20.00
Colonial Homestead Pieces	1.00
Fast Food Glasses	1.00
Heath Co. Bottles	5.00
Holly Hobby Items (mostly ceramic)	up to 5.00
Horse Models	up to 5.00
Indian Dolls	2.00
Lady Head Vases	up to 5.00
L.E. Smith Glassware	up to 5.00
Marigold Piggy Banks, Ohio Oil Co.	5.00
Marx Toy Sets	up to 10.00
Prints, old color	up to 10.00
Prints, Gutmann or Icart	up to 20.00
Ransbottom Roseville	up to 10.00
Trolls	up to 25.00

MODEL KITS

I am seeking figure-related model kits from 1950 through the 1970s, especially Aurora monsters, super heroes, etc. Revel Rat Fink series, the Hawk Company's Weird-Ohs series, and others are wanted as well – also any product catalogs, store displays, original artwork, etc. Just a few examples are listed here.

Toy Scouts, Inc.
Bill Bruegman
137 Casteron Ave.
Akron, OH 44303
216-836-0668 or FAX 216-869-8668

We Pay

Aurora Godzilla-Go-Cart, unassembled in box ....**up to 1,000.00**
Aurora Lost in Space, unassembled in box....................................**up to 400.00**
Revel Robin Hood Fink, unassembled in box ....**up to 100.00**

MOTORCYCLES

Wanted are old motorcycles and motorcycle accessories. Of special interest are Indian motorcycles. Complete machines in any condition as well as parts are sought. Motorcycle licenses, plates, trophies, awards, photos, etc. are wanted as well.

Virginia Young
P.O. Box 42
Amherst, NH 03031; 603-673-3717

MOVIE MEMORABILIA

I am interested in all **movie trade publications** from 1900 to the present. These publications were issued by the various movie studios or publishers for use in the motion picture industry and were not for the general public.

My primary collecting interest is in movie studio publicity annuals. These were produced by the various movie studios to advertise their upcoming films to movie theatre owners. Some of these are quite large and elaborate, while others were smaller in size and less elaborate. These folios often pictured many different movies for the coming movie season of the various studios. They were sometimes done in color or black and white.

Other trade publications I'm interested in are those published by studios on a regular basis such as *The Lion's Roar, Columbia Mirror,* and other similar studio-related magazines. Also, *Moving Picture World, Motion Picture News,* and similar general trade movie publications, especially those from 1900 to the 1940s, are wanted. Several specific titles are listed here.

George Reed
7216 Kindred St.
Philadelphia, PA 19149; 215-725-3003

We Pay

Advertising the Motion Picture, Quigley Publishing, 1937.....................100.00+
Columbia Mirror, July 1st, 1935 ....75.00+
Fox Dynamo ....25.00+
Greater New Show World, Paramount, 1930-31 ....100.00+
Happy Omen for Happy Showmen, Fox, 1930-31...................................100.00+
Lion's Roar ....50.00+
Moving Picture World, 1900-30s ....15.00+
Parade of Hits, M.G.M., 1926-27 ....100.00+
Paramount Pictures 15th Birthday Group, 1926-27 ....100.00+
Pathe, 1930-31 ....100.00+
United Artists, 1927 ....100.00+
54 from Universal, Second White List, 1925-26 ....100.00+
Studio Publicity Books, ca 1920s...50.00-100.00+
Studio Publicity Books, late 1920s-early '40s ....100.00-200.00+
Studio Publicity Books, late 1940s-early '50s ....75.00-100.00+
In-House Publications (depending on publication, studio, etc.)..50.00-100.00+
Trade Publications, 1900s-30s ....15.00-50.00+
Trade Publications, 1940s-50s ....10.00-25.00+

MUSIC AND RELATED ITEMS

I am a private collector interested in purchasing all types of **antique musical boxes, phonographs, radios, etc.** I also pay finder's fees for assistance in locating these pieces. I pay top prices and guarantee a fast response to your correspondence.

John S. Zuk
666 Plainfield Ave.
Berkeley Heights, NJ 07922; 908-464-8252

We Pay

Cylinder Musical Boxes	**500.00+**
Disc Musical Boxes	**750.00+**
Wooden (carved) Whistling Figures	**500.00+**
Mechanical Singing Birds	**500.00+**
Antique (tube) Radios	**50.00+**
Wind-Up Phonographs (78 rpm)	**50.00+**
Cylinder Record (horn) Phonographs	**250.00+**

We are buying **fretted instruments of value**. We prefer them in good condition made before 1970 but will consider later models as well. We are interested in a variety of name brands and models. Call or write for a fair price quote.

Jeff Soileau
155 N College St.
Auburn, AL 36830; 205-887-7735

Martin   **We Pay**

D-18	**300.00+**
D-28	**400.00+**
D-35	**400.00+**
D-45	**800.00+**

Music and Related Items

Gibson

	We Pay
Les Paul	250.00+
Brydland	500.00+
Es Series	200.00+
Archtop	200.00+

Fender

	We Pay
Stratocaster	250.00+
Telecaster	250.00+
Broadcaster	1,000.00+
Jazz Bass	250.00+

I want to buy **American-made guitars** such as Fender, Gibson, Rickenbacker, Gretsh, and Martin. I would be interested in hearing about other fine guitars with other brand names. I am paying $100.00 and up for certain models. Please send photos if possible and an SASE for a reply when corresponding. Thank you for your consideration.

Brett Ivers
1104 Shirlee Ave.
Ponca City, OK 74601
405-762-5174 or 405-762-8697

I am buying **player panio rolls and ten-tune nickelodeon rolls of popular music only** – no foreign or classical wanted. Rolls need not be perfect but only in average playable condition with no major tears or serious edge damage.

Before sending anything, please look in the box and make sure the roll label is the same as the label on the box. Original rolls only are wanted – no recuts or reissues are needed at this time. I am offering $10.00 or more for any roll I can use.

Ed Sprankle
1768 Leimert Blvd.
Oakland, CA 94602

We Pay

Standard Player Roll (for home players), any I can use **10.00**
65-Note Pin-End Rolls (for early home players), any I can use...................**10.00**

10-Tune 'A' Nickelodeon Piano Roll Brand   **We Pay**

Clark, Automatic, or United States Music, ea....................................**25.00-40.00**
Capitol 10-Tune or 15-Tune Rolls, ea **45.00-65.00**
Capitol Rolls, all blues, ea **150.00**

NEON SIGNS AND ART

I collect old neon pieces including clocks, signs, or unusual symbols. Some of these have metal framework with no art behind the glass tubing, and some have painted or printed artwork on a background piece with the tubing outlining only parts of the design. Clocks often have the neon tubing enclosed within the clock itself. The neon tubing must be unbroken and still connected at the transformer for a premium price. Lower prices will be paid for a neon that needs work.

B.J. Summers
Rt. 6, Box 659
Benton, KY 42025

NIPPON

I am wanting to buy chocolate pots with or without cups, lemonade sets, vases, or anything else with hand-painted decoration as long as they are not chipped or cracked. I will pay good prices for a desirable piece (depends on mark as well). No reproductions are wanted. Please state asking price with first writing.

Rhonda Hasse
566 Oak Terrace Dr.
Farmington, MO 63640

NORTH DAKOTA COLLECTIBLES

We live in a small rural community in southwest North Dakota and are interested in buying items originating in North Dakota, South Dakota, and Montana prior to the 1950s. Wanted are souvenir items with town names (especially North Dakota towns of Bowman, Rhame, Marmarth, Scranton,

Reeder, Amidon, Haley, and Griffin).

Items of most interest with these names are souvenir glassware in red, green, blue, or white; advertising mirrors; and crocks. No alcohol or tobacco promotional items please. We also buy Dakota Territory memorabilia, small artifacts or calvary items, books by North Dakota or regional authors, pottery by Messer, and old salt and pepper collections.

We pay from $5.00 to $25.00 for most items with no cracks or chips. Please send a photo or a detailed description. We will try to pay your asking price, or we will make you an offer.

Stan & Carrie Soderstrom
003-3rd St. SW
Rt. 2, Box 300
Bowman, ND 58623

We Pay

Advertising Mirrors	**5.00+**
Cavalry Items	**2.00+**
Dakota Territory Memorabilia	**1.00+**
Salt & Pepper Sets	**2.00+**
Souvenir Glass, clear or colored	**8.00+**
Messer Pottery	**2.00**

NAUTICAL MEMORABILIA

Nautical Memorabilia

I am buying all nautical or navy-related items as well as anything relating to the United States Naval Academy located at Annapolis, Maryland. I am seeking anything nautical from any era such as Wedgewood and Spode china, glasses with the Naval Academy insignia, uniforms, medals, swords, yearbooks, and the like. Please send a picture with a stamped self-addressed envelope. Include your asking price, or feel free to call.

Walnut Leaf Antiques
Joel Litzky
50 Maryland Ave.
Annapolis, MD 21401; 410-263-4885

Nautical Instruments

	We Pay
Sextants	50.00+
Octants	50.00+
Telescopes	25.00+
Compasses	10.00+
Binnacles	100.00+

Ship Models

	We Pay
Freestanding	25.00+
In Bottles	10.00+
In Picture Frames	25.00+
Half Hulls	25.00+

Naval Academy Memorabilia

	We Pay
Wedgwood Cup & Saucer	10.00+
Wedgwood Plate	20.00+
Wedgwood Serving Pieces, ea	35.00+
Spode Cup & Saucer	10.00+
Spode Plate	20.00
Spode Serving Pieces, ea	35.00
Glasses, any type or size	3.00+
Uniform, any era	25.00+
Sword, any era	50.00+
Yearbook (Lucky Bag)	3.00+
Sports Memorabilia	5.00+
Diploma	5.00+

OCCUPIED JAPAN

I will buy certain types of Occupied Japan collectibles. All items must be marked. Salt and pepper sets or paper products are not wanted. Listed below are some categories I am particularly interested in buying. However I will consider other items of an unusual nature.

Mary Zuzan
Rt. 2, Box 65
Denton, MD 21629

We Pay

Planters	**5.00+**
Mugs, Steins, or Tobies	**10.00+**
Metal Items	**2.00+**
Teapots or Tea Sets	**Write**

Occupied Japan items for private collection and resale are wanted. Items may be made of china, metal, or paper; nearly all items from rugs to figurines are wanted. Fair prices will be paid for a single item or for a whole collection. No damaged items please. Other interests for resale are costume jewelry, glass, and pottery.

Brent Dilworth
89 W Pacific
Blackfoot, ID 83221; 208-785-7109

OPTICAL-RELATED ITEMS

I am buying eyeglasses and other eyewear. I prefer items from the 1700s through 1920s – one piece or a collection. Some of the things I am looking for are listed here. I also look for unique opera glasses.

Kayla Conway
4500 Napal Ct.
Bakersfield, CA 93307

We Pay

Gold-Filled Glasses w/Chain..**5.00+**
Opera Glasses ....**25.00+**
Reading or Sunglasses Charm ....**10.00+**
Monocular, any kind...**25.00+**
Lorgnettes ....**25.00+**

PAPERWEIGHTS

Private collector buying one or entire collections of antique (pre-1900s) glass paperweights. French, American, English, Bohemian, millefiori, and flowers and fruit designs are preferred. Please, no rectangular glass-covered photos unless it shows an old glass factory. Also desired are modern, artist-signed paperweights such as Stankard, Ysart, and Kazian as well as modern Baccarat, St. Louis, and Perthshire limited-edition paperweights.

On older paperweights, surface wear and minor chips to base are not a problem. Please write or call first with description or photo together with your asking price.

Andrew Dohan
49 E Lancaster Ave.
Frazer, PA 19355; 215-647-3310

PEN DELFIN RABBIT FIGURINES

I'm interested in purchasing quality retired Pen Delfin rabbit figurines and display pieces. Quality is extremely important. Please send picture and/or description along with price desired. I respond to all inquiries. Listed below are some of the items I am interested in buying.

George Sparacio
P.O. Box 791
Malaga, NJ 08328

We Pay

Aunt Agatha	**750.00+**
Cha Cha	**200.00+**
Cyril Squirrel	**900.00+**
Father (old)	**600.00+**
Gussie	**150.00+**
Lollipop	**150.00+**
Margot	**200.00+**
Midge (original)	**150.00+**
Mother (old)	**600.00+**
Mother Mouse	**600.00+**
Robert (original)	**125.00+**
Uncle Soames	**175.00+**

PENCIL SHARPENERS

As an avid pencil sharpener collector for over thirty years, I am always interested in finding unusual ones to add to my collection. Small pencil sharpeners were first developed for the pocket or purse in the 1890s. The typical design consisted of small steel tubes containing a cutting blade which could be adjusted by screws.

Mass-produced novelty pencil sharpeners became popular in the late 1920s. The most detailed figurals were made in Germany. The German sharpeners originally sold for less than a dollar. Disney and other character pencil sharpeners have been produced in Catalin, plastic, ceramic, and rubber. And for over fifty years, pencil sharpeners have been used as advertising giveaways. As you see, there are many facets to collecting pencil sharpeners. Listed below are the minimum prices I will pay for pencil sharpeners in excellent condition.

Marth Hughes
4128 Ingalls St.
San Diego, CA 92103; 619-296-1866

We Pay

Turn-of-the-Century Mechanicals	**50.00**
German Metal Figurals	**25.00**
Japan Metal Figurals	**10.00**
Catalin Items	**10.00**

PHOENIX GLASS

I am researching the Phoenix Glass Company of Monaca, Pennsylvania, in an effort to write a detailed and accurate history of the company since its beginning in 1880. Over the years, Phoenix has produced a wide variety of utilitarian and decorative glassware including Webb-style art glass, colored cut glass, hand-decorated oil lamps, hotel and barware, gas and electric light shades, and the line of 'sculptured' vases, bowls, etc., for which they are best known. I am especially hunting original company catalogues and advertising brochures, magazine ads showing glassware, unusual pieces, and related items such as post cards of Monaca. I'd Like to hear from retired workers and other people who are willing to share their knowledge and love of Phoenix with me. Mini-biographies of 'the Phoenix family' will be included in my book.

The price I can pay for an item varies, depending on pattern, color, and condition of each piece. Please price and fully describe each item. Photos are helpful. I answer all letters.

Kathy Hansen
1621 Princess Ave.
Pittsburgh, PA 15216; 412-561-3379

PHOTOGRAPHICA

SABONY, 60L BROADWAY.
BUFFALO BILL

I will buy **all types of photos: daguerreotype, ambrotype, CDV, cabinet card, long regimental photos, etc.** I especially want all types of military photos and prefer outside shots. Good, clear photos with uniforms and equipment are worth more. I am very interested in photos of Black soldiers and photos of early U.S. Cavalry. Condition and content decide how much the photo is worth. Please send a xerox copy if possible. I am a collector and will pay more than any dealer, so contact me first. Below are just some examples of prices but the final price is decided by the photo itself. I will answer all inquiries.

David L. Hartline
P.O. Box 775
Worthington, OH 43085

We Pay

Cabinet Card, cavalry man on horse **25.00-100.00**
CDV, soldier w/equipment...**20.00-100.00**
Tintype, Civil War soldier w/equipment...**25.00-100.00**
Tintype, soldier w/gun, sword, knives, etc. **50.00-300.00**
Tintype, Black soldier **35.00-150.00**
Black Cavalryman on Horse **50.00-250.00**

Charles has been buying old photographs for the past twelve years. His interests are in American subjects from the 1800s to the early 1950s. Strongest interests are in those from the 19th century and early 20th century. Only original photos (no reprints) in excellent condition are purchased. When writing him, please indicate the size and subject of the photo, condition, identifying markings, any known historical information about the photo, and the type of photo (tintype, CDV, cabinet card, real-photo post card, etc.). A photocopy is essential in evaluating the photograph's desirability. Mr. Hatfield does not accept items sent on approval.

The following is a list of photos with prices he is willing to pay.

Charles L. Hatfield
1411 S State St.
Springfield, IL 62704

We Pay

Abe Lincoln CDV	**12.00**
Civil War Soldier Tintype	**25.00**
Civil War Soldier CDV	**10.00**
Horace Greeley CDV	**12.00**
U.S. Grant CDV	**10.00**
Grover Cleveland Cabinet Card	**8.00**
Benjamin Harrison Cabinet Card	**7.00**
William Jennings Bryan Cabinet Card	**8.00**
William McKinley Cabinet Card	**7.00**
Black Person Tintype	**9.00**
Black Person Cabinet Card	**7.00**
Fireman Tintype	**15.00**
Fireman Cabinet Card	**10.00**
Fire Company Cabinet Card or Real-Photo Post Card	**8.00**
Lawman (w/badge) Tintype	**12.00**
Lawman (w/badge) Cabinet Card	**10.00**
American Indian Tintype	**15.00**
American Indian CDV or Cabinet Card	**10.00**
Baseball Player Tintype	**15.00**
Baseball Player Cabinet Card	**12.00**
Baseball Player Real-Photo Post Card or Regular Photo	**4.00**
Child (w/toy) Tintype	**10.00**
Child (w/toy) in Any Other Type of Photo	**5.00**

Photos Through Early 20th Century   **We Pay**

Circus Parades	**4.00**
Country Store Interior or Exterior View	**5.00**

Photographica

Dry Goods Store Interior or Exterior View...**5.00**
Meat Market Interior or Exterior View..**6.00**
Non-Soldier Subjects (w/guns)..**3.00**
Telegraph Office Interior or Exterior View **6.00**
War Scenes (w/blimps present)..**4.00**
Western Town Street Scenes (w/people) **4.00**

I am interested in **photography of commercial establishments and artifacts, any date**; specifically of coin machines in location use, pre-Prohibition saloons (inside and out), 'speakeasies' of the 1920s, early 'repeal' taverns ca 1933-41, can openers being used in kitchens, ornate ceiling fans in restaurants and hotels, and similar commercial interiors. The coin machines can be coin-op scales in front of stores, vending machines attached to walls or on counters, peep shows and amusement machines in Penny Arcades, slot machines in resorts and casinos, jukeboxes and pinball games in roadhouses or taverns, etc. Send copy and price first.

Richard M. Bueschel
414 N Prospect Manor Ave.
Mt. Prospect, IL 60056

Subject   **We Pay**

Slot Machine, large floor or counter type, before 1900.............................**35.00+**
Slot Machine, cast iron, in use before 1910...**25.00+**
Saloon, interior w/coin machine on bar ....**20.00+**
Saloon, interior, pre-prohibition...**5.00+**
Saloon, exterior w/saloon name...**7.50+**
Any 'Speakeasy,' interior or exterior view, ea..**25.00+**
Vending Machine, mounted on wall outside of store ....**15.00+**
Scale (image at least 1¼" high), inside or outside store ....**15.00+**
Jukebox or Pinball Games, in resort or roadhouse, ea..............................**10.00+**
Coin Machine, professional advertising type ....**5.00+**
Interior w/ornate ceiling fan, commercial type...**10.00+**
Restaurant or Home Kitchen, w/can opener in use, ea ....**10.00+**
Penny Arcade, showing machines, any date ....**15.00+**
Snapshots, showing background beer signs or coin machines...................**1.50+**
Wooden Folding Chairs, any situation ....**2.50+**
Wooden Folding Chairs, used as photo props, large image.......................**5.00+**

I am buying clear, clean **stereoviews featuring American artists and American paintings of the 19th century and early 20th century**. I am also interested in any stereoviews having to do with American art such as art exhibit interiors, art museum interiors featuring paintings, and artists at their work (interior or exterior views). Prices paid depend on the scene and condition. Please send photocopy of slide.

H.A. Milton
P.O. Box 224
Bound Brook, NJ 08805

PICKLE CASTORS

Pickle castors were always found on the Victorian dinner table. They consist of a decorated, silverplated frame that held either a fancy, clear pressed-glass insert or a decorated art glass insert and a pair of silver tongs. I prefer pieces in very good to excellent condition; glass jars must be mint. A close-up photo is most helpful. Prices can range from $50.00 to $750.00. I will make offers and answer all replies.

Bill Sinesky
7228 McQuaid Rd.
Wooster, OH 44691

PIE BIRDS

Pie birds and pie funnels are wanted for my collection. I am seeking the older pie birds and funnels – either singly or a collection. Listed below are some examples wanted. Prices paid depend on condition and rarity.

Lillian M. Cole
14 Harmony Rd.
Flemington, NJ 08822; 908-782-3198

	We Pay
Pie Boy (US)	30.00+
Eaton's Improved Pie Funnel (Canadian)	30.00+
Servex Pie Chef (possibly New Zealand/Australia)	30.00+
Puff-Chested Canary (US)	30.00+
Rooster, long S-curved neck (Pearl China)	30.00+
Rooster, cream-colored body w/pink & blue details	30.00+

I am a dealer and want to offer a large selection of pie birds. Prices paid depend on condition and detail. I also want to buy all kinds of kitchen collectibles.

Christina Caldwell
Rt. 1, Box 336
Hawkins, TX 75765; 903-769-3862

We Pay

Pie Birds..**up to 30.00+**

POLITICAL ITEMS

Political buttons of all kinds, new and old are collectible; but the most desirable are the celluloid-coated pin-backs ('cellos') produced between the 1890s and 1920s. Many of these are attractively and colorfully designed, which enhances their value as historical artifacts. Most but not all buttons since then have been produced by lithography directly on metal discs ('lithos').

Collectors generally favor presidential buttons – especially picture pins from 1960 or earlier. 'Jugates' featuring presidential and vice-presidential candidate photos are even more desirable, but there are numerous other specialties within the hobby including state and local, third party, and 'cause' types.

Value depends on scarcity, historical significance, design, and condition – buttons with cracked celluloid, deep gouges or scratches, and/or rust-colored stains ('foxing') are not collectible. Reproductions exist, and many are marked as such; but a certain amount of expertise is needed to distinguish real from fake.

Although my own specialty is celluloid state and local buttons from 1925 or earlier, I am interested in purchasing all kinds of buttons in nice, clean condition only. Send me a clear photocopy of whatever you have, and I will either make an offer to purchase or, if not, give an informal appraisal. I will respond promptly to any and all inquiries, whether one button or a thousand. Prices below are for picture pins unless stated otherwise.

Michael Engel
29 Groveland St.
Easthampton, MA 01027; 413-527-8733

Presidentials 1896-1960   **We Pay**

Alton B. Parker, James Cox, or John W. Davis...**25.00+**
Theodore Roosevelt or Woodrow Wilson..**10.00+**

Political Items

Herbert Hoover or Harry Truman...**10.00+**
William J. Bryan, William McKinley, or Charles E. Hughes....................**5.00+**
W.H. Taft, Harding, Coolidge, Al Smith, Willkie, Landon, FDR, or JFK (1½" or larger)...**10.00+**
W.H. Taft, Harding, Collidge, Al Smith, Willkie, Landon, FDR, or JFK (smaller than 1½").. **up to 10.00**
Buttons w/Name Only...**up to 10.00**
Jugates...**up to 100.00+**

Third Party 1896-1960   We Pay

Socialist, Communist, or Prohibition Candidates ....**10.00+**
Eugene V. Debs..**50.00+**

State and Local   We Pay

Older Celluloid Pins for Governor, U.S. Senator, or Congress.........**up to 25.00**
Other Older State & Local ....**up to 10.00**

Cause   We Pay

Early Labor Union Items...**5.00+**
Civil Rights or Vietnam...**up to 10.00**

Charles began collecting **U.S. presidential campaign paper memorabilia** twenty years ago and has been at the forefront of this hobby since. Mr. Hatfield has become widely known as the top collector of this material in the United States. Materials he collects must be made of paper and used to promote a candidate for U.S. presidency; pamphlets, leaflets, flyers, tickets, electoral ballots, and hand cards are examples of his collecting pursuits. All campaigns are of interest, but he especially searches for 19th-century and early 20th-century items. When writing him, indicate which candidate, the year (if known), the size, condition, and description (any slogans, messages, and pictures that appear on the item). A photocopy of the item(s) is helpful. Mr. Hatfield does not accept items sent on approval. He does not buy buttons, bumper stickers, or daily newspapers.

The following is a list of items with prices he is willing to pay.

Charles L. Hatfield
1411 S State St.
Springfield, IL 62704

We Pay

Henry Clay Electoral Ballot **20.00**
Abe Lincoln Electoral Ballot **25.00**
U.S. Grant Electoral Ballot..**15.00**
James Blaine Campaign Trade Card **4.00**
Grover Cleveland Leaflet **12.00**
Benjamin Harrison Leaflet...**12.00**
William Jennings Bryan Campaign Post Card.................................**8.00**
William McKinley Leaflet..**10.00**
Theodore Roosevelt Sheet Music **8.00**
William Howard Taft Campaign Hand Card.....................................**5.00**
Woodrow Wilson Leaflet **7.00**
James Cox Brochure **15.00**
Warren Harding Pamphlet..**8.00**
Calvin Coolidge Booklet **6.00**
John W. Davis Brochure..**10.00**
Alfred E. Smith Leaflet **8.00**
Herbert Hoover Pamphlet...**5.00**
Franklin D. Roosevelt Flyer..**6.00**
Alf Landon Brochure **4.00**
Wendell Willkie Pamphlet **4.00**
Thomas Dewey Ticket **3.00**
Harry Truman Campaign Card **5.00**
Dwight Eisenhower Pamphlet **3.00**
Adlai Stevenson Leaflet..**3.00**
John F. Kennedy Brochure **3.00**
Barry Goldwater Pamphlet **2.00**

Political Items

Items used in **presidential campaigns** are the most sought after by collectors. Of all items used, the pin-back button seems to be most popular. Ribbons, license attachments, and posters are also collected. I'm interested in buying good single items or collections. Below is a listing of prices that I'll pay. Keep in mind that certain items are rarer than others. A pinback that pictures Coolidge and Dawes may be worth $25.00 – or $500.00 – depending on size, color, wording, design, and condition.

Dave Beck
P.O. Box 435
Mediapolis, IA 52637

Pin-Back Buttons   We Pay

Lincoln Ferrotype ....150.00+
Truman for Senator...100.00
John W. Davis..100.00
Taft, ⅞"..10.00
Taft, riding an elephant 1,000.00
Parker, 1¼" ....35.00+
Hoover, ⅞" 25.00
Wilson, celluloid fob 50.00

I am buying **Ross Perot Campaign '92 political memorabilia** such as badges, hats, shirts, posters, signs, bumper stickers, coffee mugs, etc. If it says 'Ross Perot,' I want it! I'm also looking to obtain **old firecracker packs and labels as well as other 4th of July items** such as post cards, posters, catalogs, etc. Finally, I'm interested in collecting **any pinball machine from 1950 to 1965** – either operating or non-working.

Rob Berk
2671 Youngstown Rd. SE
Warren, OH 44484
216-369-1192 or 800-323-3547
FAX 216-369-6279

Perot Campaign '92

We Pay

Badges	**1.00+**
Hats	**5.00+**
Shirts	**5.00+**
Mugs	**5.00+**
Posters	**3.00+**
Signs	**3.00+**

July 4th Novelties

We Pay

Firecracker Packs	**5.00+**
Firecracker Labels	**3.00+**
Post Cards	**3.00+**
Posters	**3.00+**
Signs	**3.00+**

Pinball Machines (1950-65)

We Pay

Operable	**50.00+**
Non-Working	**25.00+**

I am an advanced collector of **Willkie for President items** with over 2,500 pieces in my collection. I have no interest in newspapers or magazines. Prices given are for pieces having normal wear or use. Some mint-condition items bring a premium price. Xerox or sketch along with dimensions helpful.

James C. Bernard
1023 S Anderson St.
Elwood, IN 46036

We Pay

Auto License Plate Attachments	**5.00-40.00+**
Books, hardcover	**8.00+**

Political Items

Chalkware .... **5.00-30.00+**
Glassware .... **5.00-30.00+**
Hats, Ties, or Handkerchiefs .... **10.00-25.00+**
Metal 3-Dimensional Items .... **5.00-30.00+**
Paper Ephemera or Decals.. **1.00-5.00**
Pin-Backs, Lapel Pins, or Other Jewelry.. **1.00-65.00+**
Posters **5.00-12.00**
Signs, cardboard **5.00-12.00**
Song Sheets .... **6.00+**

I pay top prices for **all types of political items from political buttons and pins, posters, post cards, dolls, banks, mechanical toy-type items, etc.** I buy single items, whole collections, or one hundred of the same item. My primary interest is presidential items but also am interested in older Senate and governor items – particularly items from early races for people who later became president (such as Lyndon Johnson's Congress or Senate items). Send a photocopy of item for quick offer, or call me!

Ronald E. Wade
229 Cambridge
Longview, TX 75601; 903-236-9615

We Pay

Abe Lincoln Silk Ribbon .... **500.00+**
Abe Lincoln Flag, Banner or Campaign Lamp, ea................................ **1,000.00+**
'Me & Roosevelt for Johnson' Photo Button.. **1,000.00**
Landon 'Land on Washington' Photo Button w/Plane.......................... **2,000.00**
Theodore Roosevelt (on horseback) Beer Tray **250.00**
Theodore Roosevelt (on horseback) Button **400.00**
Theodore Roosevelt (shaking hands w/Taft) Button **350.00**
Bryan & Stevenson (w/photos & Miss Liberty) Beer Tray **25.000**
Bryan or McKinley Whiskey Flask, w/photo label, ea **200.00**
James Cox & Roosevelt Photo Buttons .... **10,000.00+**
John Kennedy poster, cardboard... **20.00+**
John Kennedy, Jackie, or Robert Kennedy Bobbing-Head........................ **50.00**
John Kennedy Poster, for Congress **350.00**
Jimmy Carter Poster, for Senator **200.00**
Lyndon Johnson Poster, for Congress **350.00**
George McGovern Button, w/Barbara Streisand **100.00**
John W. Davis for President Photo or Word Button, ea........................... **100.00+**
Eugene V. Debs (Socialist) Photo Post Card.. **100.00**

PORCELAIN

I am buying exceptional porcelain vases, plates, and bowls. I prefer pieces from the late 1700s through the 1920s. Slightly damaged pieces (restorable) are preferred. I will purchase single items or complete collections. Please send a photo with description of damage (if applicable) and price desired.

Val Arce
23029 Cerca Dr.
Valencia, CA 91354

We Pay

Capo Di Monte	20.00+
Chelsea	20.00+
Dresden	20.00+
Haviland	20.00+
Meissen	20.00+
Nippon	20.00+
Noritake	20.00+
Rosenthal	20.00+
Royal Dux	20.00+
Royal Worcester	20.00+
Staffordshire	20.00+
Victorian	20.00+

POST CARDS

I am buying old or unusual post cards. I prefer **comic or advertising art as well as political cards.** Listed below are some of the types of cards of interest, but I will consider any kind.

Mary Zuzan
Rt. 2, Box 65
Denton, MD 21629

We Pay

Advertising	**1.00+**
Carmichael	**2.00-4.00**
C.F.L. (Monogram)	**1.00-3.00**
Dwig	**3.00-5.00**
Political	**1.00+**
Bernhardt Wall	**3.00-6.00**
Walter Wellman	**1.00-2.00**

I am the foremost collector of **ice cream and soda fountain-related real-photo post cards.** If you have any of these cards to sell, think of me first. I am looking for strong images where the primary image is ice cream or soda-fountain related. The following list will give you an idea of what I am looking for.

Interiors: Entire soda fountain with people behind the counter and/or children or people eating ice cream in front of the fountain.
People: Making or eating ice cream.

Animal-Drawn Vehicles: Ice cream truck with ice cream shipping barrels and name of ice cream company on side.
Trucks: Ice cream with name of truck on side and people eating ice cream.
Carts: Showing street vendors selling ice cream (can be from United States or foreign).
Advertising: Ice cream or a product used in the manufacture or serving of ice cream.

Please send a photocopy and your price. Don't send me exterior scenes where there is just an ice cream sign in the distance.

Allen 'Mr. Ice Cream' Mellis
1115 W Montana
Chicago, IL 60614

POTTERY

I am buying **American art pottery – preferably hand-painted items made before 1960 and foreign art pottery made before 1930**. I will buy any number of pieces and want only those in mint condition. Please send pictures for price offers.

Frank Bernhard
2791 Fiesta Dr.
Venice, FL 34293

We Pay

Rookwood	20.00-100.00+
Roseville	20.00-75.00+
Weller	20.00-75.00+
Owens, hand-painted	50.00+
George Ohr	100.00+

As an ardent collector of **lustreware pottery and porcelains**, I am seeking pieces to add to my collection. Lustre on pottery and porcelains goes back as far as the Roman and Greek civilizations. The ancient Chinese were also known to have produced lustre pieces. Josiah Wedgewood experimented and developed lustered pieces in the late 1790s. Copper is the most common; however pieces can also be found in silver, pink, purple, canary yellow, blue, black, and cobalt blue (which is rare). The majority of lustre that we know about today originated in England, but it was also made by the French, Belgiums, Germans, Italians, and Americans. Lustre was in its 'heyday' from the early 1800s to about 1840. There is also a later period (called by some the 'modern period') from the early 1920s to the early 1940s. My main endeavor is to find pieces 4" tall or smaller of all shapes, designs, and colors. I am also interested in plates, cups and saucers, mugs, and any odd-designed pieces.

Forward a full description (be sure to include any markings or transfers, color, etc.). A photo would be helpful and would be returned. Please, don't ask me to make offers. Price depends on piece, maker, and color. I pay from $5.00 to $250.00. All replies are answered.

The Trunk Shop
C.W. Gray
123 W 3rd St.
Hermann, MO 65041; 314-486-2805

We live in a small rural town in southwest North Dakota and are interested in buying pottery made in North Dakota before 1965. Items may be marked **Dickota, Messer, Rosemeade, WPA (Ceramics Project, Works Project Administration) or UND (University of North Dakota, School of Mines)** and have paper stickers with incised or ink-stamped marks.

Items wanted include shaker sets, figurines, sugar/creamer sets, vases, knickknacks, flowerpots, and miscellaneous pieces. Items must have no chips or cracks. Send a photo of your item or collection, if possible, along with a good description and your asking price.

Stan & Carrie Soderstrom
003-3rd St. SW
Rt. 2, Box 300
Bowman ND 58623

We Pay

Most Items, ea **5.00-100.00**

I am buying **19th-century relief-moulded jugs of stoneware or parian**. They must be undamaged and unrestored. Of particular interest are pieces potted by Charles Meigh, Samuel Alcock, Masons, Minton, Copeland, Wedgwood, etc. Listed below are a few examples of prices I can offer.

Kathy Hughes
1401 E Blvd.
Charlotte, NC 28203

We Pay

Fox & Hounds, Minton **180.00**
Bacchanalian Dance, Meigh **150.00**
Two Drivers, Minton..**180.00**
Distin, Alcock..**200.00**
Musical Instruments, Minton **200.00**

I am collecting **old crockery whiskey jugs with brewery names and artwork under the glaze.** I am especially interested in crockery from Kentucky and Southern Illinois. Prices will depend on item and its condition.

B.J. Summers
Rt. #6, Box 659
Benton, KY 42025

I am buying **pottery of all kinds from 1900 through 1970**. I prefer vases, cookie jars, figures, salt and pepper shakers, teapots, and creamer and sugar sets.

I'll buy one item or a whole collection of items. All items must be in perfect condition with no chips or cracks of any size. So please check your items very carefully. I'm not interested in anything made in Mexico, Taiwan, or Italy. No Indian pottery is wanted.

Enclose a photo of your item(s) listing any words or numbers on each piece (please specify). Make a drawing of any mark on the piece. Give a price and a phone number where you may be reached.

James Goad
1152A S Eagle Circle
Aurora, CO 80012; 303-745-7068

We Pay

Roseville	20.00+
Van Briggle	20.00+
Royal Doulton	20.00+
McCoy (no planters)	1.00+
Vases	5.00+
Elephant, Pigs or Blacks Salt & Pepper Shakers	5.00+
Miscellaneous Salt & Pepper Shakers	1.00+
Elephant, Pigs or Blacks Cookie Jars	20.00+
Other Figural Cookie Jars	10.00
Miscellanous Cookie Jars	5.00+
Teapots, marked USA or England	3.00+
Figurines, marked USA	5.00+
Figurines, marked England	10.00+
Figurines, marked Spain	10.00+
Figurines, marked Germany	5.00+

PURSES

We collect **metal mesh purses painted with multicolored designs**. These bags were made by the Whiting & Davis Co. and the Mandalian Manufacturing Co. in the 1920s and early 1930s. There are three basic types of mesh: Dresden or chain-link type, Armor-Mesh or flat-link type, and Bead-Lite which is a flat link-and-bubble mesh.

Especially wanted are purses featuring figural designs, scenic or landscape designs, elaborate geometric or floral patterns, ornate frames with polished stones, faux jewels or enameled decorations, painted frames, and Art Deco frames with painted inserts. We do not collect the plain gold or plain silver clutch-type bags made in the 1940s and 1950s.

We are interested only in purses in mint or near-mint condition. The uniqueness of the design and condition of the paint on the mesh are the most important factors in determining desirability. On mint condition bags, the paint will be virtually perfect. Near-mint purses will have few or no missing fringe chains or drops and will show only minor paint wear.

Sherry & Mike Miller
303 Holiday Dr.
R.R. 3, Box 130
Tuscola, IL 61953; 217-253-4991

We Pay

Child's Size (2¼x3", 2½x3½", or 3x4¾")..**40.00-75.00**
Small Size (3¼x5¾", 3½x6¼", or 4x7")...**60.00-95.00**
Medium Size (4½x7¾", 5x6¼", or 5¼x8")......................................**75.00-150.00**
Large Size (4½x10", 5x9", or 6x9¾")..**100.00-175.00**
Extra-Large Size (7x12", 8x9", or 9¼x12")...**200.00+**
Compact & Mesh Combination Vanity Bags **160.00-500.00**
'Celebrity' Bags (Clark Gable, Marion Davies, Charlie Chaplin, etc.).**250.00-600.00**

———————————

Collecting **vintage purses** is my passion: mesh, beaded, enameled, Bead-Lite, crocheted, vanity bags, compact purses, compacts with chains or tassels, along with any unusual items. I also collect **'go-withs' such as perfumes, makeup containers, talc shakers, tins, rouge boxes, compacts, lipsticks, and coin holders**.

Purses should be in good to mint condition with no tears on sides or any major defects and should have original chain handle (if there was one). Cherubs, ornate frames, compact purses, tangos, and beaded bags are favorites. I will buy parts of purses and beads at minimum prices. Also wanted are Victorian and ladies' boudoir items for resale. Photos are helpful. Ornate frames, gems, fancy designs, and original boxes all add to prices paid.

Antiques & Treasures
908 E Maywood Ave.
Peoria, IL 61603

We Pay

Vanity Purse..**15.00-100.00+**
Compact Purse ....**15.00-150.00+**
Beaded Purse ....**25.00-125.00+**
Crochet Purse ....**5.00+**
Tango's ....**2.00+**
Accessories, ea ....**2.00+**
Compacts..**5.00+**

———————————

I am buying **vintage beaded and mesh bags and purse frames of the Victorian era (and earlier) through the 1930s and '40s**. Frames must have tiny holes for sewing and be elaborate in design with either enameling, imitation pearls, or glass 'jewels' or a combination; they might be celluloid or Bakelite with some type of design or carving. Bags or purses should be in good condition, and I sometimes buy in 'as is' condition and pay accordingly. I especially like unusual and fancy bags with elaborate designs and pay good prices for these.

Flat enameled-mesh bags should have either a bright floral design, enameled birds, scenes, or celebrity faces. Or they could be a plainer design with jewels in the frame or the body of the bag. Another type of mesh bag I purchase does not have to have an unusual design on the body but must have a compact top or middle as part of the frame. These bags are usually approximately 3" to 7" long.

Beaded bags should be beaded allover with tiny glass beads and have scenes of people, houses, castles, animals, mountains, or unusual subjects. I also buy beaded geometric or rug motifs and sometimes floral bags if they have fancy, jeweled, or enameled frames. I also buy bags with watches in the frame or in the bag design itself, or Mickey Mouse or Disney motifs. I also buy dance purses that are made in unusual shapes and sometimes have metal tassels and jewels in the body of the bag. They may be made of metal or early plastic.

I am interested in one piece or a collection and pay postage if contacted first. This is a permanent want. I also buy compacts, costume jewelry, and ladies' accessories.

The Curiosity Shop
Lynell Schwartz
P.O. Box 964
Cheshire, CT 06410; 203-271-0643

We Pay

Vintage Purse Frames	35.00+
Mesh Bags w/Scenes	200.00+
Mesh Bags w/Compacts	125.00+
Mesh Bags w/Glass 'Jewels'	100.00+
Mesh or Beaded Bags w/Mickey or Disney	100.00+
Bags w/Watches (as part of the bag)	100.00+
Dance Purses	140.00+

I am buying **many types of purses.** Please see list below for examples.

Kayla Conway
4500 Napal Ct.
Bakersfield, CA 93307

I collect antique purses. Preferred are finely beaded scenics or florals dating **from the 1800s to the early 1900s or enameled mesh evening purses (primarily by Mandalian Mfg., although some were made by Whiting & Davis, too) dating from the 1920s through the '30s.** I'm also interested in unique or unusual types. They must be in very good condition, although not necessarily perfect. The amount I am willing to pay depends on condition and rarity. Color photos are preferable, or send photocopies with color and condition description.

Linda Fancher
1118 Park Ave.
Alameda, CA 94501; 510-865-2503

PUZZLES

I am buying jigsaw puzzles with outer space scenes from the 1940s and 1950s only. These puzzles are either interlocking or in a frame-tray format. They are children's puzzles that are usually radio or TV related but can be generic scenes containing rockets, spaceships, and space-suited people.

I am also interested in buying 1940s Superman puzzles and 1930s through '40s Tarzan puzzles.

Don Sheldon
P.O. Box 3313
Trenton, NJ 08619; 609-588-5403

We Pay

Buck Rogers, 1940s	**45.00**
Flash Gordon, 1940s	**40.00**
Rockey Jones, 1950s	**25.00**
Dan Dare, 1950s	**25.00**
Superman, 1940s	**35.00**
Tarzan, 1940s	**35.00**
Generic Space Scenes	**20.00**

RADIOS

I buy radios made from 1915 through 1985. Small 1950s transistor sets with civil defense markings on the dial, novelty sets shaped like advertising items and characters, plastic and Bakelite radios in unusual or Deco shapes, wooden radios in black and chrome, and Deco radios or those with unusual styling are also wanted. Lucite, Plexiglas, and mirrored radios or those with see-through cabinets are wanted. I buy novelty tube radios (shaped like bottles, baseballs, globes, etc.) and character radios (Mickey Mouse, Rudolph, Lone Ranger, etc.). Electronic items and clocks in unusual shapes or made of Bakelite or plastics are wanted. I buy old radio tubes with less than seven pins on the bottom. Please send a photo or photocopy, color, brand, model, and defects – I will make offers (a SASE helps). I've published an illustrated price guide.

Harry Poster
P.O. Box 1883 WB
S Hackensack, NJ 07606

We Pay

Transistor (Regency, Mantola, Mitchell, Raytheon)	**100.00-1,000.00**
Transistor (Sony TR-55, TR-63, Toshiba, Ruby)	**50.00-1,000.00**
Colored Bakelites (Air King, Fada, Emerson, RCA, DeWald)	**250.00-10,000.00**
World's Fair, Mickey Mouse, Charlie McCarthy	**200.00-1,000.00**
Novelty Tube Type (baseball, bowling ball, globe)	**100.00-1,000.00**
Novelty Transistor (gun, porcelain lady, oil can)	**20.00-150.00**
Table Top Models, blue or peach mirror	**250.00-2,000.00**
Sparton Floor Model #1186 Nocturne (mirror type)	**5,000.00-10,000.00**
Transistor, Tube Advertising & Dealer Displays	**Write**
Old Tubes, w/4, 5 or 6 pins on bottom, ea	**1.00+**

I am buying two types of radios: oriental-styled cabinet radios (usually lacquered and decorated with paintings of figures, flowers, and landscapes) and radio/furniture combinations (radios that are also working lamps, tables, appliances, etc.). All radios must be in fine, original cabinet condition and complete.

Gerald Schneider
3101 Blueford Rd.
Kensington, MD 20895-2726; 301-929-8593

We Pay

RCA 75x17, 75x19, etc. (1948)	**75.00+**
Sharp PF-116 (ca 1950)	**75.00+**
Crosley Gemchest Model 609 (1929)	**150.00+**
Emerson Model 350AW (1933)	**100.00+**
Federal Model 1540T (1946)	**75.00+**
Westinghouse Model H-188 or H-204 (1948)	**50.00+**
Toshiba Transister, Model 6TR-92 (1959)	**100.00+**
Philco Lamp Radio, Model 53-706 (1953), w/original shade	**100.00+**
Radio Lamp Company of America Series	**100.00+**

Crosley Refrigerator w/Radio in Door (1939-1941) ....**150.00+**
Other Oriental-Style or Radio-Furniture Combination......................**Negotiable**

RAILROADIANA

The term 'railroadiana' is meant to cover all collecting facets of the golden age of railroading. Depending upon the railroadiana collector's interest, items such as lanterns, tools, locks and keys, dining car wares (china, glass, silver, linen), advertising, timetables, signs, watches, and many other items are eagerly sought.

Our particular area of interest is authenticated patterns of dining car china. We prefer those pieces which have a top or side logo and/or a designated railroad backstamp. In addition we seek to buy railroad station restaurant and eating house wares, examples of china and silver from street and electric railways, and also pieces from railroad-related ferryboat and steamship systems.

This listing represents only a sampling of railroadiana items we seek to buy. We respond to all offerings by telephone or letter.

Fred & Lila Shrader
202 Hwy. 199 (Hiouchi)
Crescent City, CA 95531; 707-458-3525

Railroad China   **We Pay**

Bowl, bouillon; CMStP&P, Traveler...**15.00**
Bowl, cereal; CMStP&P, Peacock, 6½" **20.00**
Bowl, cereal; WP, 6½" **25.00**

Railroadiana

Butter Pat, ATSF, California Poppy, no backstamp.................................**13.00**
Butter Pat, B&O, Centenary **15.00**
Butter Pat, UP, Historical...**100.00**
Creamer, SP, Sunset...**100.00**
Cup & Saucer, Alaska, McKinley **150.00**
Cup & Saucer, ATSF, Adobe, top logo **50.00**
Cup & Saucer, demitasse; WP..**150.00**
Cup & Saucer, SP, Prairie-Mountain Wildflowers....................**40.00**
Plate, C&O, Train/Ferry, 9½" **30.00**
Plate, C&NW, Flambeau, 10½"...**250.00**
Plate, IC, Pirate, 10"...**110.00**
Platter, D&RG, Curecanti, 11x8" **200.00**
Teapot, UP, Historical...**250.00**
Teapot, UP, Winged Streamliner...**65.00**

Glassware   We Pay

Ashtray, ATSF, oval, 2¼x4"...**14.00**
Cordial, ATSF, script logo **35.00**
Juice Glass, SP, Sunset logo...**35.00**
Water Glass, UP (in script), 4½" **7.00**
Wine, stem; ATSF, script logo..**20.00**

Linen   We Pay

Blanket, D&RG, wool, logo in center...**35.00**
Headrest, GN, 'Rockie' logo **15.00**
Napkin, D&RG, white on white **9.00**
Napkin, UP, pink on pink w/small rose on edge.........................**12.00**
Place Mat, UP, Winged Streamliner..**12.00**
Tablecloth, SP, white on white w/Sunset logo............................**15.00**
Towel, SP, 'Southern Pacific' on vertical blue stripe.................**10.00**

Silverplate   We Pay

Butter Pat, SP, 'Southern Pacific' in script **15.00**
Coffeepot, UP, side logo...**125.00**
Creamer, D&RG, side logo, w/lid...**75.00**
Knife, ATSF, 'Santa Fe' in script..**10.00**
Menu Holder, SP, ball & wing finial **90.00**
Sugar Tongs, SL&SF, top mark...**50.00**
Teapot, UP, silver frame w/ceramic insert..................................**150.00**
Tray (for tips), PRR, w/Keystone logo, 4" square.......................**75.00**
Tray (for tips), SP, w/Sunset logo, 6"...**75.00**

I am buying **railroad china and glassware** with special interest in Great Northern, B&O, Chesapeake & Ohio, and Chicago, Milwaukee, St. Paul & Pacific Railways. All other railroads will be considered. Single pieces or an entire collection are wanted.

Lisa Nieland
1228 W Main St.
Redwing, MN 55066

We Pay

Great Northern Tableware ....15.00+
Great Northern Serving Pieces ....25.00+
Great Northern Children's Dinnerware..50.00+
B&O Tableware ....10.00+
B&O Serving Pieces..30.00+
Chesapeake & Ohio Chessie Items..25.00+
Chesapeake & Ohio Children's Dinnerware...35.00+
Chesapeake & Ohio George Washington Items......................................35.00+
Chesapeake & Ohio, other pattern pieces ....20.00+
Milwaukee Road Peacock..20.00+
Milwaukee Road Traveler (w/flying goose)..20.00+

I am interested in buying **railroad memorabilia from obsolete railroads**. Listed below are some of the items I am looking for.

David H. Ward
20406 Little Bear Cr. Rd. #25
Woodinville, WA 98072; 206-485-1437

We Pay

Lanterns, marked ....20.00+
Lantern Globes, marked..15.00+
Padlocks, brass ....25.00+
Switch Lock Keys...8.00+
China, w/company marks...15.00+
Silverplate Dining Car Items, w/company marks.....................................5.00+
Steam Whistles..100.00+
Miscellaneous Paper Items ....**Call or Write**

I buy **railroadiana whether a single item or an entire collection.** I will pay top price for good quality, marked pieces of china, silver, flatware, and glassware. I am also looking for decks of playing cards, timetables, brochures, menus, annual passes, hat and breast badges, wax sealers, service pins, brass keys, brass locks, lanterns with marked globes, mechanical pencils, calendars, and advertising promotional items. Due to the wide range of prices of items, please contact me for fair and honest quotes.

Special Interest Items:
  Hiawatha Memorabilia
  Milwaukee Road Memorabilia
  Santa Fe Mimbreno China
  Marked Individual Creamers, Cream Pitchers, Butter Pats
  Marked Demitasse Cups and Saucers

Dean D. Collins
P.O. Box 9623
Madison, WI 53715; 608-271-2727

RECORDS

The following listed records are wanted. I desire nearly-new to excellent copies if possible and will pay the prices listed for them. Records in lesser condition will be considered. Also wanted is the 16" radio transcription of *The Bluebird of Happiness* by Jan Peerce made circa the late '30s (not the later '50s RCA Victor commercial recording). I will pay $40.00 for this or will accept a good cassette copy for $15.00.

John S. Montemore
700 Beacon Ave.
Paulsboro, NJ 08066

45 rpm **We Pay**

Peerce, Jan; Oh Holy Night, The Holy City, + two songs; red vinyl, extended play **25.00**
Breen, Bobby; Rainbow, Chic 1013 ....**10.00**

LP **We Pay**

Countess Maritza, Opperetta Anton Paulik, RCA LSC2406 ....**15.00**

78 rpm **We Pay**

Bluebird 7320, Bobby Breen, Hawaii Calls...**20.00**
Decca 18560, Dick Haymes, There's a Star-Spangled Banner....................**10.00**
Decca 22317, Dick Haymes, Look for the Silver Lining **7.50**
Decca 23434, Dick Haymes, Some Sunday Morning...................................**5.50**
Decca 23481, Dick Haymes, Gimme a Little Kiss **5.50**
Decca 23611, Dick Haymes, Why Does It Get So Late So Early..................**5.50**
Decca 23944, Dick Haymes, Til We Meet Again **7.50**

Listed below is a small portion of the records I am seeking to buy along with prices I will pay. Records should be in nice, playable condition: not cracked, badly worn, or scratched. I buy thousands of records by mail each year and travel to purchase large, worthwhile collections. For the convenience of sellers by mail, I offer (for $2.00, refundable when I buy) *Shellac Shack's Want List of 78 rpm Records*, a 72-page, fully illustrated catalog listing thousands of 78 rpm records on commonly found labels (Bluebird, Columbia, Decca, Victor, etc.), individually listed with specific prices I pay for each disc. It also contains information on scarce and preferred labels (78s and 45s), shipping instructions, etc. This want list is a 'live' offer to buy, backed by enough cash to handle any possible offering and not just a vague reference.

It is not necessary, however, to buy anything from me in order to sell me records. Lists are welcome but should include record labels and numbers, names of artists/bands, and song titles. Return postage should accompany lists.

Wanted: **scarce and unusual labels** (a listing follows with my record wants). These are some records wanted regardless of performers, music content (or lack thereof). If labels are clean, many of these will be bought even if playing surface is impaired. All are pre-1935 and should not be confused with other, more recent labels of the same or similar names. Note: prices quoted are **minimums** for the label.

My book, *American Premium Record Guide*, may be useful to those seeking to learn more about popular record collecting. It identifies and prices more than seventy thousand records (78s, 45s, LPs) in the major categories of popular record collection: dance bands, jazz, blues, hillbilly, rhythm and blues, rock 'n' roll, rockabilly, etc. Ask your bookseller, or write for further information.

L.R. 'Les' Docks
P.O. Box 691035
San Antonio, TX 78269-1035

Records   **We Pay**

All Star Quartet, Perfect 14513, 14525, ea	**10.00**
Danny Altier, Vocalion 15740	**100.00**
Arcadia Peacock Orch. of St. Louis, Okeh 40264, 40372, 40440, ea	**25.00**
Arcadian Serenaders, Okeh 40562	**30.00**
Bailey's Lucky Seven, Gennett 3075	**10.00**
Ben Bernie's Orch., Brunswick 3145, 3887, ea	**5.00**
Tommy Bohn's Orch., Okeh 41372	**15.00**
Bolton & Cipriani's Orch., Columbia (Personal) 93-P	**25.00**
Broadway Bell-Hops, Harmony 140-H, 450-H, 546-H, ea	**5.00**
Broadway Broadcasters, Cameo 839	**10.00**
Ted Brownagle's Orch., Columbia 1741-D, Victor 20262, ea	**15.00**
Merritt Brunies' Orch., Okeh 40579, 40593, ea	**35.00**
Hale Byers' Orch., Brunswick 3108, Vocalion 15370, ea	**10.00**
California Ramblers, Edison 11042	**150.00**
California Ramblers, Edison 14083	**50.00**
Joe Candullo's Orch., Gennett 3385, 3405, ea	**20.00**
Joe Candullo's Orch., Perfect 14841, 14874, ea	**10.00**
Carolina Club Orch., Diva 2639-G, Harmony 639-H, ea	**10.00**
Jack Chapman's Orch., Victor 19775	**100.00**
Chicago Loopers, Perfect 14910	**50.00**
Jerome Conrad's Orch., Diva 2738-G, Harmony 738-H, ea	**10.00**
Frank Dailey's Och., Bell 497	**10.00**
Walter Davison's Louisville Loons, Columbia 1031-D	**10.00**
Bob Deikman's Orch., Gennett 3196	**20.00**
Dixie Jazz Band, Jewel 5446, Oriole 1396, ea	**15.00**
Dixie Jazz Band, Oriole 517, 619, 705, 778, ea	**10.00**

Jerry Fenwyck's Orch., Clarion 11503-C...**20.00**
Frankie & Johnnie Orch., Bluebird 6499...**10.00**
Frisco Syncopators, Puritan 11244, 11271, ea..**25.00**
Jack Gardner's Orch., Okeh 40501, 40518, ea...**25.00**
Lou Gold's Orch., Perfect 14549, 14584, ea...**10.00**
Golden Gate Orch., Perfect 14500, 14542, ea...**10.00**
Ross Gorman's Virginians, Gennett 6132...**25.00**
Ross Gorman's Orch., Columbia 615-D..**5.00**
Earl Gresh's Orch., Columbia 693-D **10.00**
Earl Gresh's Orch., Columbia 1031-D **10.00**
Earl Gresh's Orch., Perfect 14818...**15.00**
Fred 'Sugar' Hall & His Sugar Babies, Okeh 40410, 40437, 40482, 40496, ea **20.00**
Fred Hall's Orch., Marathon (7", any), ea..**15.00**
Mal Hallett's Orch., Edison 14080 ....**100.00**
Henry Halstead's Orch., Victor 19513, 19514, ea **30.00**
Harmonians, Harmony 185-H, 746-H, 774-H, 777-H, ea **8.00**
Phil Hughes' High Hatters, Perfect 14586 ....**10.00**
Ipana Troubadours, Columbia 2117-D **10.00**
Billy James' Dance Orch., Oriole 1250...**10.00**
Jimmy Joy's Orch., Okeh 40627...**50.00**
Art Kahn's Orch., Columbia 624-D **10.00**
Irving Kaufman, Banner 6015..**10.00**
Hal Kemp's Orch., Columbia 671-D **15.00**
Roy King's Orch., Romeo 369...**15.00**
Kirby's Kings of Jazz, Bell 589, 591, 592, 598, ea **25.00**
Knickerbockers, Columbia 549-D..**10.00**
Sam Lanin's Orch., Perfect 14544 ....**10.00**
Joie Lichter's Orch., Paramount 20428 ....**25.00**
Ernest Loomis' Orch., Victor 20755 ....**50.00**
Los Angeles Biltmore Hotel Trio, Okeh 41064 ....**5.00**
Bert Lown's Orch., Diva 2853-G, Harmony 853-H, ea............................**10.00**
Marathon Dance Orch., Okeh 40625, 40686, ea **10.00**
Mike Markel's Orch., Okeh 40625, 40686, ea **10.00**
Mendello's Dance Orch., Banner 6214..**15.00**
Vic Meyers' Orch., Cameo 576 ....**10.00**
Vic Meyres' Orch., Columbia 1168-D, 1456-D, 1516-D, 1530-D, 1678-D, ea.**10.00**
Missouri Jazz Band, Banner 7140..**10.00**
New Orleans Jazz Band, Banner 1318...**15.00**
George Olsen's Music, Victor 19633 ....**15.00**
Original Indiana Five, Harmony 134-H **10.00**
Original Indiana Five, Perfect 14601 ....**15.00**
Original Memphis Five, Perfect 14746 ....**15.00**
Original Memphis Five, Vocalion 15712, 15805, 15810, ea **50.00**
Glen Oswald's Serenaders, Victor 19733..**30.00**
Jack Pettis' Pets, Vocalion 15703, 15761, ea **50.00**
Red Hot Dogs, Banner 6057, 6059, ea **20.00**
Fred Rich's Orch., Harmony 84-H...**8.00**
Albert Short's Orch., Vocalion 14600 ....**10.00**

Al Siegel's Orch., Paramount 20314 ....**30.00**
Six Black Diamonds, Banner 1428 ....**20.00**
Six Black Diamonds, Banner 6076 ....**10.00**
Six Jelly Beans, Challenge 571 ....**10.00**
Six Jumping Jacks, Brunswick 3095, 4362, ea **10.00**
Six Jumping Jacks, Brunswick 4498 ....**15.00**
Southern Melody Serenaders, Marathon (7", any), ea **10.00**
Paul Specht's Orch., Columbia 577-D, 627-D, ea **8.00**
Charley Straight's Orch., Paramount 20244, 20264, ea **25.00**
Frankie Trumbauer's Orch., Okeh 41421 ....**15.00**
University Six, Harmony 134-H, 160-H, 619-H, ea **10.00**
Van's Hotel Half Moon Orch., Perfect 14860 ....**15.00**
Don Voorhees' Orch., Cameo 1134 ....**15.00**
The Whoopee Makers, Vocalion 15763, 15768, 15769, ea **75.00**
Julie Wintz's Orch., Harmony 1169-H **20.00**
Bill Wirges' Orch., Perfect 14443 ....**10.00**
Yankee Six, Okeh 40335, 40348, ea **30.00**

Labels   We Pay

Autograph (Marsh Labs., Chicago) **5.00**
Black Patti (Chicago Record Co.) **50.00**
Blu-Disc **30.00**
Buddy **15.00**
Carnival (John Wanamaker, New York) **10.00**
Clover (Nutmeg Record Co.) **4.00**
Edison (Needle-Cut Electric) **6.00**
Electradisk **3.00**
Everybody's **3.00**
Golden (Los Angeles) **3.00**
Herschel Gold Seal **6.00**
Herwin (St. Louis) **5.00**
Homestead **5.00**
Marathon (7") **10.00**
Meritt (Kansas City) **20.00**
National (Iowa City) **3.00**
New Flexo **5.00**
Nordskog **6.00**
Odeon (American 'ONY'- series **only**) **5.00**
Parlophone (American 'PNY'- series **only**) **5.00**
Q.R.S. **5.00**
R.C.A. Victor 'Program Transcriptions' ....**Varies**
R.C.A. Victor picture discs (early 1930s) ....**Varies**
Rialto (Chicago) **10.00**
Sunrise (R.C.A. Victor product, early 1930s) **20.00**
Sunset (California) **2.00**
Superior **5.00**

Timely-Tunes (R.C.A. Victor product)..**8.00**
Tremont **3.00**
Up-To-Date (early 1920s)...**20.00**

I collect older records by lesser-known artists in any speed – 78 rpm, 45 rpm, or LP. Also needed are empty picture sleeves. I collect only blues, early rock, and rockabilly. Please describe fully and state desired price in first letter. Enclose SASE for a speedy reply.

G.F. Wade
1320 Ethel St.
Okemos, MI 48864-3009

RED WING POTTERY

Needed items include cookie jars, ashtrays, animals, and figures (ladies). All items must be in perfect condition. If you are in doubt about whether your items are Red Wing or not, a photograph or drawing is helpful.

Lisa Nieland
1228 W Main St.
Redwing, MN 55066

Cookie Jars   **We Pay**

Bakers, Katrina (Dutch Girl), or Monk (yellow, green, or blue)................**30.00+**
Bakers, Katrina, Monk, King of Hearts, Fruit (apple, bananas, grapes, pear), Jack Frost, Drummer Boy (colors other than yellow, green or blue)........**40.00+**
Any Pink Jars...**50.00+**
Any Stoneware...**30.00+**
Any Stoneware w/Sponging...**50.00+**
Hand-Decorated (multicolored) Pottery...**50.00+**
Ashtrays..**25.00**
Ashtray, w/advertising ....**40.00+**

Red Wing

I am interested in buying Red Wing pottery and **Stuart Nye sterling silver jewelry.** Listed are some of the items I am interested in finding. Please send a description of others you may have.

Paul L. Trentz
126 E McKinley
Stoughton, WI 53589

We Pay

Red Wing Jug, Beehive, 4-gal	300.00+
Crock, salt-glazed butterfly	75.00+
Crock, salt-glazed leaf	75.00+
Red Wing Bowl, Etc. w/Wisconsin Advertising	35.00+
Stuart Nye Jewelry, sterling silver	10.00+

ROOKWOOD

I am a serious collector wanting to buy Rookwood pottery. Perfect condition items only with no chips, repairs or X marks. Return privilege guarantee requested.

Joe Brell
607 Center Ave.
Pittsburgh, PA 15215; 412-784-9437

We Pay

Artist Signed Pieces	**up to 600.00**
Unusual Production Pieces	**up to 300.00**
Blue Ship Dinnerware	**up to 150.00**
Human or Animal Figures	**up to 300.00**
Plates	**up to 300.00**
Plaques & Tiles	**up to 600.00**

ROOT BEER COLLECTIBLES

Collector searching for root beer and soda fountain items will buy single items or collections. I've listed many of the brands I'm looking for, but the list is far from complete. Please write!

Jan Henry
Rt. 2, Box 193
Galesville, WI 54630

Brand   **We Pay**

American	**50.00-100.00**
B & R	**50.00-100.00**
Bardwell's	**200.00+**
Berry	**50.00-100.00**

Big Top	50.00-100.00
Bowey	50.00-100.00
Buckeye	20.00-50.00
C.P.	50.00-100.00
Connors	50.00-100.00
Croce	50.00-100.00
Dr. Murphy's	50.00-100.00
Dr. Swett's	100.00-200.00
Faust	50.00-100.00
Fox's	50.00-100.00
Graf's	50.00-100.00
Gehring's	50.00-100.00
Gold Bond	50.00-100.00
Greene's	50.00-100.00
Hall & Lyon	100.00-200.00
Hennesey	100.00-200.00
Hires (common)	20.00-50.00
Hunters	50.00-100.00
Jim Dandy	50.00-100.00
Kravemor	50.00-100.00
Lash's	20.00-50.00
McKinnon's	50.00-100.00
Mettlach, salt-glaze Hires	100.00-200.00
Miner's	200.00+
Murray's	50.00-100.00
Papoose	200.00+
Paramount	50.00-100.00
Pixie	50.00-100.00
Richardson's	50.00-100.00
S & H	50.00-100.00
Schuster's	50.00-100.00
Standard	50.00-100.00
Stite's	50.00-100.00
Wiedeman's	50.00-100.00
Zarembo	50.00-100.00
Zipp's	50.00-100.00

Other Items

We Pay

Glass, early etched or embossed	15.00-50.00
Glass, unusual painted labels	5.00-25.00
Pottery, root beer bottles	25.00-150.00
Soda Fountain Glasses, advertising, early	10.00-50.00
Soda Fountain Dispensers	300.00-1,500.00

Root beer was known in colonial America and was one of the earliest flavors available at the pharmacy soda fountains of the 1850s and '60s. Charles Hires popularized root beer at his concession stand at the Philadelphia Centennial in 1876 and led its commercial success. By 1900 many companies made root beer syrup and promoted their product with advertising, mugs, pitchers, and bowls. During this period, root beer was usually served from chilled pitchers (as the time in the pitcher gave a chance for the foam to subside). Our interest is the mugs and pitchers it was served in.

Harold & Joyce Screen
2804 Munster Rd.
Baltimore, MD 21234

We Pay

Bardwell, blue-glazed root beer mug	**100.00**
Dr. Swett's, mug	**150.00**
Jim Dandy, pottery mug	**40.00**
Hires, salt-glazed mug	**150.00**
Liquid Carbonic (or similar), crockery mugs	**40.00**
Miners, salt-glazed mug	**125.00**
Stite's, mug	**50.00**
Root Beer, blue-glazed pitchers	**400.00+**

ROSEMEADE POTTERY

231

Rosemeade Pottery

Rosemeade pottery was produced by the Wahpeton Pottery Company of Wahpeton, North Dakota, from 1940 to 1961. Items made include salt and pepper sets, large and small figurines, jewelry, and lamps. I buy both to collect and to resale items. Prices paid are for mint-condition items only with postage and insurance charges included. No broken or repaired items will be accepted.

Call about other Rosemeade pieces not listed or ship insured for my offer. I am buying other North Dakota pottery including Dickota, W.P.A., Messer, and U.N.D.

Clayton D. Zeller
R #2, Box 46
Grand Forks, ND 58203; 701-772-4995

We Pay

Ashtray, w/lg figure	75.00
Bank, bear or buffalo figural, ea	90.00
Bank, fish, hippo, pony or rhino figural, ea	135.00
Dealer sign	400.00
Creamer & sugar bowl, Mallard duck, pr	75.00
Figurine, alligator	155.00
Figurine, buffalo, lg	125.00
Figurine, donkey	65.00
Figurine, koala	100.00
Figurine, pheasant, 10¾"	90.00
Figurine, pheasant, 12½"	115.00
Figurine, walrus, lg	200.00
Jardiniere, Egyptian	45.00
Lamp, chicken	475.00
Lamp, doe	300.00
Lamp, dog	300.00
Lamp, horse	150.00
Lamp, pheasant	265.00
Lamp, panther	300.00
Lamp, stag	350.00
Planter, koala	60.00
Plaque, fish	70.00
Plaque, pheasant	110.00
Plaque, sea gull, set of three	235.00
Sailboat, lg	80.00
Wall pocket, Egyptian	45.00

ROSEVILLE POTTERY

I am buying Roseville pottery. I prefer items in perfect condition – either a single piece or an entire collection. This is only a partial listing.

Lisa Nieland
1228 W Main St.
Redwing, MN 55066

We Pay

Jardiniers	**50.00+**
Novelty Steins	**65.00**
Wall Pockets	**35.00+**
Juvenile	**25.00+**
Rozane	**75.00+**
Dogwood, sm pieces	**15.00+**
Dogwood, lg pieces	**40.00+**
Pine Cone, sm pieces	**25.00+**
Pine Cone, lg pieces	**50.00+**

SALESMAN'S SAMPLES

I am actively buying salesman's samples and anything small and well made – dollhouse items are not wanted, however. If the item is in miniature and is complete, I would be interested, whether it is a salesman's sample or not. Hundreds of different types of salesman's samples were made – too many to list. I see examples that are new to me constantly, so if you have something you think might be a sample or that is fine and well made, please feel free to contact me.

John B. Everett
P.O. Box 126
Bodega, CA 94922; 707-876-3513

We Pay

Barber Chairs	**10,000.00+**
Gas Stoves	**1,500.00+**
Bank Vault Doors & Deposit Vault Gates	**2,000.00+**
Store Display Cabinets	**500.00+**
Ladders	**200.00+**
Dental Cabinets	**5,000.00+**
Signs	**500.00+**
Hires Muni Makers	**10,000.00+**
Wooten Desks	**5,000.00+**
Home Comfort Stoves	**5,000.00+7**

SALT AND PEPPER SHAKERS

We are serious collectors of **antique art and pattern glass salt and pepper shakers**. As authors of two books dealing with the Victorian shakers, we are interested in obtaining the following shakers for our collection and a possible future book publication. We will pay fair retail prices for either a single shaker or a pair. Please send a full description and photograph of your items for sale and state each item's condition along with your selling price. Please note that we do not collect the so-called novelty type salt and pepper shakers made of porcelain, plastic, etc.

Art Glass
C.F. Monroe Nakara & Kelva
Chocolate Glass (all types)
Cranberry or Rubina (especially hand decorated)
Custard Glass (all types, pattern or free-blown)
Findlay Onyxware (ruby, orange, yellow, green, or black)
Mt. Washington, Peachblow
Mt. Washington/Pairpoint, Napoli
Mt. Washington/Pairpoint, Mother-of-Pearl (satin glass)
Mt. Washington/Pairpoint, Rose Amber (amberina)
New England Glass Co., Agata
New England Glass Co., Decorated Amberina
New England Glass Co., New England Peachblow
New England Glass Co., Opaque Green
New England Glass Co., Plated Amberina
New England Glass Co., Pomona (1st or 2nd grind)
Opalescent Glass (cranberry or blue)
Spatter Glass
Stevens & Williams Peachblow
Tortoise Shell (molded or free-blown)
Webb Peachblows
Unidentified Types of Mother-of-Pearl (satin glass)
Unidentified Types of Peachblow (shading from red to pink/white)

Pattern Glass
Amethyst Glassware (decorated or undecorated)
Black Glass (decorated or undecorated)
Opalware (milk glass) w/Hand-Painted House, Windmill, or Snow Scenes
Tree of Life
Unusual Figural Shakers (crystal or colored glass)

Mildred & Ralph Lechner
P.O. Box 554
Mechanicsville, VA 23111; 804-737-3347

I am buying **figural salt and pepper shaker sets**. My top wants include Disney and other comic and advertising characters, personalities in fact or fiction, and nursery rhymes. I especially want figural nodder shakers, unusual condiment sets, Black Americana sets, nudes and naughties, mermaids, dinosaurs, miniatures, Ceramic Arts Studio sets, Twin Winton sets, Goebel sets, and more. I'll buy one set or entire collections!

Judy Posner
R.D. #1, Box 273 WB
Effort, PA 18330: 717-629-6583

We Pay

Vintage Mickey Mouse Condiment Sets	250.00+
Unusual Figural Nodder Salt & Pepper Shakers	40.00+
Unusual Black Americana Sets	40.00+
Goebel Sheraton Bellhop Set	75.00+
Shmoo Salt & Pepper Shakers	75.00+
Twin Winton Salt & Peppers	15.00
Ceramic Arts Studio Black Sambo & Tiger	150.00
Dean Martin & Jerry Lewis Shakers on Tray	75.00+
Nursery Rhyme Condiment Sets	35.00+

I collect **old novelty salt and pepper shakers**. I am mainly interested in Blacks, storybook and comic figures, fruit and vegetable people, and Parkcraft state sets. All figural and novelty sets will be considered. I also collect **Ceramic Arts Studio and Rookwood.**

Gene A. Underwood
909 N Sierra Bonita Ave., Apt. 9
Los Angeles, CA 90046-6562; 213-850-6276

We Pay

Blacks on Vegetables (peas, turnips, etc.), pr	30.00+
Seated Black w/Watermelon Shakers on Shoulders	30.00+
Celery People	12.00
Mushroom People	12.00
Banana & Pineapple Boxers, pr	12.00
Dinosaurs, any ca '50s through '60s, pr	15.00
Office People, pr	12.00+

SALTS, OPEN

Called salt cellars, salt dips, open salts, celery salts, salt dishes, salters, trencher salts, and salt dips, these are the tiny dishes used for individual servings of salt at each place setting before salt shakers were common tableware. They have been made of sterling silver, silverplate (often with colored glass liners), china, porcelain, and other materials. Some have metal stands holding glass or china inserts, some are tiny, round, shallow dishes, some are basket shaped, others are figural. They are usually 1" high for individual salts but may be larger for master salts or when combined with a holder of some type.

I am interested in buying single salts, sets, and collections. I buy pieces in perfect condition only. I do not buy reproductions. Prices vary greatly due to type of salt, age, rarity, and collector appeal. I also buy the small spoons used with open salts. These may be sterling, silverplate, enameled, glass, etc. Please contact me giving a complete description and your asking price. An SASE would be appreciated. You may call about collections you may have for sale (I live in the Pacific Time Zone).

I am interested in any of the following open salts and any others you have.

Salts from Countries and Manufacturers Include:

Austria	Belleek
Bavaria	Flow Blue
England	Lenox
France	Limoges
Germany	Nippon

Wanted, Salts of These Materials:

Metal w/glass or china inserts	Early American Pattern Glass
Figurals	Cut Glass
Porcelain or Bisque	Cranberry Glass
Colored Glass	Cobalt Glass
China w/Hand-Painted	Vaseline Glass
or Transfer Decoration	Art Glass

Open salts (sometimes called salt cellars or salt dishes) are tiny bowls (some are covered) designed to serve salt. They average 2" to 3" but may be larger or smaller, depending on style. They were often made in sets and are usually found with a tiny spoon. Shapes are varied: round, oval, square, octagon, figural, etc. Some are double with a center handle, while others are paired with a pepper shaker and/or mustard pot. These little dishes are the forerunners of our modern salt shaker and are made of glass, silver, china, brass, etc.

I am especially interested in art glass, Czechoslovakian items, silver with colored glass liners, figurals, complete sets, and anything fancy or unusual. Prices range from a few dollars to a few hundred dollars, depending on rarity. I also buy unusual salt and pepper shakers, sugar shakers, and talcum shakers. Describe items carefully, noting any damage. Photos are helpful, and an SASE insures a reply.

Betty Bird
107 Ida St.
Mount Shasta, CA 96067

SCOTTIE DOG MEMORABILIA

The hobby of collecting Scottie dog memorabilia is not new, as some collectors have been engaged in this field for over thirty years. However, the popularity of Scottie collecting has been brought to the attention of dealers in recent years through the promotion of Donna and Jim Newton of Columbus, Indiana. In 1983 the Newtons began publishing the *Scottie Sampler*, a quarterly newspaper offering historical data, current market prices, features, photos, and ads. As a free bonus, subscribers of the *Scottie Sampler* are encouraged to participate in a collectors' fellowship called Wee Scots. This group holds an annual collector's show and informal, regional meetings across the United States. The aim of the unorganized group is to provide programs which include education, acquisition, and fellowship.

Donna and Jim Newton have been collecting for fourteen years. They have a large, comprehensive collection and are currently looking for unique Scottie items. The Newtons do not make initial offers and request photos on all items before purchasing. They prefer items from the 1930s and 1940s. All prices paid depend on condition.

Donna Newton
c/o Wee Scots, Inc.
P.O. Box 1512, Dept. 93-1
Columbus, IN 47202-1512

We Pay

Advertising Tins	**5.00-15.00**
Buster Bean Comic Strips	**1.00-4.00**
Magazine Covers	**1.00-6.00**
Post Cards or Trade Cards	**2.00-6.00**
Cambridge Glass	**Write**
Rosenthal Figurines	**Write**

SCOUTING COLLECTIBLES

I am buying scouting items for display. Needed are many boy and girl scout pieces from 1911 through the 1950s. Listed below are some items currently needed.

Edward J. Quirk, Jr.
46 Kelsey Ave.
W Haven, CT 06516

We Pay

Arm Band, guide, 1953	**15.00+**
Patch, 369/WWW, felt	**50.00+**
Patch, rank, pre-1950	**2.00+**

Patch, Order of the Arrow, pocket ....**2.00+**
Patch, Camp Sequassen, felt...**3.00+**
Merit Badge Sash ....**3.00+**
Medal, Eagle Scout..**25.00+**
National Jamboree Ring, 1935 or 1937..**25.00+**
National Jamboree Flag, 1935 or 1937 ....**35.00+**
National Jamboree Shoulder Tab, NJ, 1935, felt.....................................**15.00+**
National Jamboree Shoulder Tab, 1937 ....**10.00+**
National Jamboree Stickers...**5.00+**
Jamboree Armband ....**8.00+**
Jamboree Baggage Tag...**1.00+**
Jamboree Pennant ....**5.00+**
Jamboree Pillow Cover...**5.00+**
Jamboree Printed Material..**3.00+**
Jamboree Souvenir Item..**2.00+**
Jamboree Troop Flag...**10.00+**
N.O.A.C. Button, 1946 ....**10.00+**
N.O.A.C. Patch, 1948, felt...**20.00+**
N.O.A.C. Chorus, staff material ....**5.00+**
World Jamboree Medal, 1920 ....**100.00+**
World Jamboree Patch, pre-1967...**20.00+**
World Jamboree, any other item..**5.00+**

We buy the unusual items associated with boy or girl scouting. Did you know the B.S.A. had watch fobs, gardening medals with ribbons, and Liberty Loan awards? Did you know the G.S.A. had farm aides, hospital aides, and Liberty Loan medals? We buy scouting materials such as sheet music, dolls, banks, games, posters, flags, plates, toys, puzzles, pocket watches, wing pins or patches, pre-1940 uniforms, World Jamboree items, etc. All letters answered, or FAX us a list.

Memory Tree
P.O. Box 9462
Madison, WI 53715
414-261-6641 or FAX 414-261-9461

We Pay

Jamboree Troop Flag..**10.00+**
Jamboree Printed Material..**1.00+**

SEWING MACHINES

I collect primitive hand-turned sewing machines with the latest patent dates prior to 1870. The machines below are a sampling of those I buy. Please accompany your offer with a photo, or call with a description.

Mike Brooks
7335 Skyline Blvd.
Oakland, CA 94611; 510-339-1751 (evenings)

Manufacturer's Name   **We Pay**

Bartholf...**200.00**
Blodgett & Lerow..**250.00**
Elliptic..**150.00**
Finkle & Lyon..**150.00**
Globe...**100.00**
Ladies' Companion **200.00**
Lathrop **250.00**
Leavitt...**200.00**
Little Monitor **100.00**
Morey & Johnson..**200.00**
Paradox..**100.00**
Pratt **200.00**
Robertson..**250.00**
Williams & Orvis **200.00**

SEWING TOOLS

Before the advent of the sewing machine, garments and household goods were made by hand. High-quality needlework tools were used by generations of needleworkers during the 18th, 19th, and early 20th centuries. Tools were made of gold, silver, ivory, mother-of-pearl, and other fine materials as well as of wood, brass, leather, and silk. Forms of decoration included tartanware and transfer ware from Scotland, inlays of ivory and mother-of-pearl on horn and ivory, hand-engraved and carved decoration, embossed designs, and many others.

I am especially interested in **tools and work boxes of the 19th and early 20th centuries.** Figural pieces (tape measures, needlecases, etc. in the form of animals, buildings, flowers, birds, people, etc.) are of special interest as are items from the Victorian era. I buy single items, sets, and collections. Prices paid reflect the rarity, condition, age, and material of individual pieces and would be impossible to generalize here.

If you have any of the following items for sale or other hand needlework tools I may have omitted, I would appreciate hearing from you with a complete description and your asking price. I do not buy reproductions or broken tools.

Bodkins & Ribbon Threaders
Chatelaines (complete or individual pieces)
Crochet Ball Holders
Darning Eggs & Glove Darners
Emeries
Fitted Needlework Boxes
Hem Gauges
Knitting Needle Sheaths & Guards
Needle Books
Needlecases
Needlework Clamps
Pin Disks
Pincushions & Pin Cubes
Scissors
Spool Knaves
Tape Measures
Tatting Shuttles
Thimbles, Thimble Holders & Cases
Thread Containers, Winders, Reels, & Stands
Thread Waxers
Victorian Brass Needlecases & Tape Measures
Other Tools Wanted

Marjorie Geddes
P.O. Box 5875
Aloha, OR 97007; 503-649-1041

I am interested in any antique sewing items, especially **sewing and pincushion birds, miniature sewing machines, and other sewing tools**. I also collect **items relating to herbs** such as posters, pictures, boxes, wood items, medicine containers, etc. (items picturing herbs, etc.).

Dorothy VanDeest
494 Saint Nick Dr.
Memphis, TN 38117-4118; 901-682-4040

We Pay

Sewing Birds ....**up to 50.00**
Miniature Sewing Machines ....**up to 50.00**
Old Sewing Tools ....**up to 50.00**

Tatting is a process by which a fabric akin to lace is made of thread with a small hand shuttle and the fingers. It was once a widely practiced craft, known in Italy as occhi and in France as 'la frivolite'. Unlike knitting and crochet, tatting stitches are composed of knots and are very difficult to undo. The resulting product appears to be quite fragile but is indeed strong and durable. The resulting knots form rings or semicircles that can be used for edging, insertions, doilies, etc. The thickness of the finished product is determined by the size of the shuttle and the thread. In tatting, twisted threads are tied around or through small, pointed shuttles that are made of ivory, mother-of-pearl, tortoise shell, wood, steel, or celluloid. In addition to **tatting shuttles, thimbles, 'special' crochet hooks, patterns, and miscellaneous sewing items** are wanted. Please, no new metal shuttles that can be purchased at stores today.

Hicker' Nut Hill Antiques
Genie & Robert Prather
Rt. 2, Box 532-Y
Tyler, TX 75704

Tatting Shuttle **We Pay**

Metal	**.50¢+**
Wood	**2.00+**
Ivory	**Write**
Mother-of-Pearl	**10.00+**
Advertising	**Write**
Celluloid	**.50¢+**
Tortoise Shell	**5.00+**
Unusual	**Write**

Wanted: **darners** – wooden, all shapes and sizes. Unpainted items preferred; paying $1.00 and up.

C. Erling
285 Wilbur Cross Hwy.
Suite #128
Kensington, CT 06037

SHAVING MUGS

I am hungry for **figural or character shaving mugs** which also may be in relief and paper literature about them. These shaving mugs come in ceramic or metal and also have matching brushes. While condition, age, and rarity usually determine the price, a general price listing (for items assumed to be in very good condition) is given below. The list below has some of the mugs I am looking for. I will pay the highest price. If I already have your mug, I will steer you to another character collector. I have other character shaving mug friends. Please call me! Thank you!

David C. Giese
1410 Aquia Dr.
Stafford, VA 22554; 703-659-5984

Character Shaving Mug	We Pay
Dachshund, entire figure	300.00-500.00
Owl, entire figure	150.00-400.00
Tiger, head	150.00-400.00
Pig, head	150.00-250.00
Rhino, head	150.00-250.00
Bear, entire figure	150.00-400.00
Man's Boot	150.00-250.00
Buffalo, head	150.00-400.00
White Elephant, head	90.00-200.00
Goat, head	150.00-300.00

Figural–Handled Mugs	We Pay
Barber Pole	60.00-90.00
Razor	60.00-90.00
Snake	90.00-150.00
Scuttle Mug, w/devil handle	150.00-200.00

SHAWNEE POTTERY

My love and my specialty is this adorable pottery made between 1937 and 1961. Primarily, I am seeking other collectors who would like to meet fellow Shawnee-aholics nationwide. We have a national club with a monthly newsletter just chock full of pictures, information, ads, current prices, and much more! Chartered in 1990, we have reached over 650 Shawnee collectors. Just $25.00 per year opens a whole new world of Shawnee for you. We buy, sell, and trade Shawnee pottery.

Shawnee Pottery Collectors
c/o Pamela D. Curran
P.O. Box 713
New Smyrna Beach, FL 32170-0713; 904-345-0150

We Pay

Cookie Jars	**Listed Price**
Creamers	**Listed Price**
Flora Ware	**Listed Price**
Kitchen Ware	**Listed Price**
Pitchers	**Listed Price**
Planters	**Listed Price**
Salt & Pepper Shakers	**Listed Price**
Sugar Bowls	**Listed Price**
Teapots	**Listed Price**

I am interested in buying Shawnee cookie jars, teapots, and pitchers. Of special interest are Granny Anns and items with gold trim.
Mrs. John Hathaway
N Main St.
Bryant Pond, ME 04219; 207-665-2124

SHELLEY

We wish to buy Shelley china to better accommodate our Shelley china replacement service. We particularly wish to buy 6-flute (Dainty shape), 12-flute, 14-flute, Oleander shape, and the more 'modern' shapes of Eve, Mode, Regent, Vogue, and the graceful Queen Anne. Individual pieces, luncheon sets, dessert sets, and full dinner sets are sought. We respond to all offerings by telephone or letter.

Fred & Lila Shrader
2025 Hwy. 199 (Hiouchi)
Crescent City, CA 95531; 707-458-3525

	We Pay
Bowl, oval vegetable, 10½"	**55.00+**
Butter Dish, round w/lid	**55.00+**
Butter Pat	**20.00+**
Cake Plate, pedestal, 3½" tall	**75.00+**
Chamber Set (pitcher, bowl & accessories)	**150.00+**
Children's Cup & Saucer	**35.00+**
Children's Egg Cup	**25.00+**
Children's Plate, various sizes	**30.00+**
Coffeepot, various sizes	**90.00+**
Cup & Saucer, various sizes	**35.00+**
Plate, various sizes	**35.00+**
Platter, various sizes	**50.00+**
Teapot, various sizes	**90.00+**

I am buying English bone china dinnerware marked Shelley, Dainty Blue. Please, only mint condition pieces wanted.

Betty Zimkowski
2566 Thoman Place
Toledo, OH 43613

Dainty Blue	We Pay
Teapot	**45.00+**
Dinner Plate, 10¾"	**25.00+**
Luncheon Plate, 8"	**15.00+**

Sauce Boat w/Underplate ....30.00+
Platter 35.00
Coffeepot 45.00
Teacup & Saucer 20.00
Demitasse Cup & Saucer 20.00
Other Patterns, cup & saucer set...20.00

SHEET MUSIC

I collect sheet music no one else wants – **the 1950s-70s rock and roll**. Please send list of items. List must include the artist, tell whether or not a picture of the artist is featured on the front, and the title. Please include desired price in the first letter. Send SASE for a speedy reply.

G.F. Wade
1320 Ethel St.
Okemos, MI 48864-3009

We are buying **2-piano/4-hand sheet music, moderate to difficult arrangements**. Arrangement must be complete (not necessarily two copies, but the entire arrangement must be intact). We are paying from $5.00 and up per arrangement. There were also some collections published with multiple titles. These will be considered also. These items are not for resale. All titles will be considered. Titles from the 1940s and 1950s are preferred, but we will consider whatever you have. Please call or write if you have any question about the music!

Bill & Beverly Rhodes
N 4820 Whitehouse
Spokane, WA 99205; 509-328-8399

SODA FOUNTAIN

Soda fountain and ice cream collectibles are one of the most enjoyable categories for a hobby. These items take you back to wonderful memories and can still be acquired at reasonable prices. We have an association, *The Ice Screamers*, with over five hundred members and publish a quarterly newsletter and have an annual convention.

I have been collecting ice cream and soda fountain memorabilia for over twenty years and am known as 'Mr. Ice Cream.' I look for unusual items that have as their primary image either ice cream or soda fountains and are graphically interesting. Please send a photocopy of the item, your price, and SASE.

Allan 'Mr. Ice Cream' Mellis
1115 W Montana
Chicago, IL 60614

We Pay

Advertising Booklets, pre-1925, w/colorful covers....................................**10.00+**
Advertising Fans, picturing ice cream or people eating ice cream.............**10.00**
Advertising Trade Cards, for ice cream parlors & freezers........................**10.00+**
Ephemera, pre-1920, graphic billheads, letterheads, covers, etc..............**10.00+**
Match Covers, only those w/ice cream or soda fountain scenes ....**3.00+**
Novelties (clickers, rulers, tops, whistles, tape measures, etc.)................**20.00+**
Photographs, old soda fountains & ice cream trucks................................**20.00+**
Pin-back Buttons, pictorial, advertising ice cream...................................**20.00+**
Pocket Mirrors, showing ice cream, excellent condition ....**50.00+**
Post Card, especially real photo & advertising ....**10.00+**
Soda Fountain Supply Catalogs, pre-1920, except *Mills* #31...................**30.00+**

Soda Fountain Catalogs: *Tufs, Matthews, Lippincott, Green* ....**100.00+**
Trade Magazines, pre-1920 *Soda Fountain & American Druggist* (April 1931
  & other ice cream covers)..**20.00+**
Valentines, showing soda fountain scenes ....**5.00+**
Watch Fobs, showing ice cream or soda fountains ....**40.00+**

    We collect early soda fountain material and prefer items from the last century, but interests extend up to the 1930s. We have progressed to where the history of the industry is more important than the artifacts, hence our interest in paper items: trade catalogs, trade magazines, recipe (formula) books, original old photos showing the fancy marble soda fountains, etc. Hardware interests include builders' nameplates from the fountains, pink glass ice cream sodas and footed banana split dishes, etc. We have a favorite company and collect any advertising from the J. Hungerford Smith Co. ('True Fruit') of Rochester, New York.

    We have two books in process on the history of the industry. We will answer your questions about this subject if you include SASE (no appraisals).

Harold & Joyce Screen
2804 Munster Rd.
Baltimore, MD 21234

We Pay

Trade Catalogs, pre-1900, per illustrated page **1.25**
Trade Catalogs, post-1900, per illustrated page...**75¢**
Photographs, original, showing old soda fountains, ea............................**10.00+**
Soda Fountain Magazine, early issues ....**up to 25.00**
Soda Dispenser Magazine, early issues...**up to 20.00**
Spatula Soda Water Guides, editions 1, 3, 4 or 5, ea **35.00**
Stereoview Cards, showing old soda fountains..**25.00**
Nameplates, from old soda fountains...**up to200.00**
Straw Jar, opalescent swirl, w/original lid..**500.00**
Hand-Held Fans, cardboard, showing soda fountain scenes **20.00**
Any Original Business Paper, relating to soda fountains ....**Write**

    I buy **soda fountain and pharmacy items** made before 1920. Always looking for unusual and early items.

Ron White
6924 Teller Ct.
Arvada, CO 80003

We Pay

Syrup Dispensers, china, early 300.00-800.00
Show Globes, hanging 100.00-300.00
Bottles, brown or blue glass w/label 20.00-25.00
Straw Holders 80.00-200.00

STAMPS

I am paying from one-half Scott to five times Scott for certain Mushroom stamp issues. Please send offers (lists) or call.

William J. (Bill) Long
8653 Afton Rd.
Afton, MI 49705; 616-525-8400

STANGL

I would like to buy Stangl serving pieces. Patterns wanted include Country Garden, Fruit and Flowers, Rooster, Thistle, and Magnolia. Also wanted are vases and birds. Items must have no chips or cracks.

G.D. Johnson
7565 Roosevelt Way NE
Seattle, WA 98115; 206-524-1698

We Pay

Teapot..**25.00+**
Coffeepot ....**20.00+**
Vase ....**20.00+**

STATUE OF LIBERTY

As early as 1875, eleven years before she was unveiled on Bedloe's Island, images of the Statue of Liberty began to appear in magazines and lithographs, souvenir medals and miniature statues, trade cards, booklets, fliers, and countless other forms. She was a national symbol long before her arrival from Paris. Companies formed throughout the Eastern United States that adopted her name and image to promote their wares.

I collect Liberty in all her early forms. The material listed is just a sampling. I suggest that paper and other small items (such as watch fobs and medals) be photocopied. Photos of larger items are helpful, or you may wish to first inquire with a telephone call. If I already have an item, I will gladly offer advice and a free appraisal. Please include a SASE when writing.

Mike Brooks
7335 Skyline Blvd.
Oakland, CA 94611; 510-337-1751 (evenings)

We Pay

Books & Booklets, pre-1900	**25.00**
Buttons	**5.00-10.00**
China	**25.00+**
Donor Certificates, 1880s, American & French	**100.00+**
Fobs	**25.00+**
Invitations to Inauguration or Early Fund-raising Benefits	**100.00+**
Lithographs	**50.00+**
Medals, Centennial (1876) & Columbian (1892) Expostitions	**50.00+**
Pamphlets & Fliers, pre-1890	**20.00+**
Statues, American & French, pre-WWI	**50.00-500.00**
Tins (food & medical)	**30.00+**
Trade Cards	**5.00-25.00**
Vases, pressed glass	**100.00+**

STEAMSHIP

I buy **Great Lakes steamship collectibles** – whether a single item or entire collection. I pay top price for good quality, marked pieces of china, silver, flatware, and glassware. Also wanted are decks of playing cards, timetables, brochures, deck plans, etc. Due to the wide range of prices of Great Lakes steamship memorabilia, I cannot list prices; contact me for fair and honest quotes.

Special Items of Interest Include:
Goodrich Steamship Memorabilia
Crosby Steamship Memorabilia
Chicago & South Haven Steamship Memorabilia
Milwaukee Clipper Steamship Line Memorabilia
Pere Marquette Steamship Memorabilia
Side-Marked State Room China Water Pitchers (any Great Lakes
Line)

Dean D. Collins
P.O. Box 9623
Madison, WI 53715

STERLING SILVER AND

SILVERPLATE

We buy new store stock, estate and used items, good-condition items as well as damaged, with or without monogram. Items made by Gorham, International, Kirk, Stieff, Tiffany, George Jensen, Lunt, Towle, Reed & Barton, Wallace, Westmoreland, and Whiting are wanted along with others.

We will be pleased to do our best to give you a quote over the telephone. These details will help us give you an accurate quote: number of pieces for sale, manufacturer's name or symbol, pattern (if known), condition, and presence of monogram (if any). If the item is silver, please give size, weight, and purity as well. All price quotes are subject to visual inspection. Please call or write for quotes.

Antique Silver House
8976 Seminole Blvd.
Seminole, FL 34642
800-745-8375 or 813-392-7250

We are buying the following silverplate patterns for resale: **Vintage, Charter Oak, Berkshire, Mosselle, and First Love**. Pieces must not be worn and must be in excellent condition (they do not have to be cleaned, we will do that). We will consider other patterns. We are interested in place settings and other pieces that were manufactured for the pattern.

We are also buying **silverplated holloware by Wallace in the Baroque pattern** for our own collection. Pieces cannot be dented or terribly scratched. Pieces do not need to be cleaned but must be in excellent shape otherwise. The Baroque holloware is almost always marked on the bottom 'Wallace Baroque.'

Sterling flatware patterns (Grande Baroque, King Louis, Rosepoint, Crown Baroque, Medici, Violet) are wanted for resale. The same conditions we gave for silverplated items apply here.

If you have silver and do not know the pattern, please send a photocopy. Lay the largest piece you have with the pattern down on a copy machine. Send the copy to us, and we will attempt to identify it. Tell us how many pieces you have to sell and your asking price; we will get back to you with the information as soon as possible. Please include your phone number with anything you send.

Bill & Beverly Rhodes
N 4820 Whitehouse
Spokane, WA 99205; 509-328-8399

STOCKS AND BONDS

Wanted: old stocks and bonds. These stocks and bonds are worthless because the companies that issued them have gone bankrupt; however, I collect them for their beauty and history and will pay a good price for them.

What I want are stocks and bonds that are dated 1899 (or before), have been issued (meaning they were issued to someone) with the signature of the president or secretary of the company, and have the company seal on the document. They also need to have one or more nice vignettes (pictures) on them. Plain stocks and bonds are worth much less than beautiful ones.

I will buy all stocks, but the price for post-1900 ones is much less than pre-1900 ones, unless the company is one that did not exist prior to 1900 (such as automobile, airplane, or radio companies). I will buy unissued stocks, but at a lower price. I also want **letters by famous people.**

There are millions of companies that have gone broke since 1830 (that is when the first vignetted stocks were issued), so the few examples that are mentioned here are just that – examples – of what I would consider nice. So please phone, or send me photocopies of what you find.

Examples of some subjects would be: railroads, mining companies, 1860s oil companies, telegraphs, any industry, iron and steel, insurance companies, airplane, zoos, circus, automobile, submarine, etc.

David M. Beach
Paper Americana
P.O. Box 2026
Goldenrod, FL 32733
407-657-7403 or FAX 407-657-6382

Certificates   We Pay

Any, before 1900	5.00-50.00
Auto, after 1900	5.00-70.00
Airplane, after 1900	6.00-60.00
Others, after 1900	1.00-60.00

Signed by Famous People or Businessmen   We Pay

Andrew Carnegie	1,000.00+
Any U.S. President	500.00-10,000.00+
John D. Rockefeller	1,000.00+
Alexander Graham Bell	750.00
Albert Einstein	1,500.00
Samuel F.B. Morse	1,000.00
Frank W. Woolworth	350.00
Commodore C. Vanderbilt	500.00+

SURVEYING EQUIPMENT

I buy old surveying and engineering equipment and books. Items preferred date to 1940. I am interested in all items at all prices.

Transits	Chains
Levels	Books
Tripods	Drafting Equipment
Compasses	

Richard C. Price
Professional Land Surveyor
Box 219
Arendtsville, PA 17303; 717-677-6986

TEDDY BEARS

I am buying teddy bears made through the 1950s. Single items or entire collections are wanted. Below are examples of prices paid. Old, unusual, and growler bears are preferred.

Sherry Thornhill
Rt 1, Box 32
Hawk Point, MO 63349

We Pay

1940s-50s, ea	**20.00+**
1920s-30s, ea	**45.00+**
Earlier than 1920s, ea	**75.00+**
Artist Signed, ea	**35.00+**

TELEVISIONS

I am the world's largest vintage TV dealer and can afford to pay the most for many sets! We stock several hundred vintage TVs from 1920 through 1970, and we can pick up your set or hundreds of sets from old TV shops. Many televisions from before World War II are worth over $1,000.00; but many 1940s wooden sets with 3", 7", 10", or 12" screens are of value as well. Unusually shaped plastic TVs from 1965-75 are wanted, as are early transistor TVs and 15-19" color sets from the mid to late 1950s. Sets need not work and need not be complete! I will buy empty cabinets and cabinet repair parts for many early sets. Send a photo along with model information and condition – I will make offers (SASE helps). We repair early TVs and publish an illustrated price guide.

Harry Poster
P.O. Box 1883 WB
S Hackensack, NJ 07606

We Pay

Any 1920-42 Television, mostly complete **1,000.00-7,000.00**
1946-49 Wooden TVs, w/3" to 12" tube **25.00-500.00**
1950-57 Color TVs, 15" to 19" & color wheels **250.00-3,000.00**
Philco Predictas (unusually styled sets) **100.00-500.00**
Philco Safari, Sony 8-301W (or other early transistor models)...............**100.00+**
1970s (JVC Pyramid, Panasonic 'Flying Saucer,' etc.).............................**100.00+**
TV Displays, Dealer Items, Neons, & Signs ....**Write**
Books & Literature on Televisions, 1920-45 ....**Write**

TIFFANY

I am buying art glass, lamps, and desk pieces made by Tiffany Studios from 1890 through 1930. Most pieces are signed L.C.T., Favrile, or Tiffany Studios-New York. There is a large variety of items available today that were made by Tiffany Studios. Color determines the price of the glass pieces and condition is very important. I also want Quezal art glass and Rookwood and Newcomb art pottery.

William Holland Fine Arts
1708 E Lancaster Ave.
Paoli, PA 19301; 215-648-0369

We Pay

Desk Pieces...**75.00-1,500.00**
Desk Lamps w/Glass Shades **1,000.00-5,000.00**
Lamps w/Leaded Shades, small...**2,000.00+**
Lamp Bases, small..**300.00+**
Lamp Bases, large...**2,000.00+**

TOASTERS

I am a private collector interested in purchasing vintage electric toasters ca 1908 through 1940. I am interested in old and unusual models that are in very good condition without cracks or corrosion and with all parts intact. Prices listed are for toasters in excellent condition. I am also interested in other unusual models not listed below.

Joe Lukach
7111 Deframe Ct.
Arvada, CO 80004; 303-422-8970

We Pay

Armstrong Automatic **40.00**
Bersted #78..**30.00**
Bigelow Electric **35.00**
Birtman Single Slice **45.00**
Cadillac Electric **40.00**
Cookenette...**40.00**
Cutler Hammer..**35.00**
Dalton Electric Heater **50.00**
D.A. Rogers Self Timing **80.00**
Delco...**40.00**
Thomas A Edison 'Edicraft'...**50.00**
Electric Specialties 'Okeco' **35.00**
Electro Mfg. Co. Automatic Toaster **50.00**
Excelsior Twin Reversible **75.00**
Hewitt..**40.00**
Landers, Frary & Clark #E 3941 or #E 1941 ....**25.00**
Landers, Frary & Clark #E 1942...**35.00**
Landers, Frary & Clark #E 943 ....**100.00**
Landers, Frary & Clark #E 9410...**75.00**
Landers, Frary & Clark #E 7732...**45.00**

Landers, Frary & Clark #E 2122 ....**40.00**
Manning Bowman #1209 to #1223, ea **30.00**
Manning Bowman #1209 to #1223, w/toast rack, ea **55.00**
Mattatuck Commander #101 ....**55.00**
Mecky **110.00**
Mesco...**70.00**
Millar **40.00**
Pan Electric **100.00-300.00**
Paragon **40.00**
Pelouse **60.00**
Perm-Way Electric **40.00**
Phelps Mfg. Co. 'Cozy Toaster'..**65.00**
Plant & Co. 'Double Ray' **45.00**
Porcelier **150.00**
Radion Helion **50.00**
Simplex #T 215 ....**50.00**
Sprite Automatic 4-Slice **50.00**
Steelcraft...**35.00**
Superior Electric 'Super Lectric 55' **35.00**
Toast-O-Lator Models A to H, ea...**40.00-100.00**
Trimble **40.00**
Truit **40.00**
Wicks **50.00**
White Beauty **40.00**

TOKENS

'Don't take any wooden nickels' has been said many times but not by Norm Boughton. He collects the crazy things.

Most pieces advertising businesses are not wanted, but there are exceptions: Sambos resturants (those that say 'Good Anywhere' are not wanted), Dairy Queen, and McDonald's. The most desirable are the flat pieces from the 1930s that served as script when the banks were closed. Next come the early pieces (again 1930s) made for civic celebrations. Most of these pieces are oblong, while most of the circular pieces we know today started being used in the 1950s.

You may either write describing what you have and what you would like for them (if you have access to a copier most woods will copy well), or you may ship for my offer. If you ship for offer and you don't accept my offer, I will reimburse your postage and return your woods at my expense.

Think you might be interested in collecting wood? Contact R. Quinn, Secretary, International Order of Wooden Money Collectors, at P.O. Box 153, Mexico, IN 46958-0153, or write me for a membership application.

Norm Boughton
1356 Buffalo Rd.
Rochester, NY 14624

TOOLS

I am a mechanical engineer and collector of **early machinist tools**. I especially like tools that are pre-1915, although there are later tools that I enjoy. Factory-made tools with patent dates are preferred. I also want catalogs, displays, fobs, what have you. I have listed typical prices paid for tools that are complete and in excellent condition.

I also collect **small patented vises and advertising anvils**. The anvils must be small (under five inches long). The vises should be small also and have jaws 2½" wide or smaller. I only collect factory-made tools and am not interested in handmade ones. Many vises I am interested in use a lever for clamping rather than screwing shut as other vises do. Anvils should be decorative and must be marked with the maker's name. I have listed typical prices paid for tools that are complete and in excellent condition.

If you have one of these tools but want more money, please contact me anyhow. On occasion I have been known to go an extra mile for that special tool. I am also willing to make offers on tools that are of interest to me. Please do not clean your tools, I prefer items that are in old, as-found condition. All letters answered.

John R. Treggiari
5 Pioneer Circle
Salem, MA 01970-1225; 508-744-2897

Anvils   **We Pay**

Parker's, jeweler's type w/swivel jaws...**45.00**
Detroit Stove Works, advertising..**35.00**

Fisher or Stuart, advertising **35.00**
Billings & Spencer, clamp onto table tops **35.00**
Starrett No. 240, vise-pliers **30.00**
Iron Deficiency...**20.00**

Machinist Tools   We Pay

Grimshaw & Baxter, equivalents micrometers w/dial..............................**350.00**
A.J. Wilkinson, micrometers w/shifting screw..**275.00**
Walker's, surface gauges **155.00**
Church, micrometers **140.00**
Ciceri Smith, micrometers w/digital readout **135.00**
C.E. Billings, surface gauges **100.00**
Pat. Apr. 23 1878, micrometers w/visible thread (only wanted)..............**75.00**
Standard Tool Co., surface gauges **70.00**
Stevens, surface gauges...**65.00**
Standard Tool, caliper gauges **60.00**
Davis or Stratton, metal pocket levels...**50.00**
Starrett No. 175, micrometers...**50.00**
The Universal Testometer, indicator **40.00**
Pat. Apr. 23 1878 or Pat Jan. 22 1884, micrometers **20.00**

Vises   We Pay

Hall's Patent, lever-operated **70.00**
Loery's Patent, Pat. July 23 1889, lever-operated **65.00**
Stephens Patent, lever-operated...**60.00**
Parker's Quick-Action, lever-operated...**55.00**
Lewis Patent, Pat. July 25 1893 (OK in large sizes) **50.00**

Old **tools of many trades** such as carpentry, cabinetmaking, etc. are wanted. Any unusual, handmade tool made of wood, metal, or a combination of materials will be considered. Tools in good condition are preferred. Send a sketch or photo and description along with your asking price. I will not make appraisals.

Larry Smith
2432 S Park Rd.
Bethel Park, PA 15102; 412-831-9169

TOOTH FAIRY

I am looking for artifacts related to the Tooth Fairy — books, pillows, banks, letters from children, stories, cartoons, dolls, etc. My collection currently contains over five hundred items, many one-of-a-kind done on commission. Others are commercial. I'm willing to talk with artists who feel they can make special Tooth Fairy items for a fee and will negotiate with anyone owning and wishing to sell Tooth Fairy artifacts. Books in which the Tooth Fairy appears are also wanted. While I currently own over forty Tooth Fairy books, there may be others of which I am not aware. Specific books (I'm willing to pay 30% or more over original price, depending on condition) are listed below.

Rosemary Wells
Tooth Fairy Consultant
1129 Cherry St.
Deerfield, IL 60015

Dodge, Dan F. (1963). *Tu-Tu and the Joy Bell: The Story of How the Tooth Fairy Came To Be*. Fort Dodge, IA: The Fort Press.

Greene, Jacqueline Dembar. (1980). *The Hanukkah Tooth*. Wellesley, MA: Pascal Publishers. (ISBN: 0-938836-02-1)

Henry, Gilson. (1987). *How the Tooth Fairy Got Her Job*. Seattle, WA: Purple Turtle Books, Inc. (ISBN: 0-943925-03-7)

Miner, Carl E. (1985). *The Original Tooth Fairy Story*. OR: Grant's Pass. (Illustrated by Melva Teeter). (ISBN: 0-9615985-0-6).

Park, W.B. (1977). *Jonathan's Friends. New York, NY: G.P. Putnam's Sons. (ISBN: 0-399-2006604-3)*.

Quin-Harkin, Janet. (1983). 'Hattie and the Tooth,' in *Helpful Hattie*. San Diego, CA: Harcourt Brace & Jovanovitch, Publishers. (ISBN: 0-15-233756-3).

Robbins, John. (1988). *The Tooth Fairy Is Broke*. Darnestown, MD: Clark-Davis Publishing Co. (ISBN: 0-945938-01-2).

Whittaker, Otto. (1968). *The True Story of the Tooth Fairy (And Why Brides Wear Engagement Rings). Anderson, SC: Droke House. (Distributed by Grosset & Dunlap)*.

TOYS

We are looking for **toys and child-related items of the 'Baby-Boom' era (1948-72)** – especially character-related items from TV, playsets, Colorforms, paint sets, cartoons, space, monsters, super heroes, games, dolls, lunch boxes, gum cards, etc. Also **food packaging** such as cereal boxes, candy and gum wrappers and boxes, instant drinks, etc. are wanted. Cloth items such as bed-spreads, curtains, pajamas, etc., if they are character-related or evident of that era (e.g., space designs, cowboys and Indians, etc.); school/public literature on the atom bomb and fall-out procedures; select schoolbags, school books, and ephemera; children's magazines, mail-order club memberships, comic books, etc.; cereal and bubble gum giveaways, store displays, product catalogs; original artwork; gun sets; robots; model kits; coloring books...**Anything!**

Toy Scouts, Inc.
Bill Bruegman
137 Casterton Ave.
Akron, OH 44303
216-836-0668 or FAX 216-869-8668

We Pay

Creepy Crawler Thingmaker Set...**up to 25.00**
Marx Great Garloo Robot, plastic, 36" ....**up to 300.00**
MAD Scientist Laboratory Set ....**up to 200.00**
Howdy Doody Sweater Vest ....**up to 50.00**
Quisp/Quake Cereal Rings ....**up to 50.00**
Mystery Date Board Game...**up to 15.00**
Mattel Fanner Fifty Gun Set..**up to 100.00**
Marx Fort Apache Cowboy & Indian Playset ....**up to 100.00**
Gilbert Atomic Energy Lab...**up to 200.00**

Wanted to buy: **Cracker Jack & Checkers items** such as prizes, store displays, and boxes. Market items only; no plastic examples wanted.

Wanted to buy: **radio and cereal box premiums** such as rings, decoders, manuals, paper items; cereal boxes wanted with Tom Mix, Buck Rogers, Dick Tracy, Green Hornet, Space Patrol, Superman, Operator 5, Lone Ranger, etc.!

Wanted to buy: **toys related to 1950-60s TV and rock and roll** such as playsets, cap guns, lamps, space toys, models, games, lunch boxes – anything child-related from that period of time!

Old Kilbourn Antiques
Phil Helley
629 Indiana Ave.
Wisconsin Dells, WI 53965; 608-254-8659

Cracker Jack and Checkers   **We Pay**

Prizes	**10.00+**
Store Displays	**100.00+**
Signs	**50.00+**
Boxes	**10.00+**

Radio Premiums   **We Pay**

Rings	**20.00+**
Decoders	**15.00+**
Manuals	**30.00+**

TV-Related Toys   **We Pay**

Paper Dolls	**10.00+**
Toys, in original box	**15.00+**

Collector is buying **boys' toys from the 1950s through the 1980s.** I collect old, 12" tall G.I. Joes, Captain Action, and Johnny West figures. These are all scaled similar to Barbie dolls and feature military, science fiction and comic book, and western themes, respectively. I also want Major Matt Mason (a 6", bendable astronaut) and many of the 8" dolls from Mego. Mego had a huge line of posable dolls with cloth outfits. There were comic book characters, Star Trek, movie, and TV figures. I collect Star Wars toys as well as the new 4" G.I. Joes. I am also looking for all kinds of robots and spaceships, movie monsters, and comic book character dolls. Outfits, gear, and vehicles are important, too! Condition and scarcity affect price greatly.

Here are some broad price ranges for some of these toys. Some categories, however, are too broad to give an accurate price range. For the highest price, send me a photo of what you have. I am interested in all loose clothing, equipment, and vehicles – often these pieces are more valuable than the dolls! Please send your description and/or photos and include a phone number. I will make an offer promptly, and all letters are answered.

Paul Ivy
702 Mangrove #125
Chico, CA 95926

We Pay

G.I. Joe, 12", painted hair...**10.00-30.00**
G.I. Joe, 12", fuzzy hair **5.00-15.00**
G.I. Joe, 4"..**50¢-2.00**
Johnny West **5.00-20.00**
Captain Action **20.00-50.00**
Major Matt Mason...**5.00-25.00**
Mego Dolls **5.00-30.00**
Star Wars, 4" figures...**50¢-2.00**
Star Wars, 10" or 15" figures..**5.00-30.00**

I am buying **1950s outer space children's items** such as puzzles, card and board games, coloring and punch-out books, greeting cards, records, wallets, drinking glasses and mugs, drink mixers, clocks, lamps, blankets, drapes, and clothing. Sample prices are given below.

Don Sheldon
P.O. Box 3313
Trenton, NJ 08619; 609-588-5403

We Pay

Blankets...**25.00+**
Card & Board Games ....**10.00+**
Clocks ....**20.00+**
Clothing...**15.00+**
Drapes...**20.00+**
Drinking Glasses & Mugs ....**10.00+**
Drink Mixers ....**15.00+**
Greeting Cards...**5.00+**

Toys

Lamps ....**25.00+**
Puzzles ....**15.00+**
Records...**8.00+**
Wallets..**10.00+**

I am a collector of **Breyer plastic horses and other animals**. I prefer older models from the 1950s through 1970s in very good to excellent condition. Wanted are models, models on lamps or clocks with riders, old catalogs, etc. Especially wanted are unusual items. Please note that not all Breyer figures are marked. Also collected are Hartland plastic models and Hagen-Renaker ceramic animals. Many other figures are wanted besides those listed below.

Elle Deen
P.O. Box 8631
Redlands, CA 92399-2648
or call Denise Deen
714-795-1246 or 909-795-1246

We Pay

Blue & White or Metallic Gold & White Model, any condition **10.00-50.00**
Glossy Finished Model..**15.00-30.00**
Woodgrain Model **10.00-30.00**
Pearly Plastic Model **10.00-15.00**
Red Roan, heavily red freckled **10.00-18.00**
Indian Pony, buckskin or white & gray w/war paint.....................**20.00**
Unicorn, lying down..**7.00**
Bucking Bronco, bay or gray **15.00-20.00**
Models with Riders, Breyer or Hartland, ea **10.00-40.00**
Breyer Dogs, ea..**5.00-20.00**
Kitten, sitting...**20.00**
Dahl Sheep (white Bighorn ram)..**20.00**
Pronghorn Antelope...**20.00**
Cow w/Horns & Calf, all wanted but black pinto..........................**10.00-20.00**
Elephant, pink, blue or woodgrain, ea **25.00**

We buy **all types of transportation toys** – individual items or complete collections. Areas of special interest include Hubley, Manoil, Tootsietoy, and toys of cast iron. We also buy toys with missing parts or just parts. See partial listing below.

Gary Reed
P.O. Box 342
Fenton, MO 63026

We Pay

Pre-War Tootsietoys (Graham)	**40.00-200.00**
Post-War Tootsietoys	**10.00+**
Manoil	**15.00-100.00**
Hubley	**20.00-600.00**
Cast Iron	**50.00-2,000.00**

We pay a premium for **toys made before 1960** in mint condition and in their original boxes. We buy all toys made of iron, tin, wood, etc. You may send us a photo and description of the toy, or you can mail us the toy (insured for your protection), and we will make you an offer. If you accept our offer, we will mail you a check. If you do not accept our offer, we will mail back your toy at our expense.

Lor-Wall Antiques
P.O. Box 142
S Jamesport, NY 11970; 516-722-4829

We Pay

Cap Guns (except plastic)	**5.00-100.00+**
Cast Iron Toys (all types)	**10.00-100.00+**
Tin Toys (all types)	**5.00-100.00+**
Model Kits (all types), in original box	**10.00-100.00+**
Erector Sets (all types), in original box	**10.00-200.00+**
Toys by Hubley (all types)	**10.00-200.00+**

I am buying **old toys made from 1870 through 1950**. I am interested in many different items – the more unusual the better. I will buy a single piece or a collection. Listed below are some of the toys I prefer.

David A. Smith
1142 S Spring
Springfield, IL 62704; 217-523-3391

We Pay

Tin Toys, ea	10.00+
Cast Iron Figures & Banks, ea	20.00+
Promo Cars & Trucks, ea	5.00+
Disney Items, ea	10.00+
Wind-ups, tin or plastic, ea	10.00+
James Bond Items, ea	10.00+
Miscellaneous Toy-Related Advertising, ea	10.00+

I will buy your **character toys from the 1960s through the 1990s**. Super hero, science fiction, monster, advertising, television, and movie characters are wanted. If the item is figural and/or articulated, I want it. I will purchase items in mint condition and in their original packaging, loose but complete, (and in many cases) incomplete, or even broken.

Michael Paquin
That Toy Guy
57 N Sycamore St.
Clifton Heights, PA 19018
315-626-5688 or 315-DYG-TOYS

Dolls　　　　　　　　　　　　　　　　　　　　　　**We Pay**

Advertising, Mr. Clean, vinyl, 8"	25.00+
Alien, Kenner, 1978, 18"	100.00+
Caption Action	up to 100.00+
G.I. Joe, 12"	up to 100.00+
G.I. Joe Nurse	up to 500.00
Hans Solo, Star Wars, 12", mint in original box	75.00+
IG-88, Star Wars, 12", mint in original box	100.00+
Super Hero, Mego	up to 100.00

Other Toys Wanted　　　　　　　　　　　　　　　**We Pay**

Aurora Monster Models	up to 100.00
Cereal Boxes, premiums, or advertising pieces, before 1980	up to 50.00
Chucky Child's Play, cardboard standup (promotional)	35.00+
Creature from the Black Lagoon Items	25.00+
Green Hornet Halloween Costume	35.00+
Green Hornet Miscellaneous Items	20.00-100.00
Manor Matt Mason, Colorform Outer Spacemen	up to 100.00

Original Movie Props ....**up to 1,000.00**
Pez Candy Dispensers ....**up to 100.00**
Store Displays, for 1960s dolls & toys ....**up to 200.00**
Rom the Space Knight ....**25.00+**
Underdog, 1970s cartoon items..**25.00+**

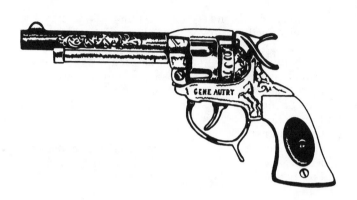

As a collector of **TV show collectibles**, I am interested in endless numbers of items and toys produced as promotions for the TV shows. Below is a listing of some of the items I am searching for and the prices I am willing to pay for excellent-condition items. I would be paying less for items in lesser condition. Mint-in-the-box items would be worth more. If possible, please send photos along with your inquiry. An SASE is necessary for a reply.

Terri Mardis-Ivers
1140 Shirlee Ave.
Ponca City, OK 74601
405-762-5174 or 405-762-8697

We Pay

Cap Guns or Holster & Gun Sets for Gunsmoke, Gene Autry, Roy Rogers, Lone Ranger, Wyatt Earp, Paladin, Bonanza, Wagon Train, & other Westerns or detective shows..**20.00+**
Other Cap Gun or Holster Sets ....**10.00+**
Hopalong Cassidy Named Items: clothes hampers, chaps, guns, holsters, bicycles, tricycles, saddles, figurines, dolls, lamps, other named items.....**50.00+**
Elvis Presley Enterprises Items: scarfs, jewelry, overnight cases, dolls, guitars, autograph books, record cases, wallets, handbags, shoes, pillows, as well as newer dolls & liquor decanters..**20.00+**
Playsets: Fintstones, Blue & Gray, etc. ....**40.00+**

Realistic Cowboy or Horse, or Sports Figures Marked Hartland Plastics or
Breyer Molding Co. ....**10.00+**
Promotional Cars (given away or sold at car dealerships) and other cars,
planes, tractors, or boats that look real...**5.00+**

Many other items related to the already mentioned TV shows as well as
others listed below are wanted. Any toy or character item will be considered
for purchase or trade.

American Bandstand	Paladin
Beany & Cecil	Robots
Beatles	Space Patrol
Brady Bunch	Star Trek
Daniel Boone	Steve Canyon
Davy Crockett	Supercar
Dark Shadows	The Rifleman
Flintstones	Tom Corbett
Green Hornet	Underdog
Howdy Doody	Universal Movie Monsters
Jetsons	Many Others Wanted
Lost in Space	

We are interested in **small or large consignments for our auctions** of toy
trains (pre-war Lionel, American Flyer), tin toys (Japanese, German, Italian),
G.I. Joe figures (large), movie figures, and pre-1970 Matchbox or Hot Wheels.

D. Lerch Promotions
P.O. Box 586
N White Plains, NY 10603
Phone or FAX 914-761-8903

We Pay

Lionel, rolling stock ....**up to 60.00**
Engines...**up to 500.00**
Lampposts..**up to 80.00**
Tunnels ....**up to 80.00**
Buildings..**up to 80.00**
Tin Toys...**up to 500.00**
G.I. Joe, movie figures ....**up to 150.00**
Matchbox or Hot Wheels, pre-1970 ....**up to 50.00**

I need the following items to complete my collection of **Care Bears and Care Bear cousins**. Please send a description of the item along with your asking price.

Wish Bear (green w/shooting star on tummy) Playful Heart Monkey
Funshine Bear (yellow w/smiling sun on tummy) Proud Heart Cat
Loyal Heart Dog Cozy Heart Penguin
Loyal Heart Pig

Marion Parsons
Box 92
Ashland, AL 36251; 205-354-3743

Wanted: **antique toys, early-painted (tole) tin toys, cast iron toys, toys with clockworks or bells, and banks**. I will buy broken and incomplete examples; I buy, broker, and sell toys. Call or write, and send a photo.

Dr. 'Z'
1350 Kirts, Suite #160
Troy, MI 48084; 313-8129

Toys   **We Pay**

Antique Tin Toys	**50.00-5,000.00**
Clockwork Toys	**250.00-10,000.00**
Bell Toys	**250.00-7,000.00**

I am currently buying **toys from all periods** that are in decent condition made of pressed steel, cast iron, plastic, and much more. **Pedal cars to small toys** are of interest to me. The original box is very important, so be sure when you write to mention whether or not you have the box. My specialty is toy motorcycles, but I buy everything. Character toys are also high on my list.

Kimball M. Sterling
125 W Market
Johnson City, TN 37604; 615-928-1471

We Pay

Toy Motorcycles	50.00-200.00
Buddy L Trucks	20.00-1,000.00
Robots	50.00-2,000.00
Japan Tin Toys	20.00-500.00
Battery-Operated Toys	30.00-1,000.00
Cast Iron Toys	20.00-500.00
Homemade Toys	20.00-5,000.00
Any Toy	20.00 to ?

We are always interested in buying **old pedal cars, trucks, planes, or coaster wagons, also smaller pressed steel or cast iron toys from the 1920s-60s**. Mainly wanted are unrestored items that need not be complete as well as broken or rusty items for parts. Please send pictures and your asking price. We pay from $50.00 to $2,500.00 for items.

Merle U. Von Drasek
409 N Hampton-A
De Soto, TX 75115

TRADE CATALOGS AND MAGAZINES

I am looking for old consumer and trade magazines that deal with cigars, saloons, show business, vending machines, and mechanical music and juke-boxes, circa 1880-1965. I'm interested in single copies, whole runs and bound copies by years, or other time units. While condition is important and gets top dollar, magazines in poor condition that have most of their interior pages intact are useful to me. I am also looking for other trade publications that deal with these subjects, such as professional drink mixers' guides issued prior to 1920. Describe and price in a letter first.

Richard M. Bueschel
414 N Prospect Manor Ave.
Mt. Prospect, IL 60056
Phone or FAX 708-253-0791

Bound Volumes   We Pay

Tobacco Leaf, 1880-1925 ....150.00+
National Police Gazette, 1880-1919 ....125.00+
New York Clipper, 1885-1910 ....100.00+
Judge, 1892-1900 ....80.00+
Puck, 1892-1900 ....60.00+
The Billboard, 1894-1965 ....25.00+
Automatic Age, any date ....40.00+
Coin Machine Journal, 1931-50 ....40.00+

Single Issues   We Pay

Bar & Buffet, 1905-20 ....10.00+
New York Clipper, 1892-1905 ....7.00+
The National Police Gazette, 1880-1919 ....5.00+
Tobacco Leaf, 1880-1925 ....5.00+
Judge, 1892-1905 ....3.00+
Automatic Age, any date ....5.00+
The Coin Machine Journal, 1932-65 ....4.00+
Automatic World, any date ....3.50+
Pacific Coin Machine Review, any date ....3.00+
The Billboard, 1894-1940 ....1.00+

TRAMP ART

Tramp art may be found in many forms, however, is generally associated with folk art and pieces made from cigar boxes and labels. Most are carved in a diamond-shaped design and layered. We are interested in all pieces, large or small, simple or complex. Due to the many types available, it is difficult to offer a pricing guide. However, we are interested in all pieces and will pay fair market price. Pricing varies from $30.00 to over $500.00. Give us a call or send a photograph.

Sam Kennedy III
P.O. Box 168
Clear Lake, IA 50428
515-357-7151 or 515-357-8850

TROLLS

Collector paying high prices for trolls from the 1960s – any condition. I buy any size troll from ½" to 24". Also wanted are troll-related items. Look in your attic or cellar; maybe you have a troll that needs a good home.

Especially wanted are the troll pig, alligator, reindeer, large gray elephant, small brown white-faced cow, small and large brown horse, small horse with a felt saddle, and any size troll with a tail made by Dam Things (paying $100.00 and up).

Roger M. Inouye
2622 Valewood Ave.
Carlsbad, CA 92008-7925; 619-729-8739

Trolls

	We Pay
3"	8.00+
5½"	35.00+
6"	40.00+
8"	50.00+
11"	75.00+
13"	100.00+
Trolls by Dam, small	30.00+
Trolls by Dam, large	100.00+
Monkey Troll, marked Dam	100.00+
Viking Troll, marked Dam, small	30.00+
Chuck-O-Luck Troll	20.00+

Santa Claus Troll, marked Dam, 11" ....**100.00+**
Mermaid Troll, any size..**40.00+**
Sitdown Troll by Royalty Designs of Florida ....**40.00+**
Troll Store Displays ....**100.00+**

Troll Houses

We Pay

Batcave by Ideal ....**200.00+**
Troll Magic Mountain..**20.00+**
Wooden Troll House...**20.00+**
Troll Traveling Bag ....**25.00+**
Troll Cottage...**25.00+**
Troll Wishnik Plastic Log Car by Irwin ....**45.00+**

Troll-Related Items

We Pay

Wishnick Troll Halloween Costume by Uneeda ....**100.00+**
Troll Handle Bar Grips for a Bike..**50.00+**
Troll Cookie Cutters...**25.00+**
Troll Records (Moonitiks & Music for Long Hairs) ....**50.00+**
Troll Decanter ....**50.00+**

TYPEWRITER RIBBON TINS

I collect any tin containers for typewriter ribbons – the kinds of things that most people throw away! The majority of these are for ½" ribbons and are either square or round. More unusual are the 'tall' tins for wider ribbons (1" to 1½"), or flat tins used to hold ribbons without spools. Please xerox your tins and send me a copy with an SASE for reply. I prefer large quantities but will be happy to look at any tin.

Darryl Rehr
2591 Military Ave.
Los Angeles, CA 90064; 310-477-5229

We Pay

Most ½" Ribbon Tins...**2.00-5.00**
Most Tall Ribbon Tins **4.00-10.00**

Flat Tins, ½x1½x4"...**10.00-30.00**
Triangular Tins **10.00**
Large Boxes (to hold a dozen tins) **10.00-50.00**

 I buy typewriter ribbon tins regardless of condition. I also by the cardboard boxes that packaged the ribbon tins, if they are in good condition. Most of the tins in my collection were bought for $2.00 to $8.00, but I will pay more for a unique tin.

 I'm hoping to someday have the largest ribbon tin collection in the country, but I'll need your help to accomplish this goal. So please root around in your attic or basement, and send me your tins. They'll be out of your house in mine, and we'll both be happy! Please send a description and your price. To save time, ship your tins to me, and if I can use them I'll make you a fair offer or pay your price. If I can't use them, I'll return them along with your postage – so you can't lose.

Ken Stephens
12 Lloyd Ave.
Florence, KY 41042; 606-371-5907

TYPEWRITERS

During the mechanical writing machine's first quarter century (from 1875-1900) the biggest manufacturers priced their machines from $100.00 to $125.00. Working men who earned $10.00 a week could not afford these type-writers, so they usually sold to banking and law offices. Because there was demand for a writing machine which was affordable for home use, about fifty manufacturers created small machines without keys or type bars which sold at prices ranging from $1.00 to $15.00. A pointer was used to pick a letter from a row or a line of type, and these primitive devices did slow but ade-quate work.

I collect these typing devices, called index or indicator typewriters. They are very small and often confused with toys. If you have a machine listed below or other unusual-looking typewriters to offer, please send a photo or begin your inquiry with a telephone call.

Mike Brooks
7335 Skyline Blvd.
Oakland, CA 94611; 510-339-1751 (evenings)

We Pay

Automatic	300.00
Boston	500.00
Coffman	200.00
Columbia	300.00
Crown	200.00
Dollar	100.00
Edland	200.00
Edison	300.00
McLoughlin	200.00
Niagara	200.00
Pocket	200.00
Pearl	300.00
Sun	200.00
Victor	200.00

Collectible typewriters are generally those which pre-date 1920 and have mechanisms which differ from the conventional format. Look for machines which do not have four rows of keys, front-striking type bars, and a ribbon for inking. This would include machines with odd shapes, single-element print-ing mechanisms, odd keyboards – and even those with no keyboards.

Condition is very important to typewriter collectors, and the prices shown are for machines in truly excellent, fully functional condition. The list which follows is incomplete, as hundreds of different typewriters were made before 1920. If you have a question, don't hesitate to contact me.

Darryl Rehr
2591 Military Ave.
Los Angeles, CA 90064; 310-477-5229

We Pay

American	100.00
Automatic	500.00
Blickensderfer Electric	1,500.00
Brooks	500.00
Chicago	100.00
Coffman	500.00
Columbia	300.00
Crandall	300.00
Commercial Visible	300.00
Crown	300.00
Daugherty	150.00
Duplex	150.00
Edison Mimeograph	1,000.00
Emerson	100.00
Fay-Sho, bronze	200.00
Ford	500.00
Fitch	1,500.00
Franklin	75.00
Garbell	75.00
Hammond #1	150.00
Jackson	500.00
Index Visible	500.00
International	500.00
Keystone	200.00
Lambert	200.00
Merritt	100.00
Morris	300.00
McCool	500.00
National, curved	350.00
Niagara	1,200.00
Pittsburgh, #1-11	100.00
Postal	125.00
Pullman	125.00
Rapid	500.00
Rem-Sho, bronze	200.00
Sholes Visible	500.00
Sholes & Glidden	5,000.00
Sterling	200.00

Victor **300.00**
Williams **200.00**
World...**250.00**

UMBRELLAS

I am purchasing umbrellas and umbrella handles, old parasols, and walking sticks that date prior to 1930. No damaged items are wanted. Send photo with your price request.

Arthur Boutiette
410 W Third St.
Suite 200
Little Rock, AR 72201

Handle Material   **We Pay**

Gold-Filled or Gold-Plated, ea..**25.00-125.00**
10k or 14k Gold, ea **75.00-225.00**
Sterling **25.00-175.00**
Other Metals..**10.00-70.00**
Porcelain **10.00-140.00**
Horn...**10.00-70.00**
Ivory **25.00-185.00**
Jeweled **10.00-70.00**
Wood **10.00-70.00**

VAN BRIGGLE

I have collected Van Briggle pottery for over twenty-three years. I prefer older (ca 1908 through 1920s) pieces but also buy pieces made as late as the 1950s. Since the Van Briggle factory is still in business, a photo is preferred; however, all offers will be noted.

Van Briggle

All Van Briggle pottery is marked with a double A in a square box. Dated pieces of Van Briggle will bring a greater price. I am not interested in any pieces signed Anna Van Briggle. Moonglo (white color name) is usually not desired. All pieces must be in very good condition with no cracks, chips, or repairs. Please describe all marks, color of piece, and color of the clay on the bottom. Listed below are examples of prices paid.

Terrye Sue Stevens
Rt. 3, Box 97
Plainview, TX 79072

We Pay

Cups or Mugs, ea	**12.50+**
Vases, ea	**20.00+**
Candlesticks, pr	**20.00+**
Bowls, ea	**20.00+**
Animals, ea	**22.50+**
Urns or Ewers, ea	**25.00+**
Statues, ea	**50.00+**
Dated Pieces, ea	**65.00-125.00**

VETERINARY MEDICINE MEMORABILIA

I buy any type of antique veterinary medicine memorabilia including old animal medicine bottles and tins, advertising signs and calendars, store display cabinets, trade cards, pamphlets, puzzles, giveaways, surgical instruments, balling guns, portable stable medical cases, etc. Anything relative to Dr. Daniels, Dr. Claris, Dr. Lesure, Pratts, Humphrey, etc. is wanted as well.

Paul Ferraglio
4410 Lakeshore Dr.
Canandaigua, NY 14424; 716-394-7663

We Pay

Dr. Daniels Medicine Cabinets	**400.00+**
Dr. Daniels Paperweights	**150.00+**
Pratts Medicine Cabinets	**400.00+**
Pratts Wheel of Success Game	**25.00+**

VICTORIAN COLLECTIBLES

I am interested in any item from the Victorian era. I prefer flawless condition but will consider items with minor damage. Please send me a listing of what you have to offer and what you are asking. The following examples are estimated values only.

Rhonda Hallden
21958 Darvin Dr.
Saugus, CA 91350

We Pay

China, chocolate sets or tea sets, hand-painted decoration (marked items preferred)	**45.00-165.00**
Clothing, ladies' camisoles, skirts, dresses, high-top shoes, etc.	**20.00-150.00**
Doorstops, cast iron (baskets, flowers, animals, etc.)	**35.00-85.00**

Ephemera, post cards, calling cards, greeting cards, advertising items,
cutouts, scrapbooks, etc. **5.00-100.00**
Glassware, water sets, lemonade sets, vases, bride's baskets, etc...**45.00-165.00**
Handiwork, needlepoint, crochet, stitchery, etc. **1.00-60.00**
Prints, showing ladies, children, or animals **20.00-120.00**
Purses, beaded fancy florals or designs **30.00-90.00**
Silverplated Items, castor sets, etc. **65.00-175.00**
Trims, Beads, Etc. (anything suitable for sewing) **1.00-40.00**

VIEW-MASTER REELS AND PACKETS

    View-Master, the invention of William Gruber, was first introduced to
the public at the 1939-40 New York World's Fair and the same time at the
Golden Gate Exposition in California. Since then the company has produced
thousands of reels and packets on subjects as diverse as life itself. The product has been owned by five different companies: the original Sawyer's View-
Master, G.A.F. (in the middle 1960s), View-Master International (in 1981),
Ideal Toy, and (most recently) Tyco Toy Company.
    Unfortunately, since G.A.F., neither View-Master International, Ideal, nor
Tyco Toy have had any intention of making View-Master anything but a toy
item, selling only cartoons. This, of course, has made the early non-cartoon
single reels and three-reel packets desirable items. Sawyer's items are especially becoming collectible, as they produced the best quality and made this

hobby a fascinating 3-D experience. They even made two cameras for the general public which enabled them to take their own 'personal' reels in 3-D; then they designed a projector so that people could show their pictures in full-color 3-D on a silver screen.

I am a collector and dealer and can pay well for good items in nice condition. Condition is important, but please let me know what you have. The prices listed below are what I will pay for items in mint or near-mint condition.

Walter Sigg
P.O. Box 208
Smartswood, NJ 07877; 201-383-2437

We Pay

Gold-Center Reels in Gold Envelopes	**10.00**
Blue-Baked Reels	**2.50-10.00**
Early Sawyer's Single Reels (white)	**25¢-5.00**
3-D Movie Preview Reels	**25.00**
Commercial Reels	**5.00-50.00**
Scenic Packets (Sawyer's or G.A.F.)	**1.00-25.00**
TV & Movie Packets (Sawyer's or G.A.F.)	**1.00-25.00**
Belgium-Made Packets	**4.00-35.00**
Mushroom Set	**100.00**
Mushroom Set w/Book	**150.00**
Mushroom Set w/Case	**200.00**
Blue Model 'B' & Other Rare Viewers	**100.00+**
'Personal' or 'Mark II' Cameras w/Case	**100.00**
'Stereo-Matic 500' Projector	**200.00**
Film Cutter for View-Master Cameras	**100.00**
Close-Up Lenses for 'Personal' Camera	**100.00**
Tru-Vue 3-D Film Strips	**1.00-20.00**
Other 3-D Items	**Call or Write**

I have been buying View-Master and stereoscopic 3-D items since 1978. Look for View-Master reels and 3-packs, cameras which took View-Master pictures, close-ups for View-Master cameras, film punchers, and dealer displays. Tru-Vue, View-Master's competitor, sold many rolls and cards which I seek, and other 3-D items (even stereo cards) are bought. Condition is important, both of the reel and the packaging. I will buy one item or a collection worth thousands; and I will make offers. Send a brief description: items, topics, and condition (SASE helps). Most viewers and plastic projectors have little value; most kiddie and cartoon items are too current.

Harry Poster
P.O. Box 1883 WB
S Hackenscak, NJ 07606

We Pay

View-Master Reels (gold, military, or advertising subjects)................**2.00-20.00**
View-Master 3-Packs (three reels w/envelope & booklet)..................**2.00-50.00**
1953 'Movie Preview' View Master Reels, ea **50.00-100.00**
View Master Camera (w/cutter & punch)...**200.00+**
View Master Close-Up Sets (for camera)..**100.00-200.00**
Stereomatic 500 (two lens) Metal Projector, w/case..............................**200.00+**
Dealer Displays & Counter Advertising ....**Write**

WATCH FOBS

The advertising watch fob was designed with a bail to accommodate a strap which was then attached to the watch. The watch itself was kept in a special pocket, and men found it easier to remove with a gentle tug on the fob than by sticking grown-up fingers into such a small opening. Many reproductions have been made over the years, but the old, authentic fobs are very desirable collectibles. In general, the old farm-equipment fobs are the most valuable.

Many varieties were made of each brand, and some are rarer than others. Case fobs are worth from $10.00 to $300.00, depending on the variation. Send fobs on approval, if you'd like; or send photocopies for my offer. I'm interested in buying all fobs – not just those that are listed.

Dave Beck
P.O. Box 435
Mediapolis, IA 52637

We Pay

John Deere, black porcelain	**250.00**
John Deere, Centennial	**50.00**
Automotive	**35.00-100.00**
Holt Tractor	**50.00-250.00**
Gun Powder	**75.00-250.00**
Waterloo Boy	**100.00**
Insurance	**20.00-75.00**
Telephone	**60.00**
Huber	**150.00**

WATCHES

Pocket watches and vintage wristwatches wanted – dead or alive! Better watches by Patek Philippe, Vacheron & Constantin, Rolex, Howard, Illinois, Hamilton, Waltham, and many other better timepieces wanted. Non-working items O.K. We have been a leading buyer of fine watches since 1976. Unusual, historical, solid golds, hunter cases, and railroad watches of all kinds needed.

We are not interested in Timex, common, inexpensive, or modern (made after 1965) wristwatches. We desire only the earlier wristwatches and better pocket watches. If you have a watch for sale, please call us toll free or write. We also pay a finder's fee for leads on entire collections or accumulations of watches for sale. Write us if you have information leading to the purchase of a collection. Significant finder's fee paid.

Maundy International
P.O. Box 13028-BY
Overland Park, KS 66212
800-235-2866

Railroad Pocket Watches (working or not)   **We Pay**

Hamilton, 21 jewels or better	**up to 3,500.00**
Ball Railroad	**up to 5,000.00**

Illinois, 21 jewels or better..**up to 2,750.00**
Rockford, 21 jewels or better ....**up to 3,400.00**
Waltham, 21 jewels or better ....**up to 4,500.00**
Any Unusual or High-Grade Pocket Watch...**Call**
Any Patek, Older Rolex, or High-Grade Wristwatch ....**Call**

They say: the 'first' watch made was in the year 1500 A.D. The minute hand did not appear until 1687 A.D. Watches with movable figures date back to 1790 A.D. There are 195,000 watches sold per day.

We say: Dig out those watches and turn them into money. They need not be working or in good shape. Our policy is to return your watch that day if you don't like our offer. In all these years, we are proud to say that we haven't returned one watch! Examples of prices are listed below. Depending on condition, gold, diamonds, etc., prices may be much more.

James Lindon
5267 W Cholla St.
Glendale, AZ 85304; 602-878-2409

Brand	**We Pay**
Audemars Piquet	350.00
Benrus	20.00
Breitling	100.00
Bucherer	20.00
Bulova	20.00

Cyma	**20.00**
Ebel	**30.00**
Gruen	**30.00**
Hamilton	**30.00**
Heuer	**40.00**
Hyde Park	**20.00**
Illinois	**30.00**
Le Coultre	**100.00**
Longines	**50.00**
Mido	**30.00**
Movado	**80.00**
Omega	**50.00**
Patek Philippe	**1,200.00**
Rolex	**300.00**
Tiffany	**100.00**
Ulysse Nardin	**80.00**
Universal Geneva	**100.00**
Vacheron Constantin	**1,000.00**
Wittnauer	**30.00**
Any Character Watches	**Call or Write**
Any Advertising Watches	**Call or Write**

Swatch watches were first marketed in this country in 1983. They were (and still are) noted for their often unusual design. Swatches are considered an inexpensive fashion watch. I am buying them in working or non-working condition if undamaged. These are the prices I am paying for Swatch watches in average used condition. Higher offers made for unusual designs or special watches and all Swatches in original boxes with papers.

Walt Thompson
Box 2541
Yakima, WA 98907-2541; 509-452-4016

We Pay

Plastic Band, purchased before 1985	**10.00**
Leather Band, purchased before 1985	**15.00**
Plastic Band, purchased before 1990	**6.00**
Leather Band, purchased before 1990	**10.00**

WESTERN AMERICANA

We buy older Western and cowboy-related materials and pay fair prices. A premium price is paid for items in excellent condition and rare or unusual items. Give us a call for a quotation.

Sam Kennedy III
P.O. Box 168
Clear Lake, IA 50428
515-357-7151 or 515-357-8550

We Pay

Chaps	**50.00-300.00**
Cartridge or Money Belt	**30.00-100.00**
Old Holsters	**50.00+**
Saddle Bags	**50.00-100.00**
Rifle Scabbards	**50.00+**
Rawhide Ropes	**50.00+**
Spurs	**50.00-300.00**
Bits	**10.00**
Branding Irons	**20.00+**
Horsehair Bridles & Other Items	**200.00-2,000.00**
Western Photographs	**5.00-200.00**
Early Guns, Muzzle Loaders, Carbines, or Revolvers	**Varies**
Sheriff's Badges	**30.00-100.00**
Early Cowboy Hats	**30.00+**
Early Saddles	**50.00-300.00**

We are buying, selling, and restoring all kinds of old cowboy items: colorful boots, spurs, horsehair items, bits, cuffs, Western badges, leather gun holsters, old West and saloon items, guns, advertising, Indian items, chaps, horn furniture, photos, etc.

Trade Route Antiques
1907 Abrams Rd.
Dallas, TX 75214; 214-826-7721

We Pay

Chaps, batwing	100.00+
Chaps, wooly	200.00+
Gun Holsters or Rigs	50.00+
Badges, Western	25.00+
Boots, colorful	35.00+
Spurs	50.00-2,000.00
Photos	25.00+
Cuffs	20.00+
Horsehair Hatbands, Belts, Bridles	35.00+

Listed below are some of the items being sought with examples of prices. Call or write describing anything old or unusual. Please note that old Western-motif clocks in need of repair are acceptable.

Roland Folsom
Rt. 3, 10th St.
Waukon, IA 52172; 319-568-4216

We Pay

Advertising Item, pin, etc., ea	3.00+
Bookends, pr	10.00+
Statue, Gene Autry or Roy Rogers	10.00+
Statue, horse	5.00+
Lunch Box	10.00+
Clock, horse, needing repair	10.00+
Clock, celebrity figural	25.00+
Picture, mounted	20.00+

There are many types of Western Americana that are collected. But as for us, we enjoy most of the old stuff from the 1800s to the 1950s. Examples of some of our favorites are saddles, spurs, holsters, cuffs, chaps, Western-styled dishes, old photos of cowboys and cowgirls, and movie star buckaroos. It is difficult to give examples of prices due to the various styles, age, condition, and collectibility of items. Please give us the opportunity to pay you a fair price for your Western items.

Rusty & Iris Gilbert
P.O. Box 92
Adkins, TX 78101; 512-649-3849

WINCHESTER

We buy products marked with the Winchester name except guns. These generally were manufactured in the 1920s and 1930s. Items marked 'Winchester-Western' (these were made after 1936) and 'Winchester, England' are not wanted. Items must be in excellent condition with all of the Winchester name intact. Almost any product made in the 1920s and 1930s might carry the Winchester name. Many Winchester stores existed in this time period, and thousands of items were sold through stores and catalogs.

Kate's Collectibles
28-US 41 East
Nagaunee, MI 49866; 906-475-4443

We Pay

Carpenter Tools, ea	**10.00+**
Mechanics Tools, ea	**10.00+**
Farm or Garden Tools, ea	**10.00**
Baseball, Football or Tennis Equipment, ea	**75.00+**
Boxing, Basketball, or Other Equipment, ea	**50.00+**
Kitchen Tools or Equipment, ea	**15.00+**
Fishing Equipment	**20.00-75.00+**
Paint, Paste or Varnish in Containers	**50.00+**
Push Lawnmower	**50.00+**
Sales Catalog, original	**50.00+**
Salesman's Samples, ea	**100.00+**
Roller or Ice Skates, pr	**15.00+**
Flashlight	**20.00+**
Flashlight Batteries, ea	**20.00+**
Store Arrangement Blueprints, ea	**50.00+**

Winchester Store Signs, ea ....**300.00+**
Display Cases, Stands or Tables, original, ea...**200.00+**
Fan, electric, table type..**100.00+**

WORLD'S FAIRS AND EXPOSITIONS

I buy souvenirs and memorabilia from these and most other world's fairs and expositions:

       1876 Centennial Exposition (Philadelphia)
       1893 Columbian Exposition (Chicago World's Fair)
       1898 Trans-Mississippi Exposition (Omaha)
       1901 Pan-American Exposition (Buffalo)
       1904 Louisiana Purchase Exposition (St. Louis World's Fair)
       1933-34 Century of Progress Exposition (Chicago World's Fair)
       1939-40 New York World's Fair

I prefer that the owner state prices for items they wish to sell but will make offers on desirable material if adequate description is furnished. The desirablility and value of these souvenir items vary greatly, and since there are thousands of different items available, it's not possible to provide a comprehensive 'buy' list. However, the following are representative prices that I will pay for items in fine, undamaged condition from the 1904 St. Louis World's Fair (Louisiana Purchase Exposition). Comparable items from other fairs might be worth more or less.

Please note that there are many reproduction ruby-flashed glass souvenirs on the market today; common items such as lace-edge glass plates, pot metal trays, and regular post cards have little value.

D.D. Woollard, Jr.
11614 Old St. Charles Rd.
Bridgeton, MO 63044; 314-739-4662

1904 St. Louis World's Fair   We Pay

Pocket Watches **100.00-200.00**
Watch Fobs...**15.00-40.00**
Clocks **50.00-200.00**
Award Medals, bronze, 'Grand Prize' **40.00-50.00**
Award Medals, bronze, 'Gold Medal' **25.00-40.00**
Award Medals, bronze, 'Silver Medal' **20.00-30.00**
Award Medals, bronze, 'Bronze Medal'...**15.00-25.00**
Award Medals, bronze, 'Commemorative Medal' **10.00-20.00**
Any Award Medal in Original Box, add **5.00**
Badges, official..**40.00-100.00**
Badges, employee's...**20.00-50.00**
Badges, other..**5.00-20.00**
Books, hardcover **5.00-15.00**
Books, softcover **2.00-10.00**
Book, *History of Louisiana Purchase Exposition*, 800-pg **35.00-50.00**
Booklets, Phamphlets, Etc., ea **1.00-10.00**
Fans, stick type **10.00-30.00**
Fans, folding type **25.00-50.00**
Invitations, ea..**5.00-25.00**
Pin-back Buttons, celluloid **5.00-30.00**
Pin-back Buttons, w/ribbon...**5.00-40.00**
Playing Cards, complete decks..**20.00-40.00**
Pocket Mirrors, celluloid..**25.00-50.00**
Pocket Knives..**15.00-50.00**
Post Cards, hold-to-light type...**5.00-20.00**
Rings, sterling **15.00-25.00**
Straight Razors **25.00-50.00**
Scissors..**25.00-50.00**
Souvenir Spoons, sterling, full size **15.00-30.00**
Souvenir Spoons, sterling, full size w/enameled bowl...................**30.00-75.00**
Souvenir Spoons, sterling, demitasse size.........................**10.00-15.00**
Souvenir Spoons, silverplate **1.00-10.00**
Steins, stoneware w/lids...**20.00-75.00**
Steins, metal w/lids **15.00-40.00**
Stock Certificates **50.00-100.00**
Tape Measures, celluloid **20.00-30.00**
Thimbles, sterling **35.00-50.00**
Thimbles, gold **75.00-100.00**
Thimbles, other material **5.00-10.00**
Tickets, Passes, Etc. (strip tickets removed from books not wanted) ..**20.00-30.00**
Tip Trays, lithographed tin **5.00-35.00**

Also wanted are china souvenirs that picture buildings or scenes of the fairs. Listed below are examples of prices paid for china souvenirs from the 1904 St. Louis World's Fair (Louisiana Purchase Exposition).

1904 St. Louis China Souvenirs	We Pay
Banks, barrel type	20.00-35.00
Banks, piggy type	20.00-40.00
Bowls, sm	15.00-25.00
Bowls, lg	25.00-75.00
Cups, sm	10.00-20.00
Cups, lg	15.00-25.00
Pitchers, sm	15.00-25.00
Pitchers, lg	35.00-75.00
Plates or Dishes, sm	10.00-20.00
Plates or Dishes, lg	25.00-50.00
Shoes or Boots	15.00-35.00
Steins, lithophane	50.00-100.00

YARD LONGS

Yard long prints are lithographs. The ones we collect show lovely ladies dressed in fashions of the early 1900s to the late 1920s. Although called 'yard longs,' few actually were exactly a yard long and some have been trimmed to fit into smaller frames. Various yard longs range in width from 6" to 11" with lengths of around 27" to 37". Some have the artist's name on the front and most have advertising and a small calendar on the back. A few of the companies whose advertising appears on the reverse of yard longs are Pompeian Beauty Products, Diamond Crystal Salt, Pabst Extract, Walk-Over Shoes, and Selz Shoes.

We collect only prints that are in excellent condition (meaning no highly visible creases, tears, or water stains). The colors must be bright, crisp, and not noticeably faded. We prefer untrimmed original-length prints with the original frame and glass.

The following are examples of specific yard longs we would like to find for our collection. There are many others not listed that we would also like to have.

Mike & Sherry Miller
303 Holiday Dr.
R.R. 3, Box 130
Tuscola, IL 61953; 217-253-4991

YELLOW WARE

We would like to buy all yellow ware stoneware pieces except bowls. Please send description of item. Pieces don't have to be in perfect condition; a chip or crack is acceptable but will affect price.

Tom & Sandy Davis
147 Longleaf Dr.
Blackshear, GA 31516; 912-449-6243

OTHER INTERESTED BUYERS OF MISCELLANEOUS ITEMS

In this section of the book we have listed over 800 buyers of miscellaneous items and related material. When corresponding with these collectors, be sure to enclose a self-addressed stamped envelope if you want a reply. Do not send lists of items for appraisal. If you wish to sell your material, quote the price that you want or send a list of items you think they might be interested in, and ask them to make you an offer. If you want the list back, be sure to send an SASE large enough for the listing to be returned.

Buyers are listed alphabetically under bold headings. Lines in italics indicate specific interests of the individual whose name and address are directly below.

Abingdon

Vintage Charm
P.O. Box 26241
Austin, TX 78755

Adding Machines

Darryl Rehr
2591 Military Ave.
Los Angeles, CA 90064

Advertising

Cream of Wheat ads from magazines
Antiques by the Beatties
3374 Ver Buker Ave.
Port Edwards, WI 54469

Cast iron paperweights
Argyle Antiques
Richard & Valerie Tucker
P.O. Box 262
Argyle, TX 76226

Signs
Dave Beck
P.O. Box 435
Mediapolis, IA 52637

Trade cards
Bernie Berman
755 Isenberg St. #305
Honolulu, HI 96826

Porcelain signs
Michael Bruner
6980 Walnut Lake Rd.
W Bloomfield, MI 48323

Soda-pop related
Terry Buchheit
Rt. 7, Box 62
Perryville, MO 63775

Paper items
Richard M. Bueschel
414 N Prospect Manor Ave.
Mt. Prospect, IL 60056-2046

Porcelain door push plates
Edward Foley
227 Union Ave.
Pittsburgh, PA 15202

Henry H. Hain III
Antiques & Collectibles
2623 N Second St.
Harrisburg, PA 17110

Porcelain signs
Sheldon Halper
9 Walnut Ave.
Cranford, NJ 07016

Terri Mardis-Ivers
1104 Shirlee
Ponca City, OK 74601

Steve Ketcham
P.O. Box 24114
Edina, MN 55424

Robert S. Macdowall
106 Hathaway Circle
Arlington, MA 02174

Seed packets & boxes
Lisa Nieland
1228 W Main St.
Redwing, MN 55066

John Deere & Caterpillar-related items
J. Schreier
Rte. 1, Box 1147
Norwalk, WI 54648

Root beer mugs
Harold & Joyce Screen
2804 Munster Rd.
Baltimore, MD 21234

Hires Root Beer
Steve Sourapas
1413 NW 198th St.
Seattle, WA 98177

Kimball M. Sterling
125 W Market
Johnson City, TN 37604

Connie Sword
P.O. Box 23
McCook, NE 69001

Trade signs
Dr. 'Z'
1350 Kirts, Suite #160
Troy, MI 48084

Airline Memorabilia

Richard R. Wallin
Box 1784
Springfield, IL 62705

Animal Dishes

Robert & Sharon Thoerner
15549 Ryon Ave.
Bellflower, CA 90706

Antiquities

Robert C. Vincent
Rt. 1, Box 327
Manton, CA 96059

Antiques

18th - 20th C American & European
Arlene Lederman Antiques
150 Main St.
Nyack, NY 10960

Arcade Machines

Thomas J. McDonald
Neshanic Station, NJ 08853-9314

Art Deco

Greyhounds
Pamela Elkin
R.F.D. 1, Box 1
Strafford, NH 03884

Jean Griswold
1371 Merry Ln.
Atlanta, GA 30329

Figural lady flower frogs
William G. Sommer
9 W 10th St.
New York, NY 10011

Art Glass

Antique Silver House
8976 Seminole Blvd.
Seminole, FL 34642

*Especially Boyd, Summit, &
Mosser*
Chip & Dale Collectibles
3500 S Cooper
Arlington, TX 76015

Catalogs of glass companies
Kathy Hansen
1621 Princess Ave.
Pittsburgh, PA 15216

Tiffany & Quezal
William Holland Fine Arts
1708 E Lancaster Ave.
Paoli, PA 19301

Scott Roland
P.O. Box 262
Schenevus, NY 12155

Kimball M. Sterling
125 W Market
Johnson City, TN 37604

Art Nouveau

*Especially works by Alphonse
Mucha*
Donald Kutz
8471 Buffalo Dr.
Commerce Twp., MI 48382

Art Pottery

Frank Bernhard
2791 Fiesta Dr.
Venice, FL 34293

Betty Bird
107 Ida St.
Mount Shasta, CA 96067

Newcomb & Rookwood
William Holland Fine Arts
1708 E Lancaster Ave.
Paoli, PA 19301

With pheasant decoration
Delores Saar
45 - 5th Ave. NW
Hutchinson, MN 55350

Atlases

Art Source International
1237 Pearl St.
Boulder, CO 80302

Murray Hudson
Antiquarian Books & Maps
The Old Post Office
109 S Church St.
P.O. Box 163
Halls, TN 38040

Before 1870
Gordon Totty
Scarce Paper Americana
347 Shady Lake Parkway

Autographs

Ads Autographs
P.O. Box 8006
Webster, NY 14580

*Especially early businessmen &
financiers*
David M. Beach
Paper Americana
P.O. Box 2026
Goldenrod, FL 32733

Michael Gerlicher
1375 Rest Point Rd.
Orono, MN 55364

Heritage Book Shop, Inc.
8540 Melrose Ave.
Los Angeles, CA 90069

Judith Katz-Schwartz
222 E 93rd St., 42D
New York, NY 10128

Key Books
P.O. Box 58097
St. Petersburg, FL 33715

Paul Melzer Fine Books
P.O. Box 1143
Redlands, CA 92373

Gary Struncius
P.O. Box 1374
Lakewood, NJ 08701

Vintage Charm
P.O. Box 26241
Austin, TX 78755

Automobilia

Sheldon Halper
9 Walnut Ave.
Cranford, NJ 07016

Autumn Leaf

Completer pieces & tin items
Brent Dilworth
89 W Pacific
Blackfoot, ID 83221

Cookie jar
Shirley Aden
1400 4th St.
Fairbury, NE 68352

Aviation

John R. Joiner
245 Ashland Trail
Tyrone, GA 30290

John Pochobradsky
1991 E Schodack Rd.
Castleton, NY 12033

Avon Collectibles

Tammy Rodrick
Stacey's Treasures
R.R. #2, Box 163
Sumner, IL 62466

Banks

Mechanical
Darrell Bemis
Shady Lane Antique Mall
R.R. 23, Box 19
Terre Haute, IN 47802

Phil Helley
Old Kilbourn Antiques
629 Indiana Ave.
Wisconsin Dells, WI 53965

Marked 'Ertl'
Homestead Collectibles
P.O. Box 173
Mill Hall, PA 17751

Dr. 'Z'
1350 Kirts, Suite #160
Troy, MI 48084

Barbed Wire

John Mantz
American Barbed Wire Collectors
Society
1023 Baldwin Rd.
Bakersfield, CA 93304

Baseball

Especially books
Brasser's
8701 Seminole Blvd.
Seminole, FL 34642

Baskets

Sharon Hamer
P.O. Box 246
Durango, CO 81302

Battersea Boxes

John Harrigan
1900 Hennepin
Minneapolis, MN 55403

Bathroom Porcelain & Related Items

Virgina S. Morgan
P.O. Box 5345
Chesapeake, VA 23324

Especially miniature items
Rosemarie Ovellette
3510 Stanton Rd.
Oxford, MI 48371

Beatles

Michael & Deborah Summers
3258 Harrison St.
Paducah, KY 42001

Bedroom Accessories & Glassware

K. Hartman
7459 Shawnee Rd.
N Tonawanda, NJ 14120

Beer Steins

Tammy Rodrick
Rt. 2, Box 163
Sumner, IL 62466

Betty Boop

Leo A. Mallette
2309 Santa Anita Ave.
Arcadia, CA 91006-5154

Judith Katz-Schwartz
222 E 93rd St., 42D
New York, NY 10128

Big Little Books

Jay's House of Collectibles
75 Pkwy. Dr.
Syosset, NY 11791

Billiards & Pool

Alan D. Conway
1696 W Morton Ave.
Porterville, CA 93257

Black Americana

Jean Griswold
1371 Merry Ln.
Atlanta, GA 30329

Irene M. Houdek
Rt. 2, Box 231
Cresco, IA 52136

Judy Posner
R.D. #1, Box 273 WB
Effort, PA 18330

Linda Rogers
4041 A N 11th St.
Milwaukee, WI 53209

Depicting popular dance forms
William G. Sommer
9 W 10th St.
New York, NY 10011

Black Amethyst Glass

Joe Brell
607 Center Ave.
Pittsburgh, PA 15215

Black Cats

Shafford only
Doug Dezo
864 Paterson Ave.
Maywood, NJ 07607

Blacksmith's Grindstone

Jack Zimmerly, Jr.
c/o 11711 Sharp Rd.
Waterford, PA 16441

Blue Moon Girl

Bill Sinesky
7228 McQuaid Rd.
Wooster, OH 44691

Blue Ridge

Christina Caldwell
Rt. 1, Box 336
Hawkins, TX 75765

G.D. Johnson
7565 Roosevelt Way NE
Seattle, WA 98115

Robert R. Sabo
2248 Lakeroad Blvd. NW
Canton, OH 44708

Blue Willow

The Antique Emporium
P.O. Box K
214 S State St.
Athens, WV 24712

Tammy Rodrick
Rt. 2, Box 163
Sumner, IL 62466

Bookmarks

Joan L. Huegel
1002 W 25th St.
Erie, PA 16502

Books

Children's illustrated
Noreen Abbott Books
2666 44th Ave.
San Francisco, CA 94116

Anthologies of cartoonists
Abalone Cove Rare Books
7 Fruit Tree Rd.
Portuguese Bend, CA 90274

Fine antiquarian
The Book Collector
2347 University Blvd.
Houston, TX 77005

Book Den South
2249 First St.
Ft. Myers, FL 33901

Children's illustrated
Arthur Bouiette
410 W Third St.
Suite 200
Little Rock, AR 72201

Western Americana
Carroll Burcham
5546 17th Pl.
Lubbock, TX 79416

By Marie Weathermon
Pat Jackson
2804 N. Monroe
Stillwater, OK 74075

Robert L. Merriam
Rare, Used & Old Books
Newhall Rd.
Conway, MA 01341

Hugh Passow
306 Main
Eauclaire, WI 54721

Charles Shaffer
321 Prospect St.
Willimantic, CT 06226

Nancy Drew, Judy Bolton, etc.
Gloria Stobbs
906 Shadywood
Southlake, TX 76092

Norma Wadler
P.O. Box 418 - S 7th & Pacific
Long Beach, WA 98631

Modern first editions
Wellerdts
3700 S Osprey Ave., Ste. 214
Sarasota, FL 34239

Tooth Fairy & related items
Rosemary Wells
Tooth Fairy Consultant
1129 Cherry St.
Deerfield, IL 60015

Little Blue Books
Judy Wilson
10125 River Acres RD.
Scott, AR 72142

Bottles

Perfume
Betty Bird
107 Ida St.
Mt. Shasta, CA 90607

Commercial perfumes & samples
Luc A. De Broqueville
8650 S Western 2623
Dallas, TX 75206

Perfume
The Curiosity Shop
P.O. Box 964
Cheshire, CT 06410

Handmade before 1900
Michael Engel
29 Groveland St.
Easthampton, MA 01027

Perfume
K. Hartman
7459 Shawnee Rd.
N Tonawanda, NJ 14120

Ed Keeler
8 Forest Rd.
Burnt Hills, NY 12027

Steve Ketcham
Box 24114
Edina, MN 55424

Dairy & milk
O.B. Lund
13009 S 42nd St.
Phoenix, AZ 85044

Soda
Thomas Marsh
914 Franklin Ave.
Youngstown, OH 44502

James P. Skinner
5209 W Hutchinson
Chicago, IL 60641

Bowie Knives

David L. Hartline
P.O. Box 775
Worthington, OH 43085

Boy Scout

Also girl scout
Doug Bearce
P.O. Box 4742
Salem, OR 97302

Judith Katz-Schwartz
222 E 93rd St., 42D
New York, NY 10128

Brayton Laguna

Ray Vlach, Jr.
5364 N Magnet Ave.
Chicago, IL 60630-1216

Breyer Figures

Ellen Deen
34111 Ave. F, Sp. 24
Yucaipa, CA 92399-2648

Bette Robinson
Gretchen & Wildrose Playdolls
5816 Steeplewood Dr.
N Richland Hills, TX 76180-6418

Bride & Groom Figurines

For cakes, pre-1960
Jeannie Greenfield
310 Parker Rd.
Stoneboro, PA 16153

V. Schupbach
P.O. Box 64
Tuscarora, NV 89834

Bronzes

Any made before 1940
Stephen R. Carter
2101 Sheffield Ct.
Mobile, AL 36693

Buffalo Pottery

Fred & Lila Shrader
2025 Hwy. 199 (Hiouchi)
Crescent City, CA 95531

Butter Pats

Marjorie Geddes
P.O. Box 5875
Aloha, OR 97007

Commercial china
Fred & Lila Shrader
Shrader Antiques
2025 Hwy. 199 (Hiouchi)
Crescent City, CA 95531

Buttons

Gwen Daniel
18 Belleau Lake Ct.
O'Fallon, MO 63366

National Button Society
Miss Lois Pool, Secretary
2733 Juno Place
Akron, OH 44333-4317

P. Kay's Antiques & More
359 Scotland St.
Dunedin, FL 34698

Patricia Quink
Box 733
Big Piney, WY 83113

Fred & Lila Shrader
Shrader Antiques
2025 Hwy. 199 (Hiouchi)
Crescent City, CA 95531

Judith Katz-Schwartz
222 E 93rd St., 42D
New York, NY 10128

Betty I. Yates
P.O. Box 759
Greeneville, TN 37744-0759

Shirley Yoder
4983 Oak St. SW
Kalona, IA 52247

Buzza Mottoes

Antiques by the Beatties
3374 Ver Bunker Ave.
Port Edwards, WI 54469

California Raisins

Larry De Angelo
516 King Arthur Dr.
Virginia Beach, VA 23464

Candy Containers

Doug Dezo
864 Paterson Ave.
Maywood, NJ 07607

Canes & Walking Sticks

Arthur Boutiette
410 W Third St.
Suite 200
Little Rock, AR 72201

Irvin Gendler
11222 Davenport St.
Omaha, NE 68154

Capo Di Monte

Val Arce
23029 Cerca Dr.
Valenca, CA 91354

Carousel Animals

P.J.'s Carousels & Collectibles
P.O. Box 65395
W Des Moines, IA 50265

Carlton Ware

Majorie Geddes
P.O. Box 5875
Aloha, OR 97077

Camark

Vintage Charm
P.O. Box 26241
Austin, TX 78755

Cameras

Harry Poster
P.O. Box 1883 WB
S Hackensack, NJ 07606

Carnival Collectibles

Thomas W. Davis
147 Longleaf Dr.
Blackshear, GA 31516

Books & ephemera
Betty Schmid
485 Sleepy Hollow Rd.
Pittsburgh, PA 15228

Carnival Glass

Antique Emporium
214 S State St, P.O. Box K
Athens, WV 24712

John & Sandra Stafford
125 E Oak St., Box 14
Dalton, WI 53926

Cartoon Art

Jay's House of Collectibles
75 Pkwy. Dr.
Syosset, NY 11791

Cast Iron Cookware

Joel Schiff
321 E 12th St.
New York, NY 10003

David G. Smith
11918 2nd St.
P.O. Box B.
Perrysburg, NY 14129

Catalina Island Pottery

Patrice Berlin
9315 Burnet Ave.
N Hills, CA 91343

Shelby Good
4640 W Ave. L-2
Quartz Hill, CA 93536

Ray Vlach, Jr.
5364 N Magnet Ave.
Chicago, IL 60630-1216

Celluloid-Covered Boxes & Albums

Mike & Sherry Miller
303 Holiday Dr.
Tuscola, IL 61953

Ceramic Arts Studio

John Pochobradsky
1991 E Schodack Rd.
Castleton, NY 12033

Vera Skorupski
226 Deerfield Dr.
Berlin, CT 06037

Cereal Boxes & Premiums

Scott Bruce, Mr. Cereal Box
P.O. Box 481
Cambridge, MA 02140

Tammy Rodrick
Rt. 2, Box 163
Sumner, IL 62466

Marc Chagall

Paul Melzer Fine Books
P.O. Box 1143
Redlands, CA 92373

Character Collectibles

Bill Bruegman
Toy Scouts, Inc.
137 Casterton Ave.
Akron, OH 44303

Terri Mardis-Ivers
1104 Shirlee
Ponca City, OK 74601

Michael Paquin
That Toy Guy
57 N Sycamore St.
Clifton Heights, PA 19018

Cartoon Glasses
Bill & Pat Poe
220 Dominica Circle E.
Niceville, FL 32578-4068

Tammy Rodrick
Rt. 2, Box 163
Sumner, IL 62466

Chauffers' Badges

Dr. Edward H. Miles
888 - 8th Ave.
New York, NY 10019

Loren J. Snyder
6867 Navarre Rd. SW
Massillon, OH 44646

Chelsea

Val Arce
23029 Cerca Dr.
Valencia, CA 91354

Children's Books

Noreen Abott Books
2666 44th Ave.
San Francisco, CA 94116

Children's Dishes

Majorie Geddes
P.O. Box 5875
Aloha, OR 97007

Gary Reed
P.O. Box 342
Fenton, MO 63026

Judith Katz-Schwartz
222 E 93rd St., 42D
New York, NY 10128

China

Miniatures
Marjorie Geddes
P.O. Box 5875
Aloha, OR 97007

Hand-painted marked items
Rhonda Hallden
21958 Darvin Dr.
Saugus, CA 91350

Lenox
Bill & Beverly Rhodes
N 4820 Whitehouse
Spokane, WA 99205

Vintage Shoppe
24 Baytree Pl.
Remerton
Valdosta, GA 31601

Christmas

Also other holidays
Cindy Chipps
4027 Brooks Hill Rd.
Brooks, KY 40109

Pre-1950
Diane & Bob Kubicki
7636 Emerick Rd.
W Milton, OH 45383

Cigar Labels & Boxes

David M. Beach
Paper Americana
P.O. Box 2026
Goldenrod, FL 32733

Circus & Ephemera

Betty Schmid
485 Sleepy Hollow Rd.
Pittsburgh, PA 15228

Clocks

Comic character
Howard S. Brenner
106 Woodgate Terrace
Rochester, NY 14625

Irvin Gendler
11222 Davenport St.
Omaha, NE 68154

Novelty animated & non-ani-mated
Carole S. Kaifer
P.O. Box 232
Bethania, NC 27010

Antique
Mark of Time
P.O. Box 15351
Sarasota, FL 34277-1351

Tammy Rodrick
Rt. 2, Box 163
Sumner, IL 62466

Norma Wadler
P.O. Box 418 - S 7th & Pacific
Long Beach, WA 98631

Dr. 'Z'
1350 Kirts, Suite #160
Troy, MI 48084

Clothing

Victorian; also trims
Rhonda Hallden
21958 Darvin Dr.
Saugus, CA 91350

Coca-Cola

Terry Buchheit
Rt. 7, Box 62
Perryville, MO 63775

Bill Ricketts
P.O. Box 9605-WB
Asheville, NC 28805

Cocktail Shakers

Arlene Lederman Antiques
150 Main St.
Nyack, NY 10960

Steven Visakay
P.O. Box 1517
W Caldwell, NJ 07007-1517

Coin-Operated Machines

Richard M. Bueschel
414 N Prospect Manor Ave.
Mt. Prospect, IL 60056-2046

Dembecks Keys and Locksmiths
24711 Harper
St. Clair Shores, MI 48080

Hal O'Rourke
Box 47
Lanexa, VA 23089

Coins

Lor-Wal Antiques
P.O. Box 142
S Jamesport, NY 11970

Carl Vincent
Rt. 1, Box 327
Manton, CA 96059

Comic Books

Judith Katz-Schwartz
222 E 93rd St., 42D
New York, NY 10128

Passaic Book Center
594 Main Ave.
Passaic, NJ 07055

Shawn Vincent
Rt. 1, Box 327, Apt. #B
Manton, CA 96059

Windmill Antiques
315 SW 77th Ave.
N Lauderdale, FL 33068

Comic Strip Art

David H. Begin
138 Lansberry Ct.
Los Gatos, CA 95032

Compacts

The Curiosity Shop
P.O. Box 964
Cheshire, CT 06410

Mike & Sherry Miller
303 Holiday Dr.
Tuscola, IL 61953

Cookbooks

The Book Corner
113 G East Brandon Blvd.
Brandon, FL 33511

Cheryl Erling
37 Linden St.
New Britain, CT 06051

Judith Katz-Schwartz
222 E 93rd St., 42D
New York, NY 10128

Cookie Jars

James Goad
1152A S Eagle Cir.
Aurora, CO 80012

Kier Linn
2591 Military Ave.
Los Angeles, CA 90064

Judy Posner
R.D. #1, Box 273 WB
Effort, PA 18330

Debbie Yates
P.O. Box 1461
Decatur, GA 30031-1461

Gene A. Underwood
909 N Sierra Bonita, Apt. 9
Los Angeles, CA 90046-6562

Coors

Pat & Bill Ogden
3050 Colorado Ave.
Grand Junction, CO 81504

Corkscrews

Antique & unusual
Paul P. Luchsinger
104 Deer Run
Williamsville, NY 14221

Country Store Collectibles

William A. (Bill) Shaw
801 Duval Dr.
Opp, AL 36467

B.J. Summers
Rt. #6, Box 659
Benton, KY 42025

Cowan Pottery

Joe Brell
607 Center Ave.
Pittsburgh, PA 15215

Cranberry Glass

Christina Caldwell
Rt. 1, Box 336
Hawkins, TX 75765

Cracker Jack Items

Phil Helley
Old Kilbourn Antiques
629 Indiana Ave.
Wisconsin Dells, WI 53965

Credit Cards & Related Items

Walt Thompson
Box 2541
Yakima, WA 98907-2541

Crockery Jugs

B.J. Summers
Rt. #6, Box 659
Benton, KY 42025

Cupids

Especially prints & Black items
Antiques by the Beatties
3374 Ver Bunker Ave.
Port Edwards, WI 54469

Currency, Foreign Paper

James R. Kruczek
N 11584 Moore Rd.
Alma Center, WI 54611-8301

Cuspidors

Virginia S. Morgan
P.O. Box 5345
Chesapeake, VA 23324

Cybis Figurines

Bill & Beverly Rhodes
N 4820 Whitehouse
Spokane, WA 99205

Czechoslovakian Collectibles

Delores Saar
45 - 5th Ave. NW
Hutchinson, MN 55350

Danish Items

Lona Seigfried
P.O. Box 25
Carterville, IL 62918

Darners

Cheryl Erling
37 Linden St.
New Britain, CT 06051

Decanters

Homestead Collectibles
P.O. Box 173
Mill Hall, PA 17751

Decoys

Robert Lappin
Box 1006
Decatur, IL 62523

Dedham Pottery

Rose Blundell
1700 Macon St.
McLean, VA 22101

Depression Glass

Larry D. Cook
3401 SW 12th St.
Des Moines, IA 50315-7513

Judith French
1623 Troy Dr.
Madison, WI 53704

Rhonda Hasse
566 Oak Terrace Dr.
Farmington, MO 63640

Pat Jackson
2804 N. Monroe
Stillwater, OK 74075

Pat & Bill Ogden
3050 Colorado Ave.
Grand Junction, CO 81504

Vintage Charm
P.O. Box 26241
Austin, TX 78755

Pamela Wiggins
6025 Sunnycrest
Houston, TX 77087

Dick Tracy Collectibles

Larry Doucet
2351 Sultana Dr.
Yorktown Heights, NY 10598

Dinnerware

Especially Bauer, Blair, & Hull
Tori Adams
664 Jay St.
Gallup, NM 87301

Robert R. Sabo
2248 Lakeroad Blvd. NW
Canton, OH 44708

Ray Vlach, Jr.
5364 N Magnet Ave.
Chicago, IL 60630-1216

Disneyana

Paul J. Baxter
P.O. Box 176
Stronghurst, IL 61480

Cohen Books & Collectibles
Joel J. Cohen
P.O. Box 810310
Boca Raton, FL 33481

Jay's House of Collectibles
75 Pkwy. Dr.
Syosset, NY 11791

Judith Katz-Schwartz
222 E 93rd St., 42D
New York, NY 10128

Judy Posner
R.D. #1, Box 273 WB
Effort, PA 18330

Documents

David M. Beach
Paper Americana
P.O. Box 2026
Goldenrod, FL 32733

Dog Collectibles

Jan Ennis
1823 Breezewood Dr.
Akron, OH 44313

Especially Russian Wolfhound
Cynthia Greenfield
12309 Featherwood Dr. #34
Silver Spring, MD 20904

Especially books
Kathleen Rais
3901 Conshohocken Ave. #2310
Philadelphia, PA 19131

Dolls

Pincushion
Elizabeth Baer
P.O. Box 266
Perry, IA 50220

Shirley Bertrand
971 N Milwaukee Ave., Box 99A
Wheeling, IL 60090

From 1960s-70s
Jean Brown
824 N Main
Independence, MO 64050

Lulu & Tubby by Georgene
Gwen Daniel
18 Belleau Lake Ct.
O'Fallon, MO 63366

Barbie & related items
Denise Davidson
834 W Grand River Ave.
Williamston, MI 48895

Barbie & related items
Irene Davis
27036 Withams Rd.
Oak Hall, VA 23416

Shari M. Decker
289 Green St.
Martinsville, IN 46151

Pre-WW II
Marjorie Geddes
P.O. Box 5875
Aloha, OR 97007

Dresser & pincushion
K. Hartman
7459 Shawnee Rd.
N Tonawanda, NJ 14120

Manufacturer catalogs
Judy Izen
208 Follen Rd.
Lexington, MA 02173

Ralonda Lindsay
2504 E Vancouver
Broken Arrow, OK 74014

Pat Lockerby
885 Beltrees St., Apt. 2
Dunedin, FL 34698

Captain Action
Michael Paquin
That Toy Guy
57 N Sycamore St.
Clifton Heights, PA 19018

P.J.'s Carousels & Collectibles
P.O. Box 65395
W Des Moines, IA 50265

Especially Barbie & modern collectibles
Bette Robinson
Gretchen & Wildrose Playdolls
5816 Steeplewood Dr.
N Richland Hills, TX 76180-6418

Dawn Rossi
Orphans of the Attic
P.O. Box 484
Canandaigua, NY 14424

Judith Katz-Schwartz
222 E 93rd St., 42D
New York, NY 10128

Antique bisque
Mary Ellen Sparr
3213 Seventh St.
Cuyahoga Falls, OH 44221

Noreen Stayton
P.O. Box 379
Doyle, CA 96109-0379

Barbie & accessories
Beth Summers
Rt. #6, Box 659
Benton, KY 42025

Sherry Thornhill
Rt. 1, Box 32
Hawk Point, MO 63349

Monica H. Tobin
7101 W Yale Ave., #1304
Denver, CO 80227

Sandi Waddell
2791 C.R. 302
Durango, CO 81301

Dollhouse Furniture & Accessories

Judith Katz-Schwartz
222 E 93rd St., 42D
New York, NY 10128

Doorstops

Rhonda Hallden
21958 Darvin Dr.
Saugus, CA 19350

Dr. Pepper

Bill Ricketts
P.O. Box 9605-WB
Asheville, NC 28806

Dragonware

Susie Hibbard
2570 Walnut Blvd. #20
Walnut Creek, CA 94596

Dresden

Val Arce
23029 Cerca Dr.
Valencia, CA 91354

Egg Cups

Majorie Geddes
P.O. Box 5875
Aloha, OR 97007

Egg Timers

Jeannie Greenfield
310 Parker Rd.
Stoneboro, PA 16153

Elsie the Cow

Marci Van Ausdall
666 - 840 Spring Creek Dr.
Westwood, CA 96137

Elvis Presley Memorabilia

Joan & Don Komlos
1502 Windriver Dr.
Arnold, MO 63010-4619

Enamelware

Linda Hicks
3055 E Lake
Gladwater, TX 75647

Ephemera

David M. Beach
Paper Americana
P.O. Box 2026
Goldenrod, FL 32733

Victorian paper items
Rhonda Hallden
21958 Darvin Dr.
Saugus, CA 91350

All categories
Judith Katz-Schwartz
222 E 93rd St., 42D
New York, NY 10128

Eyeglasses

From 1700s-1920s
Curiosity Shop Antiques
4500 Napal Ct.
Bakersfield, CA 93307

Fans

The Fan Man, Inc.
1914 Abrams Pkwy.
Dallas, TX 75214

Judith Katz-Schwartz
222 E 93rd St., 42D
New York, NY 10128

Fast Food Collectibles

Bill & Pat Poe
220 Dominica Circle E
Niceville, FL 32578-4068

Character glasses
Tammy Rodrick
Rt. 2, Box 163
Sumner, IL 62466

Ferris Wheel

Richard M. Bueschel
414 N Prospect Manor Ave.
Mt. Prospect, IL 60056-2046

Fiesta

Kate's Collectibles
28-US 41 East
Negaunee, MI 49866

Pat & Bill Ogden
3050 Colorado Ave.
Grand Junction, CO 81504

M.C. Wills
103 Virginia St.
Dyess AFB, TX 79607

Figurines

Porcelain, ca late 1700s-1920s
Val Arce
23029 Cerca Dr.
Valencia, CA 19354

James Goad
1152A S Eagle Cir.
Aurora, CO 80012

Firefighting Memorabilia

Richard Price
Box 219, 27 Pearl St.
Arendtsville, PA 17303

Fireworks & 4th of July

Novelties
Rob Berk
2671 Youngstown Rd, SE
Warren, OH 44484

Dennis C. Manochio
4th of July Americana & Fire-
works Museum
P.O. Box 2010
Saratoga, CA 95070

Harrison Fisher

Parnassus Books
218 N 9th St.
Boise, ID 83702

Fishing Tackle

Randy Hilst
1221 Florence, Apt. 4
Pekin, IL 61554

Rick Edmisten
3736 Sunswept Dr.
Studio City, CA 91604

Robert Lappin
Box 1006
Decatur, IL 62523

T.C. Wills
103 Virginia St.
Dyess AFB, TX 79607

Flashlights

Bill Utley
P.O. Box 3572
Downey, CA 90242

Flow Blue

Arthur Boutiette
410 W Third St.
Suite 200
Little Rock, AR 72201

Fountain Pens

Glen B. Bowen
2240 N Park Dr.
Kingwood, TX 77339

Also mechanical pencils
Cliff & Judy Lawrence
1169 Overcash Dr.
Dunedin, FL 34698

Bill Majors
P.O. Box 9351
Boise, ID 83707

Judith Katz-Schwartz
222 E 93rd St., 42D
New York, NY 10128

Norma Wadler
P.O. Box 418 - S 7th & Pacific
Long Beach, WA 98631

Fostoria

Pat Jackson
2804 N.Monroe
Stillwater, OK 74075

Frames

K. Hartman
7459 Shawnee Rd.
N Tonawanda, NJ 14120

Frankoma

Phyllis & Tom Bess
14535 E 13th St.
Tulsa, OK 74108

Plates or political mugs
Joe Brell
607 Center Ave.
Pittsburgh, PA 15215

M.C. Wills
103 Virginia St.
Dyess AFB, TX 79607

Franciscan

Pat & Bill Ogden
3050 Colorado Ave.
Grand Junction, CO 81504

Fruit Jars

John Hathaway
Rt. 2, Box 220
Bryant Pond, ME 04219

Furniture

Oak
Shirley Aden
1400 4th St.
Fairbury, NE 68352

Antique Silver House
8976 Seminole Blvd.
Seminole, FL 34642

1950s designer
Ralph Frattaroli
2114 Manor Ave.
Poland, OH 44514

Mission style
Gary Struncius
P.O. Box 1374
Lakewood, NJ 08701

Gambling & Gambling-Related Items

Robert Eisenstadt
P.O. Box 020767
Brooklyn, NY 11202-0017

Gambler's Book Shop
630 S Eleventh St.
Las Vegas, NV 89101

Ron White
6924 Teller Ct.
Arvada, CO 80003

Games

Phil McEntee
Where the Toys Are
45 W Pike St.
Canonsburg, PA 15317

Judith Katz-Schwartz
222 E 93rd St., 42D
New York, NY 10128

1950s outer space
Don Sheldon
P.O. Box 3313
Trenton, NJ 08619

Shawn Vincent
Rt. 1, Box 327, Apt. #B
Manton, CA 96059

Gasoline Globes

Walter Fieger
2513 Nelson Rd.
Traverse City, MI 49684

Garden Water Sprinklers

Tom Mattingly
P.O. Box 278
Churchton, MD 20733

Gazetteers & Geographies

Murray Hudson
Antiquarian Books & Maps
The Old Post Office.
109 S Church St.
P.O. Box 163
Halls, TN 38040

Glass Animals

Lee Garmon
1529 Whittier St.
Springfield, IL 62704

Robert & Sharon Thoerner
15549 Ryon Ave.
Bellflower, CA 90706

Glass Hats

B. McCurry
c/o Terrye Stevens
Rt. 3, Box 97
Plainview, TX 79072

Glass Knives

Adrienne Esco
P.O. Box 342
Los Alamitos, CA 90720

Glass Scoops

Al Morin
668 Robbins Ave. #23
Dracut, MA 01826

Glass Shoes

All other types as well
Susan K. Holland
Springfield, OR 97478

Also china shoes
The Shoe Lady
Libby Yalom
P.O. Box 852
Adelphi, MD 20783

Glassware

Black amethyst, Mt. Pleasant pattern
Barbara Craft
202 Lincoln
Emporia, KS 66801

Black amethyst
Judy Polk Harding
604 Hwy. 1 West
Iowa City, IA 52246

Rhonda Hallden
21958 Darvin Dr.
Saugus, CA 91350

Coudersport
Tulla Majot
503 N Main St.
Coudersport, PA 16915

Glow Lights

Cindy Chipps
4027 Brooks Hill Rd.
Brooks, KY 40109

Goebel

Cat figurines
Linda Nothnagel
Rt. 3, Box 30
Shelbina, MO 63468

Friar Tuck items
Pat & Bill Ogden
3050 Colorado Ave.
Grand Junction, CO 81504

Co-Boy figurines
Bill & Pat Poe
220 Dominica Circle E
Niceville, FL 32578-4068

Golf

Norm Boughton
1356 Buffalo Rd.
Rochester, NY 14624

Early prints
Antiques by the Beatties
3374 Ver Bunker Ave.
Port Edwards, WI 54469

Pat Romano
32 Sterling Dr.
Lake Grove, NY 11755

Virginia Young
P.O. Box 42
Amherst, NH 03031

Gone With the Wind Collectibles

Patrick McCarver
5453 N Rolling Oaks Dr.
Memphis, TN 38119

Grapette

Hicker' Nut Hill Antiques
Robert & Genie Prather
Rt. 2, Box 532-Y
Tyler, TX 75704

Connie Sword
P.O. Box 23
McCook, NE 69001

Graniteware

Daryl D. Alpers
P.O. Box 2621
Cedar Rapids, IA 52406

Betty Martin
Box 41B, Rt. 4
Eolia, MO 63344

Greeting Cards

1940s Superman
Don Sheldon
P.O. Box 3313
Trenton, NJ 08619

Griswold

Denise Harned
P.O. Box 330373
Elmwood, CT 06133-0373

Hall China

Red Poppy & Cameo Rose
Bonnie Neely
Rt. 1, Box 47A
Purdy, MO 65734

Pat & Bill Ogden
3050 Colorado Ave.
Grand Junction, CO 81504

Hallmark Ornaments

Susan K. Holland
6151 Main St.
Springfield, OR 97478

Rosie Wells Enterprises, Inc.
R.R. #1
Canton, IL 61520

Halloween

Diane & Bob Kubicki
7636 Emerick Rd.
W Milton, OH 45383

Hammersley of England

All pieces of Gulliver's Travels Series
Ray Vlach, Jr.
5364 N Magnet Ave.
Chicago, IL 60630-1216

Hartland Figures

Ellen Deen
34111 Ave. F, Sp. 24
Yucaipa, CA 92399-2648

Hatpins & Hatpin Holders

K. Hartman
7459 Shawnee Rd.
N Tonawanda, NJ 14120

Judith Katz-Schwartz
222 E 93rd St., 42D
New York, NY 10128

Haviland

Val Arce
23029 Cerca Dr.
Valencia, CA 91354

Head Vases

Jean Griswold
1371 Merry Ln.
Atlanta, GA 30329

Tammy Rodrick
Rt. 2, Box 163
Sumner, IL 62466

Herbal Items
Dorothy Van Deest
494 Saint Nick Dr.
Memphis, TN 38117-4118

Heisey

Floyd F. Gilmer
P.O. Box 13983
Roanoke, VA 24038

Homer Laughlin China

Darlene Nossaman
5419 Lake Charles
Waco, TX 76710

Ray Vlach, Jr.
5364 N Magnet Ave.
Chicago, IL 60630-1216

Hull

Antiquity Collectibles
3714 Lexington Rd.
Michigan City, IN 46360

Daryl D. Alpers
P.O. Box 2621
Cedar Rapids, IA 52406

Early stoneware
Joe Brell
607 Center Ave.
Pittsburgh, PA 15215

House 'N Garden
The Trunk Shop
C.W. Gray
123 W 3rd St.
Hermann, MO 65041

Pat & Bill Ogden
3050 Colorodo Ave.
Grand Junction, CO 81504

Especially baskets & vases
Beth Shank
956 E Riddle
Ravenna, OH 44266

Vintage Charm
P.O. Box 26241
Austin, TX 78755

Hummel Figurines

Linda Seboe
1242 Moorhead Rd.
Cloquet, MN 55720

Fred & Lila Shrader
2025 Hwy. 199 (Hiouchi)
Crescent City, CA 95531

Ice Cream Scoops

Lillian M. Cole
14 Harmony School Rd.
Flemington, NJ 08822

Illustrator Art

Antiques by the Beatties
3374 Ver Bunker Ave.
Port Edwards, WI 54469

Imperial Porcelain

Geneva D. Addy
P.O. Box 124
Winterset, IA 50273

Indian Art & Artifacts

Rose Blundell
1700 Macon St.
McLean, VA 22101

Carl Vincent
Rt. 1, Box 327
Manton, CA 96050

Len & Janie Weidner
13706 Robins Rd.
Westerville, OH 43081

Inkwells & Desk Items

Betty Bird
107 Ida St.
Mount Shasta, CA 96067

Jadite

Florence Hiojer
Star Rt., Box 8A
Stephenson, MI 49887

James Joyce

Paul Melzer Fine Books
P.O. Box 1143
Redlands, CA 92373

Japanese Porcelains

Robert R. Allen
P.O. Box 273
Manns Harbor, NC 27953

Jewelry

Angie's Attic
2562 S Halsted
Chicago, IL 60608

Antique Silver House
8976 Seminole Blvd.
Seminole, FL 34642

Rhinestone
Nancy Beall
1043 Greta
El Cajon, CA 92021

The Curiosity Shop
Lynell Schwartz
P.O. Box 964
Cheshire, CT 06410

Mexican sterling
Jewell Evans
4215 Cork Ln.
Bakersfield, CA 93309

Designer copper
Ralph Frattaroli
2114 Manor Ave.
Poland, OH 44514

Judy Polk Harding
604 Hwy. 1 West
Iowa City, IA 52246

Vicki Harper
410 S First St.
Trenton, OH 45067

Pat Lockerby
885 Beltrees St., Apt. 2
Dunedin, FL 34698

Judith Katz-Schwartz
222 E 93rd St., 42D
New York, NY 10128

Stuart Nye, sterling silver
Paul L. Trentz
126 E McKinley
Stoughton, WI 53589

Costume
Pamela Wiggins
6025 Sunnycrest
Houston, TX 77087

Diane Wilson
P.O. Box 561
Wexford, PA 15090

Judaica

Stanley Schwartz
1934 Pentuckett Ave.
San Diego, CA 92104-5732

Jukeboxes

Jim Dunham
4514 Maher Ave.
Madison, WI 53716-1725

Kaleidoscopes

Joan Walsh
520 Oak Run Dr. #9
Bourbonnais, IL 60914

Kansas Collectibles

Pottery, glass, & related items
Billy & Jeane Jones
P.O. Box 82
Dearing, KS 67340

Kentucky Derby & Horse Racing

B.L. Hornback
707 Sunrise Lane
Elizabethtown, KY 42701

Ron Kramer
P.O. Box 91431
Louisville, KY 91431

Jerry Newfield
1236 Wilbur Ave.
San Diego, CA 92109

Kewpies

Lillian D. Rosen
One Strawberry Hill Ave., Apt.
1F
Stamford, CT 06902

Key Chains

Marked 'Return to Sender'
Kayla Conway
4500 Napal Ct.
Bakersfield, CA 93307

Ladies' Compacts

Elizabeth Baer
P.O. Box 266
Perry, IA 50220

Roselyn Gerson
P.O. Box Letter S
Lynbrook, NY 11563

Lori Landgrebe
2331 E Main St.
Decatur, IL 62521

Lamps

Antique Silver House
8976 Seminole Blvd.
Seminole, FL 34642

Aladdin
J.W. Courter
R.R. 1
Simpson, IL 62985

Phoenix glass
Kathy Hansen
1621 Princess Ave.
Pittsburgh, PA 15216

Figural dresser type
K. Hartman
7459 Shawnee Rd.
N Tonawanda, NJ 14120

Handel
Shady Lane Antique Mall
Darrell Bemis
R.R. 23, Box 19
Terre Haute, IN 47802

Aladdin Genie
Jerry Shover
P.O. Box 10744
Portland, OR 97210

Art glass
Kimball M. Sterling
125 W Market
Johnson City, TN 37604

Motion
Deborah Summers
3258 Harrison St.
Paducah, KY 42001

Law Enforcement, Crime-Related Memorabilia

Antiques of Law & Order
Tony & Martha Perrin
H.C. 7, Box 53A
Mena, AR 71953

Lawn Sprinklers

Figural cast iron
Argyle Antiques
Richard & Valerie Tucker
P.O. Box 262
Argyle, TX 76226

License Plate Attachments

Edward Foley
227 Union Ave.
Pittsburgh, PA 15202

License Plates

Veteran
Kayla Conway
4500 Napal Ct.
Bakersfield, CA 93307

Richard Diehl
5965 W Colgate Pl.
Denver, CO 80227

Walter Feiger
2513 Nelson Rd.
Traverse City, MI 49684

Lighters

Bill Majors
P.O. Box 9351
Boise, ID 83707

Lil' Abner

Kenn Norris
P.O. Box 4830
Sanderson, TX 79848-4830

Little Golden Books

Steve Santi
19626 Ricardo Ave.
Hayward, CA 94541

Lucy Collectibles

Lucy Collector's Club
Jane Elliott, President
P.O. Box 851057
Mesquite, TX 75185-1057

Lustreware Pottery & Porcelain

The Trunk Shop
C.W. Gray
123 W 3rd St.
Hermann, MO 65041

Magazines

Dewight M. Cleveland
P.O. Box 10922
Chicago, IL 60610-0922

Country Collectibles
P.O. Box 1147
Midland, MI 48640

George & Pamela Curran
P.O. Box 713
New Smyrna Beach, FL 32170-0713

Mystery only
Grave Matters
P.O. Box 32192-08
Cincinnati, OH 45232

Men's
James R. Kruczek
N 11584 Moore Rd.
Alma Center, WI 54611-8301

Robert A. Madle
4406 Bestor Dr.
Rockville, MD 20853

Diana McConnell
14 Sassafras Lane
Swedesboro, NJ 08085

Mordida Books
P.O. Box 79322
Houston, TX 77279

Passaic Book Center
594 Main Ave.
Passaic, NJ 07055

Hugh Passow
306 Main St.
Eauclaire, WI 54721

Judith Katz-Schwartz
222 E 93rd St., 42D
New York, NY 10128

Shawn Vincent
Rt. 1, Box 327, Apt. #B
Manton, CA 96059

Maps

Art Source International
1237 Pearl St.
Boulder, CO 80302

State, pocket-type, ca 1800s
The Bookseller, Inc.
521 W Exchange St.
Akron, OH 44302

Bowie & Weatherford, Inc.
314 First Ave. S
Seattle, WA 98104

Marbles

Judy Beal
908 E Maywood Ave.
Peoria, IL 61603

Also related items
Hansel De Sousa
204 Lindbergh Rd.
Syracuse, NY 13205

Andrew H. Dohan
49 E Lancaster Ave.
Frazer, PA 19355

Gram & Me, Marbles
908 E Maywood Ave.
Peoria, IL 61603

Anthony Niccoli
823 E 25th Ave.
N Kansas City, MO 64116

Judith Katz-Schwartz
222 E 93rd St., 42D
New York, NY 10128

David Smith
1142 S Spring St.
Springfield, IL 62704

Match Covers

Bill Retskin
3417 Clayborne Ave.
Alexandria, VA 22306-1410

Match Safes

George Sparacio
R.D. #2, Box 139C
Newfield, NJ 08344

McDonald's®

Joyce & Terry Losonsky
7506 Summer Leave Lane
Columbia, MD 21046-2455

Meissen

Antique Silver House
8976 Seminole Blvd.
Seminole, FL 34642

Val Arce
23029 Cerca Dr.
Valencia, CA 91354

Metlox

Aztec
Ray Vlach, Jr.
5364 N Magnet Ave.
Chicago, IL 60630-1216

Militaria

Antique Silver House
8976 Seminole Blvd.
Seminole, FL 34642

Especially German
David L. Hartline
P.O. Box 775
Worthington, OH 43085

Dora Lerch
P.O. Box 586
N White Plains, NY 10603

Thomas Winter
817 Patton
Springfield, IL 62702

Milk Glass

Pink, by Jeannette Glass
Janie Evitts
265 Colonial Oaks
Dayton, TX 77535

Linda Seboe
1242 Moorhead Rd.
Cloquet, MN 55720

Miniatures

Judith Katz-Schwartz
222 E 93rd St., 42D
New York, NY 10128

Miscellaneous

James R. Kruczek
N 11584 Moore Rd.
Alma Center, WI 54611-8301

Tammy Rodrick
Rt. #2, Box 163
Sumner, IL 62466

Model Kits

Aurora
Bill Bruegman
137 Casterton Dr.
Akron, OH 44303

Other than Aurora
Gordy Dutt
Box 201
Sharon Center, OH 42274-0201

Moorcroft

John Harrigan
1900 Hennepin
Minneapolis, MN 55403

Bob Haynes
House of Haynes Antiques
P.O. Box 27374
Seattle, WA 98125-1874

Motorcycles & Accessories

Virginia Young
P.O. Box 42
Amherst, NH 03031

Movie Memorabilia

George Reed
7216 Kindred St.
Philadelphia, PA 19149

Dwight M. Cleveland
P.O. Box 10922
Chicago, IL 60610-0922

Moxie

E. Sargent Legard
P.O. Box 262
Stratham, NH 03885

Alphonse Mucha

Donald Kurtz
8471 Buffalo Dr.
Commerce Twp., MI 48382

Music

American-made guitars
Brett Ivers
1104 Shirlee Ave.
Ponca City, OK 74601

Marsha Lambert
1200 W University
Lafayette, LA 70506

Fretted instruments
Jeff Soileau
155 N College St.
Auburn, AL 36830

Napkin Rings

Betty Bird
107 Ida St.
Mount Shasta, CA 96067

Judith Katz-Schwartz
222 E 93rd St., 42D
New York, NY 10128

Naval Academy Memorabilia

Walnut Leaf Antiques
Joel Litzky
50 Maryland Ave.
Annapolis, MD 21401

Nautical Instruments

Walnut Leaf Antiques
Joel Litzky
50 Maryland Ave.
Annapolis, MD 21401

Neon Signs & Neon Art

B.J. Summers
Rt. #6, Box 659
Benton, KY 42025

Nickelodeon Rolls

Ed Sprankle
1768 Leimert Blvd.
Oakland, CA 94602

Nippon

Robert R. Allen
P.O. Box 273
Manns Harbor, NC 27953

Val Arce
23029 Cerca Dr.
Valencia, CA 91354

Julius Calloway
884 Riverside Dr.
New York, NY 10032

Rhonda Hasse
566 Oak Terrace Dr.
Farmington, MO 63640

Non-Sports Cards

James R. Kruczek
N 11584 Moore Rd.
Alma Center, WI 54611-8301

Noritake

Val Arce
23029 Cerca Dr.
Valencia, CA 91354

North Dakota Collectibles

Trudy E. Jorde
P.O. Box 82
Devils Lake, N.D. 58301

Stan & Carrie Soderstrom
003 - 3rd St. SW
Rt. 2, Box 300
Bowman, ND 58623

Rose O'Neill Collectibles

Lillian D. Rosen
One Strawberry Hill Ave., Apt 1F
Stamford, CT 06902

Occupied Japan

Brent Dilworth
89 W Pacific
Blackfoot, ID 83221

Pat & Bill Ogden
3050 Colorado Ave.
Grand Junction, CO 81504

Mary Zuzan
Rt. 2, Box 65
Denton, MD 21629

Ocean Liner Memorabilia

Judith Katz-Schwartz
222 E 93rd St., 42D
New York, NY 10128

Oil Paintings

Antique Silver House
8976 Seminole Blvd.
Seminole, FL 34642

New Jersey Artists
H.A. Milton
P.O. Box 224
Bound Brook, NJ 08805

Olympic Memorabilia

Ray Smith
S&S Antiques
P.O. Box 254
Elizabeth, NJ 07207

John & Virginia Torney
P.O. Box 2387
Huntington Beach, CA 92643

Organ Grinder-Related Items

Hal O'Rourke
Box 47
Lanexa, VA 23089

Oriental Rugs

Julius Calloway
884 Riverside Dr.
New York, NY 10032

Mike Epple
260 Lakewive Dr.
Defiance, OH 43512

Orientalia

Susie Hibbard
2570 Walnut Blvd. #20
Walnut Creek, CA 94596

Carl Vincent
Rt. 1, Box 327
Manton, CA 96059

Oyster Cans

Memory Tree
P.O. Box 9462
Madison, WI 53715

Paper Dolls

Judith Katz-Schwartz
222 E 93rd St., 42D
New York, NY 10128

Paperbacks

The American Dust Company
47 Park Court
Staten Island, NY 10301

Black Ace Books
1658 Griffith Park Blvd.
Los Angeles, CA 90026

Buck Creek Books, Ltd.
838 Main St.
Lafayette, IN 47901

For Collectors Only
20288 Ford Pkwy.
Dept. 136
St. Paul, MN 55116

Paperweights

Betty Bird
107 Ida St.
Mount Shasta, CA 96067

Andrew H. Dohan
49 E Lancaster Ave.
Frazer, PA 19366

Monica H. Tobin
7101 W Yale Ave. #1304
Denver, CO 80227

Parasols

Arthur Boutiette
410 W Third St.
Suite 200
Little Rock, AR 72201

Maxfield Parrish

Lisa Stroup
P.O. Box 3009
Paducah, KY 42002

Patriot China

All Disney items
Ray Vlach, Jr.
Chicago, IL 60630-1216

Pattern Glass Shakers

Mildred & Ralph Lechner
P.O. Box 554
Mechanicsville, VA 23111

Peanuts & Schultz Collectibles

Freddi Margolin
P.O. Box 512P
Bay Shore, NY 11706

Pen Delfin Rabbit Figurines

George Sparacio
R.D. #2, Box 139C
Newfield, NJ 08344

Pencil Sharpeners

Martha Hughes
4128 Ingalls St.
San Diego, CA 92103

Pepsi-Cola

Bill Ricketts
P.O. Box 9605-WB
Asheville, NC 28805

Pewter

Charles Shaffer
321 Prospect St.
Willimantic, CT 06226

Pez

Bill & Pat Poe
220 Dominica Circle E
Niceville, FL 32578-4068

Jill Russell
3103 Lincoln Ave.
Alameda, CA 94501

Beth Shank
956 E Riddle
Ravenna, OH 44266

Phoenix Glass

Kathy Hansen
1621 Princess Ave.
Pittsburgh, PA 15216

Photographica

Rose Blundell
1700 Macon St.
McLean, VA 22101

David L. Hartline
P.O. Box 775
Worthington, OH 43085

Charles L. Hatfield
1411 S State St.
Springfield, IL 62704

Judith Katz-Schwartz
222 E 93rd St., 42D
New York, NY 10128

Pickle Castors

Bill Sinesky
7228 McQuaid Rd.
Wooster, OH 44691

Pie Birds

Christina Caldwell
Rt. 1, Box 336
Hawkins, TX 75765

Also funnels
Lillian M. Cole
14 Harmony School Rd.
Flemington, NJ 08822

Pinup Art

Robert C. Vincent
Rt. 1, Box 327
Manton, CA 96059

Pinball Machines

1950-65
Rob Berk
2671 Youngstown Rd, SE
Warren, OH 44484

Hal O'Rourke
Box 47
Lanexa, VA 23089

Pink Pigs

Geneva D. Addy
P.O. Box 124
Winterset, IA 50273

Pipes

Briar, Dunhill, meerschaum, etc.
Reader's & Smoker's Den
36-42 N 4th St.
P.O. Box 1162
Zanesville, OH 43702-1162

Player Piano Rolls

Ed Sprankle
1768 Leimert Blvd.
Oakland, CA 94602

Police Officer Figurines

Tom Essary
4805 Blue Springs
Nashville, TN 37211

Political

Dave Beck
P.O. Box 435
Mediapolis, IA 52637

Rob Berk
2671 Youngstown Rd., SE
Warren, OH 44484

Michael Engel
29 Groveland St.
Easthampton, MA 01027

James C. Gernard
1023 S Anderson St.
Elwood, IN 46036

Charles L. Hatfield
1411 S State St.
Springfield, IL 62704

Judith Katz-Schwartz
222 E 93rd St., 42D
New York, NY 10128

Ronald E. Wade
229 Cambridge
Longview, TX 75601

Popeye Collectibles

Official Popeye Fan Club
5995 Stage Rd., #151
Bartlett, TN 38134

Judith Katz-Schwartz
222 E 93rd St., 42D
New York, NY 10128

Porcelains

Antique Silver House
8976 Seminole Blvd.
Seminole, FL 34642

Val Arce
23029 Cerca Dr.
Valencia, CA 91354

Post Cards

Bernie Berman
755 Isenberg St. #305
Honolulu, HI 96926

Antique to modern
S. Dobres Post Cards
Sheldon Dobres
P.O. Box 1855
Baltimore, MD 21203-1855

Sheldon Halper
9 Walnut Ave.
Cranford, NJ 07016

Margaret Kaduck
P.O. Box 26076
Cleveland, OH 44126

Judith Katz-Schwartz
222 E 93rd St., 42D
New York, NY 10128

Allan 'Mr. Ice Cream' Mellis
1115 W Montana
Chicago, IL 60614

Debby Yates
P.O. Box 1461
Decatur, GA 30031-1461

Mary Zuzan
Rt. 2, Box 65
Denton, MD 21629

Posters

Passiac Book Center
594-96 Main Ave.
Passaic, NJ 07055

Pottery

James Goad
1152A S Eagle Cir.
Aurora, CO 80012

John Harrigan
1900 Hennepin
Minneapolis, MN 55403

Pat & Bill Ogden
3050 Colorado Ave.
Grand Junction, CO 81504

Precious Moments®

Rosie Wells Enterprises, Inc.
R.R. #1
Canton, IL 61520

Prints

Antiques by the Beatties
3374 Ver Bunker Ave.
Port Edwards, WI 54469

Art Source International
1237 Pearl St.
Boulder, CO 80302

Victorian type
Rhonda Hallden
21958 Darvin Dr.
Saugus, CA 91350

Yard longs
Mike & Sherry Miller
303 Holiday Dr.
R.R. 3, Box 130
Tuscola, IL 61953

Hugh Passow
306 Main
Euclaire, WI 54721

Tammy Rodrick
Rt. 2, Box 163
Sumner, IL 62466

Purses

Judy Beal
908 E Maywood Ave.
Peoria, IL 61603

Kayla Conway
4500 Napal Ct.
Bakersfield, CA 93307

The Curiosity Shop
Lynell Schwartz
P.O. Box 964
Cheshire, CT 06410

Linda Fancher
1118 Park Ave.
Alameda, CA 94501

Beaded
Rhonda Hallden
21958 Darvin Dr.
Saugus, CA 91350

Painted mesh
Mike & Sherry Miller
303 Holiday Dr.
R.R. 3, Box 130
Tuscola, IL 61953

Veronica Trainer
P.O. Box 40443
Cleveland, OH 44140

Puzzles

Don Sheldon
3240 Nottingham Way
Trenton, NJ 08619

Radio Premiums

Phil Helley
Old Kilbourn Antiques
629 Indiana Ave.
Wisconsin Dells, WI 53965

Radios

Harry Poster
P.O. Box 1883 WB
S Hackensack, NJ 07606

Gerald Schneider
3101 Blueford Rd.
Kensington, MD 20895-2726

Raggedy Anns & Andys

Also related items
Gwen Daniel
18 Belleau Lake Ct.
O'Fallon, MO 63366

Railroadiana

Dean D. Collins
P.O. Box 9623
Madison, WI 53715

William F. Hayley
3305 Chartwell Rd.
Birmingham, AL 35226-2603

Judith Katz-Schwartz
222 E 93rd St., 42D
New York, NY 10128

China & glassware
Lisa Nieland
1228 W Main St.
Redwing, MN 55066

Fred & Lila Shrader
Shrader Antiques
2025 Hwy. 199 (Hiouchi)
Crescent City, CA 95531

Loren J. Snyder
6867 Navarre Rd. SW
Massillon, OH 44646

David H. Ward
20406 Little Bear Cr. Rd. #25
Woodinville, WA 98072

Records

Vintage
L.R. 'Les' Docks
Shellac Shack
Box 691035
San Antonio, TX 78269-1035

45 rpm
Sunrise Records
Mark Phillips
2425 S 11th St.
Beaumont, TX 77701

45 rpm, 78 rpm & LPs
G.F. Wade
1320 Ethel St.
Okemos, MI 48864-3009

Red Riding Hood by Hull

Antiquity Collectibles
3714 Lexington Rd.
Michigan City, IN 46360

Red Wing Pottery

Juanita Lind
Box 464
Columbia Falls, MT 59912

Lisa Nieland
1228 W Main St.
Redwing, MN 55066

Tom Tangen
2930 Hwy. 12
Wilson, WI 54027

Paul L. Trentz
126 E McKinley
Stoughton, WI 53589

Relief-Molded Jugs

Kathy Hughes
1401 East Blvd.
Charlotte, NC 28203

Road Maps

Oil company or states
Noel Levy
P.O. Box 595699
Dallas, TX 75359-5699

Robinson Ransbottom

Tammy Rodrick
Rt. 2, Box 163
Sumner, IL 62466

Rolling Pins

Glass or ceramic
Christina Caldwell
Rt. 1, Box 336
Hawkins, TX 75765

Rookwood

Joe Brell
607 Center Ave.
Pittsburgh, PA 15215

Roselane Sparklers

Lee Garmon
1529 Whittier St.
Springfield, IL 62704

Rosemeade

Clayton Zeller
Rt. 2, Box 46
Grandforks, ND 58203

Rosenthal

Val Arce
23029 Cerca Dr.
Valencia, CA 91354

Roseville

James Goad
1152A S Eagle Cir.
Aurora, CO 80012

Zephyr Lily (brown)
Juanita Lind
Box 464
Columbia Falls, MT 59912

Lisa Nieland
1228 W Main St.
Redwing, MN 55066

Pat & Bill Ogden
3050 Colorado Ave.
Grand Junction, CO 81504

Vintage Charm
P.O. Box 26241
Austin, TX 78755

Round Oak Stove Co. Memorabilia

Steve Saltzman
101 Spruce St.
Dowagiac, MI 49047

Royal China Co.

Currier & Ives; Colonial Homestead
Linda Flowers
1777 St. Rd. #14
Deerfield, OH 44411

Currier & Ives; Memory Lane
Pat & Bill Ogden
3050 Colorado Ave.
Grand Junction, CO 81504

Colonial Homestead
Tammy Rodrick
Rt. 2, Box 163
Sumner, IL 62466

Royal Copley

Joe Devine
D&D Antique Mall
1411 3rd St.
Council Bluffs, IA 51503

Royal Doulton

James Goad
1152A S Eagle Cir.
Aurora, CO 80012

E. Sargent Legard
P.O. Box 262
Stratham, NH 03885

Royal Dux

Val Arce
23029 Cerca Dr.
Valencia, CA 91354

Royal Haeger

Lee Garmon
1529 Whittier St.
Springfield, IL 62704

Royal Hickman

Lee Garmon
1529 Whittier St.
Springfield, IL 62704

Royal Worcester

Val Arce
23029 Cerca Dr.
Valencia, CA 91354

Russel Wright

Ray Vlach, Jr.
5346 N Magnet Ave.
Chicago, IL 60630-1216

Russian Art & Antiquities

Robert C. Vincent
Rt. 1, Box 327
Manton, CA 96059

Salesmen's Samples

John B. Everett
P.O. Box 126
Bodega, CA 94922

Saloon Memorabilia

Richard M. Bueschel
414 N Prospect Manor Ave.
Mt. Prospect, IL 60056-2046

Salt & Pepper Shakers

James Goad
1152A S Eagle Cir.
Aurora, CO 80012

Judy Posner
R.D. #1, Box 273 WB
Effort, PA 18330

James P. Skinner
5209 W Hutchinson
Chicago, IL 60641

Vera Skorupski
226 Deerfield Dr.
Berlin, CT 06037

G.A. Underwood
909 N Sierra Bonita Ave., Apt. 9
Los Angeles, CA 90046-6562

Salts, Open

M.A. Geddes
P.O. Box 5875
Aloha, OR 97007

Satin Glass

Black only
Joe Brell
607 Center Ave.
Pittsburgh, PA 15215

Scales

Irvin Gendler
11222 Davenport St.
Omaha, NE 68154

Schoolhouse Collectibles

Kenn Norris
P.O. Box 4830
Sanderson, TX 79848-4830

Shooting Gallery Targets

Argyle Antiques
Richard & Valerie Tucker
P.O. Box 262
Argyle, TX 76226

Scottie Dog Collectibles

Wee Scots, Inc.
Donna Newton
P.O. Box 1512
Columbus, IN 47202

Sewing Collectibles

Marjorie Geddes
P.O. Box 5875
Aloha, OR 97007

Dorothy Van Deest
494 Saint Nick Dr.
Memphis, TN 38117-4118

Sewing Machines

Mike Brooks
7335 Skyline
Oakland, CA 94611

Jerry Propst
P.O. Box 45
Janesville, WI 53547-0045

Shaving Mugs

David C. Giese
1410 Aquia Dr.
Stafford, VA 22554

Shawnee Pottery

John Hathaway
Rt. 2, Box 220
Bryant Pond, ME 04219

Linda Hicks
3055 E Lake
Gladwater, TX 75647

Pat & Bill Ogden
3050 Colorado Ave.
Grand Junction, CO 81504

Shawnee Pottery Collectors
Pamela D. Curran
P.O. Box 713
New Smyrna Beach, FL 32170-0713

Sheet Music

Sheldon Halper
9 Walnut Ave.
Cranford, NJ 07016

2-Piano/4-Hand Arrangements
Bill & Beverly Rhodes
N 4820 Whitehouse
Spokane, WA 99205

Relating to Black Americana
William G. Sommer
9 W 10th St.
New York, NY 10011

G.F. Wade
1320 Ethel St.
Okemos, MI 48864-3009

Shelley China

Majorie Geddes
P.O. Box 5875
Aloha, OR 97007

Fred & Lila Shrader
Schrader Antiques
2025 Hwy. 199 (Hiouchi)
Crescent City, CA 95531

Dainty Blue pattern
Betty Zimkowski
2566 Thoman Pl.
Toledo, OH 43613

Sherlockiana

The Silver Door
P.O. Box 3208
Redondo Beach, CA 90277

Shirley Temple

Gen Jones
294 Park St.
Medford, MA 02155

Sandi Waddell
2791 Country Rd. 302
Durango, CO 81301

Shot Glasses

Mark Pickvet
P.O. Box 90404
Flint, MI 48509

Silhouettes

Rose Blundell
1700 Macon St.
McLean, VA 22101

Silverplate

Rhonda Hallden
21958 Darvin Dr.
Saugus, CA 91350

Bill & Beverly Rhodes
N 4820 Whitehouse
Spokane, WA 99205

Slag Glass Animals

*Especially Imperial or Westmore-
land*
Robert & Sharon Thoerner
15549 Ryon Ave.
Bellflower, CA 90706

Slot Machines & Games
Angie's Attic
2562 S Halsted
Chicago, IL 60608

Thomas J. McDonald
2 Ski Dr.
Neshanic Station, NJ 08853-9314

Dembeck Keys and Locksmiths
24711 Harper
St. Clair, MI 48080

Smurfs

Bill & Pat Poe
220 Dominica Circle E
Niceville, FL 32578-4068

Snowdomes

Nancy McMichael, Editor
P.O. Box 53262
Washington, DC 20009

Soda Fountain Collectibles

Jan Henry
Rt. 2, Box 193
Galesville, WI 54630

Allen 'Mr. Ice Cream' Mellis
1115 W Montana
Chicago, IL 60614

Harold & Joyce Screen
2804 Munster Rd.
Baltimore, MD 21234

Ron White
6924 Teller Ct.
Arvada, CO 80003

Souvenir Tablecloths

Showing state map
Dan Kelley
P.O. Box 239
Fayetteville, AR 72702

Souvenir Spoons

Sandi Waddell
2791 County Rd. 302
Durango, CO 81301

Space Collectibles

Judith Katz-Schwartz
222 E 93rd St., 42D
New York, NY 10128

Sports Collectibles

Sports cards
Sally S. Carver
179 South St.
Chestnut Hill, MA 02167

Sports pins
Tony George
22366 El Toro Rd. #242
Lake Forest, CA 92630

Ray Smith
S&S Antiques
P.O. Box 254
Elizabeth, NJ 07207

G.F. Wade
1320 Ethel St.
Okemos, MI 48864-3009

Any baseball collectible
Windmill Antiques
315 SW 77th Ave.
N Lauderdale, FL 33068

Staffordshire

Val Arce
23029 Cerca Dr.
Valencia, CA 91354

Liberty Bell
Pat & Bill Ogden
3050 Colorado Ave.
Grand Junction, CO 81504

Stamps

William J. (Bill) Long
8653 Afton Rd.
Afton, MI 49705

Stangl

Birds
G.D. Johnson
7565 Roosevelt Way NE
Seattle, WA 98115

Birds
Pat & Bill Ogden
3050 Colorado Ave.
Grand Junction, CO 81504

Ranger & children's pieces
Ray Vlach, Jr.
5346 N Magnet Ave.
Chicago, IL 60630-1216

Statue of Liberty

Mike Brooks
7335 Skyline
Oakland, CA 94611

Peter B. Kaplan
7 E 20th St., Suite 4R
New York, NY 10003

Star Trek & Star Wars

George J. Seiger
Closet Collectibles
531 Hoyt St.
Pringle, PA 18704

Steamship

Great Lakes
Dean D. Collins
P.O. Box 9623
Madison, WI 53715

Stereoviews

H.A. Milton
P.O. Box 224
Bound Brook, NJ 08805

Sterling Silver

Antique Silver House
8976 Seminole Blvd.
St. Petersburg, FL 34642

Dressing table items
K. Hartman
7459 Shawnee Rd.
N Tonawanda, NJ 14120

Stocks & Bonds

David M. Beach
Paper Americana
P.O. Box 2026
Goldenrod, FL 32733

Prior to 1920
Irvin Gendler
11222 Davenport St.
Omaha, NE 68154

Stoneware (blue & white)

Ralonda Lindsay
2504 E Vancouver
Broken Arrow, OK 74014

Strange or Unusual Items

Carl Vincent
Rt. 1, Box 327
Manton, CA 96059

Shawn Vincent
Rt. 1, Box 327, Apt. #B
Manton, CA 96059

Strawberry Shortcake

Geneva D. Addy
P.O. Box 124
Winterset, IA 50273

Surveying Equipment

Richard Price
Box 219, 27 Pearl St.
Arendtsville, PA 17303

Talismans

Robert C. Vincent
Rt.1, Box 327
Manton, CA 96059

Tatting Shuttles

Hicker' Nut Hill Antiques
Rt. 2, Box 532-Y
Tyler, TX 75704

Tea-Related Items

Betty Bird
107 Ida St.
Mount Shasta, CA 96067

Tina Carter
882 S Mollison
El Cajon, CA 92020

Teddy Bears

Shirley Bertrand
971 N Milwaukee Ave., Box 99A
Wheeling, IL 60090

Shelby Good
4640 W Ave. L-2
Quartz Hill, CA 93536

Mary Ellen Sparr
3213 Seventh St.
Cuyahoga Falls, OH 44221

Sherry Thornhill
Rt. 1, Box 32
Hawk Point, MO 63349

Telephones

Also telegraph memorabilia
Mike Bruner
6980 Walnut Lake Rd.
W Bloomfield, MI 48323

Antique to modern; also parts
Phoneco
207 E Mill Rd.
P.O. Box 70
Galesville, WI 54630

Televisions

Harry Poster
P.O. Box 1883 WB
S Hackensack, NJ 07606

The Three Stooges

Soitenly Stooges, Inc.
Harry S. Ross
P.O. Box 72
Skokie, IL 60076

L.C. Tiffany & Tiffany Studios

Antique Silver House
8976 Seminole Blvd.
Seminole, FL 34642

Patrice Berlin
9315 Burnet Ave.
N Hills, CA 91343

Anthony Zazzarino, C.P.F.
2353 St. Georges Ave.
Rahway, NJ 07065

Toasters

Joe Lukach
7111 Deframe Ct.
Arvada, CO 80004

Tobacco Tins

Dennis & George Collectibles
3407 Lake Montebello Dr.
Baltimore, MD 21218

Clayton Zeller
Rt. 2, Box 46
Grandforks, ND 58203

Toby Jugs

John Harrigan
1900 Hennepin
Minneapolis, MN 55403

Tokens

Norm Boughton
1356 Buffalo Rd.
Rochester, NY 14624

James A. Lindsay
P.O. Box 562
Julliaetta, ID 83535

Tools

Ed Keeler
8 Forest Rd.
Burnt Hills, NY 12027

Betty Martin
Box 41B RT.4
Eolia, MO 63344

Larry Smith
2432 S Park Rd.
Bethel Park, PA 15102

Machinist
John R. Treggiari
5 Pioneer Cir.
Salem, MA 01970-1225

Flat-belt powered for shop
Jack W. Zimmerly Jr.
c/o 11722 Sharp Rd.
Waterford, PA 16441

Toys

Especially from 1948-1972
Bill Bruegman
137 Casterton Ave.
Akron, OH 44303

Especially die-cast vehicles
Mark Giles
P.O. Box 821
Ogallala, NE 69153-0821

Wind-ups
Floyd F. Gilmer
P.O. Box 13983
Roanoke, VA 24038

Cars
Sheldon Halper
9 Walnut Ave.
Cranford, NJ 07016

Trains
William F. Hayley
3305 Chartwell Rd.
Birmingham, AL 35226-2603

Phil Helley
Old Kilbourn Antiques
629 Indiana Ave.
Wisconsin Dells, WI 53965

Terri Mardis-Ivers
1104 Shirlee
Ponca City, OK 74601

Especially transformers & robots
David Kolodny-Nagy
3701 Connecticut Ave. NW #500
Washington, DC 20008; 202-364-8753

Items for consignment auctions
Dora Lerch
P.O. Box 586
N White Plains, NY 10603

Before 1960
Lor-Wal Antiques
P.O. Box 142
S Jamesport, NY 11970

Phil McEntee
Where the Toys Are
45 W Pike St.
Canonsburg, PA 15317

Slot race cars from 1960s-70s
Gary T. Pollastro
4156 Beach Dr. SW
Seattle, WA 98116

Relating to transportation
Gary Reed
P.O. Box 342
Fenton, MO 63026

Tammy Rodrick
Rt. 2, Box 163
Sumner, IL 62466

Especially from 1950s-60s
Rick Rowe, Jr.
Childhood, The Sequel
HC 1, Box 788
Saxon, WI 54559

Relating to John Deere or Caterpillar
J. Schreier
Rt. 1, Box 1147
Norwalk, WI 54648

1930s Felix & Krazy Kat
Don Sheldon
P.O. Box 3313
Trenton, NJ 08619

Especially from 1870-1950
David A. Smith
1142 S Spring St.
Springfield, IL 62704

BB guns
Loren J. Snyder
6867 Navarre Rd. SW
Massillon, OH 44646

Judith Katz-Schwartz
222 E 93rd St., 42D
New York, NY 10128

Kimball M. Sterling
125 W Market
Johnson City, TN 37604

Farm-related from 1950-1980
Edward T. Wegman
3818 Mt. Read Blvd. 'Z'
Rochester, NY 14616

Walkers, ramp-walkers, & wind-ups
Randy Welch
1100 Hambrooks Blvd.
Cambridge, MD 21613

Dr. 'Z'
1350 Kirts, Suite #160
Troy, MI 48084

Tramp Art

Judith Katz-Schwartz
222 E 93rd St., 42D
New York, NY 10128

Treenware

Judith Katz-Schwartz
222 E 93rd St., 42D
New York, NY 10128

Trolls

Rober M. Inouye
2622 Valewood Ave.
Carlsbad, CA 92008-7925

Tammy Rodrick
Rt. 2, Box 163
Sumner, IL 62466

Trunk

Sharon Hamer
P.O. Box 246
Durango, CO 81302

Patricia Quink
Box 733
Big Piney, WY 83113

TV Guides

TV Guide Specialists
Jeff Kadet
P.O. Box 20
Macomb, IL 61455

TV Lamps

Horse figurines
Trudy E. Jorde
P.O. Box 82
Devils Lake, ND 58301

Twin Winton/Winfield

Ray Vlach, Jr.
5346 N Magnet Ave.
Chicago, IL 60630-1216

Typewriter Ribbon Tins

Darryl Rehr
2591 Military Ave.
Los Angeles, CA 90064

Ken Stephens
12 Lloyd Ave.
Florence, KY 41042

Hobart D. Van Deusen
28 the Green
Watertown, CT 06795

Typewriters

Mike Brooks
7335 Skyline
Oakland, CA 94611

Jerry Propst
P.O. Box 45
Janesville, WI 53547-0045

Darryl Rehr
2591 Military Ave.
Los Angeles, CA 90064

Van Briggle

James Goad
1152A S Eagle Cir.
Aurora, CO 80012

Pat & Bill Ogden
3050 Colorado Ave.
Grand Junction, CO 81504

Terre Sue Stevens
Rt. 3, Box 97
Plainview, TX 79072

Vernon Kilns

Ray Vlach, Jr.
5346 N Magnet Ave.
Chicago, IL 60630-1216

Victorian Collectibles

Rhonda Hallden
21958 Darvin Dr.
Saugus, CA 91350

View-Master Reels & Packets

Harry Poster
P.O. Box 1883 WB
S Hackensack, NJ 07606

Walter Sigg
3-D Entertainment
P.O Box 208
Smartswood, NJ 07877

Vises

Small with patent mark
John R. Treggiari
5 Pioneer Cir.
Salem, MA 01970-1225

Umbrellas & Umbrella Handles

Arthur Boutiette
410 W Third St.
Suite 200
Little Rock, AR 72201

Unusual Items

Sheldon Halper
9 Walnut Ave.
Cranford, NJ 07016

Robert Lappin
Box 1006
Decatur, IL 62523

Wade

Ian Warner
P.O. Box 93022
499 Main St. S
Brampton, Ontario
Canada L6Y 4V8

Shirley Yoder
4983 Oak St. SW
Kalona, IA 52247

Watch Fobs

Dave Beck
P.O. Box 435
Mediapolis, IA 52637

Margaret Kaduck
P.O. Box 260764
Cleveland, OH 44126

Watches

Comic character
Howard S. Brenner
106 Woodgate Terrace
Rochester, NY 14625

Vintage
Julius Calloway
884 Riverside Dr.
New York, NY 10032

All brands & character
James Lindon
5267 W Cholla St.
Glendale, AZ 85304

Maundy International
P.O. Box 13028
Overland Park, KS 66212

Swatch
Walt Thompson
Box 2541
Yakima, WA 98907-2541

Swatch
Timesavers
Box 400
Algonquin, IL 60102

Swatch
W.B.S. Marketing
P.O. Box 3280
Visalia, CA 93278

Watt Pottery

Lona Siegfried
P.O. Box 25
Carterville, IL 62918

Tom Tangen
2930 Hwy. 12
Wilson, WI 54027

Wedgwood Jasperware

Larry D. Cook
3401 SW 12th St.
Des Moines, IA 50315-7513

Weller

Vintage Charm
P.O. Box 26241
Austin, TX 78755

Western Americana

Ephemera & unusual books
Carroll Burcham
5546 17th Place
Lubbock, TX 79416

Roland Folsom
Rt. 3, 10th St.
Waukon, IA 52172

Rusty & Iris Gilbert
P.O. Box 92
Adkins, TX 78101

Any fabric or goods
Dan Kelley
P.O. Box 239
Fayetteville, AR 73702

Cowboy gear
James A. Lindsay
P.O. Box 562
Julliaetta, ID 83535

Wicker

Sharon Hamer
P.O. Box 246
Durango, CO 81302

Windmill Weights

Richard & Valerie Tucker
Argyle Antiques
P.O. Box 262
Argyle, TX 76226

Winchester

Kate's Collectibles
28-US 41 East
Negaunee, MI 49866

Wizard of Oz

Lori Landgrebe
2331 E Main St.
Decatur, IL 62521

World's Fair

Judith Katz-Schwartz
222 E 93rd St., 42D
New York, NY 10128

D.D. Woollard, Jr.
11614 Old St. Charles Rd.
Bridgeton, MO 63044

Yellow Ware

Thomas W. Davis
147 Longleaf Dr.
Blackshear, GA 31516

Yo-Yos

Figural, advertising, etc.
Jim Marvey
5810 Salsbury Ave.
Minnetonka, MN 55345

Zeppelins

Ford U. Ross
11020 SW 15th Manor
Village of Harmony Lakes
Davie, FL 33324

Index

Schroeder's
ANTIQUES Price Guide

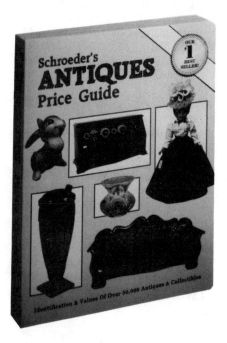

Schroeder's Antiques Price Guide is the #1 best-selling antiques & collectibles value guide on the market today, and here's why . . . More than 300 authors, well-known dealers, and top-notch collectors work together with our editors to bring you accurate information regarding pricing and identification. More than 45,000 items in almost 500 categories are listed along with hundreds of sharp original photos that illustrate not only the rare and unusual, but the common, popular collectibles as well. Each large close-up shot shows important details clearly. Every subject is represented with histories and background information, a feature not found in any of our competitors' publications. Our editors keep abreast of newly-developing trends, often adding several new categories a year as the need arises. If it merits the interest of today's collector, you'll find it in Schroeder's. And you can feel confident that the information we publish is up to date and accurate. Our advisors thoroughly check each category to spot inconsistencies, listings that may not be entirely reflective of market dealings, and lines too vague to be of merit. Only the best of the lot remains for publication. Without doubt, you'll find Schroeder's Antiques Price Guide the only one to buy for reliable information and values.

8½x 11", 608 Pages   **$12.95**

COLLECTOR BOOKS
A Division of Schroeder Publishing Co., Inc.